Contents

Preface

The evolution of performance enhancement in today's athletic world is truly amazing. Since *Jumping Into Plyometrics* was first published in 1992, there has been an explosion in the number of trainers and coaches who embrace plyometric training as an integral part of their athletes' development. Originating from track and field, this system of exercise has grown from mysterious to commonplace. The knowledge of these exercises has grown dramatically throughout the sporting world. In sports such as synchronized swimming, once far removed from the concept of power, plyometrics can now be credited for raising the level of performance.

This new book, *Plyometrics*, is an update of knowledge about plyometrics. New and exciting drills to improve footwork and basic movement skills have been included. Drills extend from beginner to more advanced skills. Additional research supporting the inclusion of plyometrics in various sport training programs has also been included. Chapter 11 features programs for new sports, including a sport-specific design for mixed martial arts (one of the fastest growing sports), and for traditional sports such as volleyball, basketball, and football. In addition, you will find chapters focused on the development of plyometric training techniques specific to the fastest growing groups of athletes, including youth (chapter 4) and female athletes (chapter 5). We have also included information regarding the latest research on using plyometric exercise to screen for injury risk (chapter 7), prevent ACL injury in females (chapter 5), and fully rehabilitate athletes in preparation for return to sport (chapter 6). The integration of these concepts into a comprehensive program for complete athletic development is outlined in chapter 10.

In this book, we provide the "nuts and bolts" of how plyometric exercise can be used to merge the physical qualities of speed and strength to produce an athlete capable of running faster, jumping higher, and achieving peak performance. Furthermore, the expansion of plyometrics to cover the multidirectional athlete provides greater variety and even more sport-specific options when designing a training program.

As the body of knowledge concerning the effects of plyometric training on performance enhancement and injury prevention expands, coaches and athletes need to keep their toolbox equipped with the latest and greatest techniques. This book demonstrates and explains the methods that will enable athletes to get the "biggest bang for their buck" in sport training. Not only do plyometrics fit into the complete training program, but a training program is not complete without the inclusion of plyometrics. Plyometric training has undergone a considerable metamorphosis over the past several years. New ideas and innovative techniques will lead athletes into a new generation of plyometric training. The coach or trainer who understands the options and opportunities available through plyometric training will find new ways to train athletes. We wish you well as you undertake the smart way (rather than the hard way) to work and train for athletic development.

Acknowledgments

We all stand on the shoulders of those who came before us and who walked alongside us. Many great European coaches and researchers deserve credit for their work with jump training, the stretch-shortening cycle, and shock training, including Veroshanksy, Boscoe, Komi, Satiskorsky, Medveydev, Javorek, Vittori, Bompa, Crisolan, MacFarlane, Francis, and many others who came before the current generation. We also recognize the many great American coaches who excelled in sport because of their quest for knowledge and adventuresome spirit, including Garhammer, Stone, Tellez, Santos, and Al Vermeil, my colleague, contemporary, and friend, who is probably the singular greatest resource in strength and conditioning the world has ever known.

I wish to thank all the NCAA Division II athletes who allowed me to use their bodies in the grandest of laboratories, the National Championships in Track and Field. I also thank the Santa Clara Aquamaids and coach Chris Carver, who believed they could go to the next level if they could find a training program no others in their sport had dreamed of risking. I am grateful to the professional and elite athletes who have been willing to challenge the odds and perform smart work instead of hard work.

My deep gratitude to my coauthor Greg Myer, who is as prodigious with a pen as any athlete is on the field. He is a key figure in the production of this project, and I am proud to have had him as a student. Now he is mentoring me.

When you want to move forward in the business of performance training, you often have to look back and recognize the roots of this tree of knowledge. It has been a pleasure to watch plyometrics grow from funny exercises used by track and field athletes to everyday, routine drills in most successful training programs. This is dedicated to those who have been and to those who will be. Compete hard and recognize that whoever wins is the best coach—today.

PART

1

KNOWLEDGE

Muscular Actions, Sport Performance, and Plyometric Training

In this chapter, we discuss the three modes of muscle action—eccentric, isometric, and concentric action—and summarize how each type of muscle action contributes to optimal performance in sport activities. We also outline techniques for plyometric exercise that will help athletes capitalize on the synergistic effects of these muscle actions.

TYPES OF MUSCLE ACTIONS

Eccentric actions, which occur when the muscle lengthens under tension, are used to decelerate the body. Eccentric muscle actions are primarily associated with the loading phase of a plyometric exercise. For example, in a runner's stride, the impact of contacting the ground on a single foot requires the body's center of gravity to drop rapidly. The runner does not collapse at this moment because the leg muscles can respond with eccentric muscle action that slows and controls this lowering motion. Eccentric muscle actions absorb force and decelerate the joint segments in preparation for the transition into isometric and, ultimately, concentric muscle action. Because eccentric muscle action is capable of generating up to 40 percent greater force than the other types of muscle action, the ability to generate eccentric muscle force is critical to successful performance in many sports.

When a runner reaches midstride, the body comes to a complete but very brief halt with no observable movement at a particular joint (e.g., knee joint). This is characteristic of isometric muscle action, or a static position in which there is no muscle lengthening or shortening visible to the observer. In sport activities, this muscle action occurs in the brief instant between the eccentric action and the subsequent concentric action (in which the muscle fibers pull together and shorten). The athlete's timing and execution of the transition through this isometric coupling phase will strongly affect whether the athlete achieves increased power in the plyometric movement. (See chapter 2 for more information about the coupling phase.) To gain benefits from the stretch-shortening cycle, the athlete must be able to generate appropriate force and properly time the coupling phase with the concentric muscle action.

After the isometric coupling phase, the payoff of dynamic movement occurs during the unloading phase of the plyometric activity. In running, this phase of plyometric movement is associated with the concentric action that results in acceleration of the limb segments. Figure 1.1 shows each of the three phases—eccentric (loading), coupling, and concentric (unloading)—for an athlete performing a jump. The synergy of the muscles as they transition through each of these muscle actions (eccentric, isometric, concentric) is ultimately what determines the benefits gained from the stretch-shortening cycle.

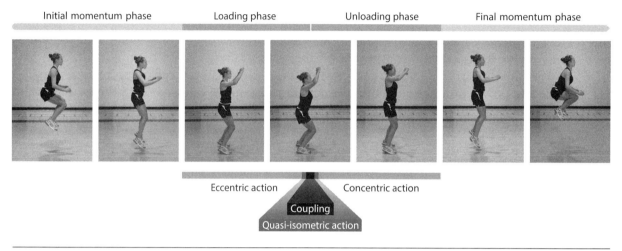

Figure 1.1 Muscle actions associated with each phase of a plyometric exercise.

The upcoming sections detail the relationship between muscular strength and the critical phases of plyometric exercise. These sections also identify techniques that can be used to target each mechanism for improved plyometric performance.

ECCENTRIC STRENGTH

The largest forces that muscles are capable of producing occur when an external force exceeds that produced by the muscle, forcing the muscle to lengthen. This is known as an *eccentric action* or *negative work*. An athlete who is running or jumping depends on eccentric actions of the lower extremities to dampen the forces when the body makes contact with the ground. If not for eccentric actions decelerating the body, the athlete would collapse to the ground every time he made foot contact. Muscles are structured so that they absorb and decelerate the body in a protective manner. In cases of rehabilitation from tendon and muscle injuries, eccentric actions are an integral part of the rehabilitation program; these actions should also be a major focus in the prevention of injuries. In strength training, eccentric-focused movements deserve the same attention to detail as concentric movements, although they may be a smaller component of total volume.

Eccentric muscle actions are the first stage of muscle work and involve the muscles acting as shock absorbers or springs; this is known as the loading phase of the plyometric movement. During the course of normal walking or running, the muscles in the lower extremities are collectively doing nearly equal amounts of eccentric (lengthening) and concentric (shortening) work. This dynamic balance between muscle actions can be seen when examining the stretch-shortening cycle (SSC) and its role in improving performance. (See chapter 2 for more information on the SSC.) The first phase (stretch or loading phase) of the SSC comes as the muscle lengthens in response to an increased load being placed on it. The load might be produced by gravity and the individual's body weight as he makes contact with the ground. As this occurs, elastic energy is produced within the muscle and may be stored for a very short period of time. If the eccentric action immediately precedes a concentric action, the muscles will stop acting as shock absorbers and will perform as if they were springs. However, if the time between the eccentric and concentric actions is too long (i.e., the subsequent shortening of the muscle does not occur immediately), the energy will be dissipated as heat within the muscle.

The storage and recovery of elastic energy within the muscles during an SSC become an important factor in performance; the energy stored can actually increase force and power production in the subsequent shortening cycle. In effect, the muscles are made up of muscle fibers, tendons, and the respective fascial tissues. All of these tissues contribute to the spring properties of the muscle-tendon system that stores and recovers elastic energy during running and jumping.

Eccentric muscle actions are particularly useful in a training program for strength development. Because eccentric actions have the unique ability to develop much greater forces, they provide greater overload to the muscle compared to when the athlete emphasizes only concentric actions. This can have an important role in preventing the muscle wasting that occurs with aging or preventing the atrophy that occurs as a result of recovery from injury or surgery.

When forces are decelerated by a limb or body segment, the entire muscle-tendon system participates. If the forces needed to decelerate the body exceed the strength of the muscle-tendon system, this can result in injury to the muscle, the tendon, or the attachment of the tendon to the bone. Athletes who experience recurring hamstring or adductor strains have been shown to have an eccentric strength deficit as great as twice a normal limb. Eccentric resistance training may prevent injury to the muscle-tendon unit by improving the unit's ability to absorb more energy before failing. Eccentric strength building has also been associated with increased hypertrophy, positive changes at the cellular level that indicate increased strength at the myotendinous (muscle-tendon) junction, and production of increased collagen for reinforcement of the tissue.

Finally, the increase of bone and muscle mass is directly related to the magnitude of muscle forces and other loads (body weight) on bone. Therefore, the strength and density of bone are influenced positively when muscle strength is developed through resistance training and eventually through plyometric training.

Training isolated muscle actions during dynamic tasks is difficult because isolating specific muscle actions can be a challenge. However, certain techniques can be used to focus on a particular muscular action at a joint. These types of exercises are often used in combination with technical instruction to help athletes improve their overall technical performance of plyometric exercise. To focus on eccentric strength in the lower extremities, an athlete could use exercises such as the assisted Russian hamstring curl (figure 1.2). Ultimately, athletes should progress from eccentric-focused exercise to speed-strength movements, but they can still employ specific plyometric movements that focus on the eccentric or loading phase, such as squat jumps (figure 1.3) or single-leg squats.

ASSISTED RUSSIAN HAMSTRING CURL

The trainer anchors the athlete by standing on the athlete's feet and provides lift assistance by using a strap that is attached around the athlete's chest (figure 1.2). The athlete performs the full eccentric (lowering) movement, getting assistance as needed to achieve the proper speed. At the end point of the movement, the athlete begins the concentric (raising) portion of the exercise; the trainer provides assistance in order to ensure the athlete's success with the movement.

Figure 1.2 Assisted Russian hamstring curl: *(a)* start; *(b)* eccentric lowering; *(c)* bottom position; *(d)* concentric raising with assistance.

SQUAT JUMPS

For a squat jump, the athlete begins in the athletic position with feet flat on the mat and pointing straight ahead (figure 1.3). Focusing on the eccentric muscle action, the athlete drops into deep flexion of the knee, hip, and ankle, touching the floor (or mat) as close to the heels as possible and then takes off into a maximum vertical jump. The athlete jumps straight up vertically and reaches as high as possible. On landing, the athlete immediately returns to the starting position and repeats the jump.

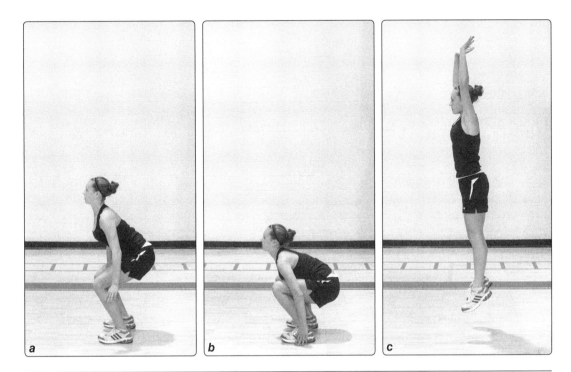

Figure 1.3   Squat jumps: *(a)* starting position; *(b)* deep flexion of the knee, hip, and ankle; *(c)* maximum vertical jump.

SINGLE-LEG SQUAT

The athlete places the heel of one foot on the back edge of a box or platform 12 to 24 inches (30 to 60 cm) tall and holds the other foot off the edge of the box. The athlete descends and slowly lowers his body until the knee on the box is fully flexed and the buttocks come to rest against the calf area of the supporting leg. The athlete then ascends at an accelerated rate until he achieves the standing starting position again. While lowering his body weight, the athlete should be mindful of keeping the knee over and in line with the second toe. The knee should not be allowed to collapse to the inside of the body, nor should it be substantially out in front of the toes. The athlete should be able to achieve 10 repetitions performed at a tempo of 8-2-2 (8-second descent, 2-second pause, and 2-second ascent). Although classified as a body weight exercise, this exercise is a definite challenge and goes a long way in helping an athlete develop eccentric strength within the lower extremity.

ISOMETRIC STRENGTH

Isometric or static muscle actions are defined as those in which no visible movement occurs; this is known as the coupling phase of a plyometric exercise. (Refer to figure 1.1 and see chapter 2 for more information about the coupling phase.) Even though studies indicate that muscle fibrils do move slightly during a static hold, the coupling phase is a point at which little or no observable joint movement occurs; thus, it is more of a quasi-isometric muscle action. In running or jumping, the coupling phase is the point at which the body "stops" for a very brief period. At this point, the joint is at a position that can be measured before the eccentric action is reversed and becomes the concentric or shortening muscle action.

In weightlifting, athletes often experience a "sticking" point within the range of motion that is difficult to overcome and may prevent them from moving the weight to the completion of a repetition. Most weightlifters know that performing isometric actions at a specific point during the exercise movement (most often the position at which the joint has the least mechanical advantage from the bony segments) can help train the muscle to deal with that specific angle or point in the range—and thus increase the lifter's ability to move the weight through that sticking point. In addition, research indicates that isometric strength is developed at specific points in the joint's range of motion; if other positions (mechanically disadvantaged positions) are ignored in training, strength in those areas will be lacking. For plyometric training, athletes can use specific exercise techniques to focus on improving their isometric strength. For example, figure 1.4 shows a single-leg balance exercise performed on an unstable surface. This exercise forces the athlete to focus on knee stabilizers and to primarily use isometric muscle action (along with a combination of eccentric and concentric corrective positioning). When athletes master this type of stabilization exercise, they can progress to more isometric-focused techniques associated with a plyometric movement, such as the single-leg hop and hold. (See the Stability Movement Progression for single-leg exercises in chapter 4.)

The brief period of static hold as the body switches from eccentric to concentric muscle actions is known in plyometric language as the *amortization phase*. This phase is brief indeed, less than .01 second in power-oriented athletes such as jumpers and sprinters. The ability to rapidly switch from an eccentric action to a concentric contracting phase is the hallmark of good athletes. The one thing we know about good athletes in general is that they don't spend a long time on the ground when running or jumping. These relatively brief ground contact times are directly related to the amortization phase of the athlete's movements.

Another way of thinking about the amortization phase is to relate it to its more traditional definition regarding a loan; the shorter the amortization phase (duration of time over which the loan is repaid), the more the borrower likes the loan. Similarly, the shorter the time that athletes spend on the ground, the more effective and faster they will be.

SINGLE-LEG BALANCE

Balance training drills are performed on a balance device that provides an unstable surface and allows the athlete to focus on the isometric hold position. The athlete stands upright on a BOSU (or other unstable device) on one leg and then bends the knee and hip of the supporting leg to achieve a low, athletic position (figure 1.4). The athlete should hold this position briefly before returning to the starting position. To optimize isometric muscle actions during balance training, athletes should focus on maintaining positions as close as possible to the athletic positions used in their sport. In addition, sport-specific actions involving implements—such as soccer kicks or ball tosses and catches to perturb the upper extremity—can be used to supplement balance training exercises.

Figure 1.4 Hold position for the single-leg balance drill.

CONCENTRIC STRENGTH

Concentric strength is the "action" portion of the SSC and is the payoff during the unloading phase of a plyometric exercise. This is the result of the muscle fiber shortening after the kinetic energy has been stored by the eccentric loading of the body and after the body has switched from eccentric to concentric modes of muscle action. Now observers see how high or far the athlete jumps, how fast she turns the legs over (stride frequency), how much ground she covers (stride length), or how far she throws the ball. Though these actions are often impressive, keep in mind that all that beautiful flowing motion is the result of the athlete firmly investing in the body's ability to absorb kinetic energy via muscle-lengthening actions under heavy loads. Think of the eccentric and isometric phases as an investment in the bank of physical performance, and think of the concentric action as the return on that investment.

Athletes can train specifically for concentric strength by using a variety of resistance training methods, including medicine ball training (figure 1.5). Ultimately, concentric-focused training should be progressed to link with the other muscle actions so that the athlete learns to capitalize on the payoff portion of plyometric training. However, the use of appropriate plyometric exercises (e.g., wall jumps; figure 1.6) that minimize the loading and coupling phases will allow the athlete to focus on the concentric portions of the movement.

BACKWARD THROW FROM SQUAT

The athlete holds a medicine ball with both hands in front at the waist and stands about 10 feet (3 meters) in front of a partner; both partners are facing the same direction. The athlete drops rapidly into a squat position with the medicine ball between the legs (figure 1.5a). After achieving a one-quarter to one-half squat position, the athlete reverses the drop, explodes vertically upward, and uses both hands to direct the medicine ball on a flight path over the head at an angle of about 45 degrees (figure 1.5b). The athlete should be careful to bend the knees, bend from the hips, and keep the back straight. Keeping the back straight means the lumbar spine and hips are locked and the torso is slightly inclined, not perfectly vertical to the ground. Locking the spine in slight extension will result in the spine being held straight. This is a maximal effort, and the athlete can be expected to leave the ground slightly at the point at which the medicine ball is released. Thus, the athlete should be prepared to recover to the starting position after the release of the ball. The athlete may also throw the ball against a wall (concrete or cinder block) or may throw it for distance. This exercise has secondary benefits such as improving muscular endurance and body coordination.

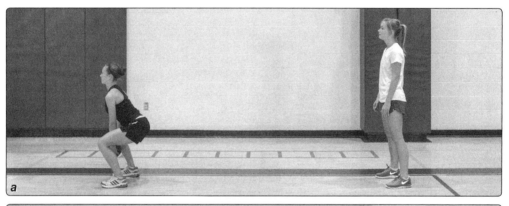

Figure 1.5 Backward throw from squat: *(a)* squat position; *(b)* release.

WALL JUMPS

The athlete stands erect with the arms semi-extended overhead. This vertical jump requires minimal knee flexion. The gastrocnemius muscles should create the vertical height. The arms should extend fully at the top of the jump (figure 1.6). This jump can be used as a warm-up or as a teaching exercise because this relatively low-intensity movement can reveal abnormal knee motion in athletes with poor side-to-side knee control.

Figure 1.6 Wall jumps: *(a)* start; *(b)* jump.

◖ SUMMARY ◗

- The three types of muscular action are eccentric, isometric, and concentric.
- Eccentric actions, which occur when the muscle lengthens under tension, are used to decelerate the body and are associated with the loading phase of plyometric movements.
- During the coupling phase of a plyometric exercise, the body comes to a complete but brief halt with no observable movement at a particular joint. This is characteristic of isometric muscle action. During this static position, there is no muscle shortening or visible change in the angle of the joint.
- The payoff of plyometric movement occurs during the unloading phase of the plyometric activity. This phase is associated with the concentric muscle action that results in acceleration of the limb segments.
- Training with plyometric exercise can help athletes capitalize on the synergistic effects of each muscle action.

Anatomy and Physiology of Plyometrics

In this chapter, we describe the science behind plyometric training and how this type of training can increase the power of movements. The chapter provides an overview of the mechanism by which plyometric training can lead to significant improvements in performance. In covering the physiology of plyometrics, the chapter details the anatomy of the stretch-shortening cycle (SSC).

DEFINING PLYOMETRIC EXERCISE

Plyometric exercise is a popular form of training used to improve athletic performance.[1] It involves a stretch of the muscle-tendon unit immediately followed by a shortening of the muscle unit. This process of muscle lengthening followed by rapid shortening during the stretch-shortening cycle (SSC) is integral to plyometric exercise.[2] The SSC process significantly enhances the ability of the muscle-tendon unit to produce maximal force in the shortest amount of time.[3,4] These benefits have prompted the use of plyometric exercise as a bridge between pure strength and sport-related power and speed.[5]

As plyometric training techniques have evolved, the description of this training and the related terminology have undergone a metamorphosis. Because the term *plyometrics* is a later creation in American training literature, much of the early physiological research on this type of training described it by other names. The term used by researchers in Italy, Sweden, and the Soviet Union for the type of muscle action involved was the *stretch-shortening cycle*. Coaches in these countries simply referred to the use of such exercises in their training programs as jump training. Based on original forms of training described by Yuri Verkhoshansky, the Russian national jump coach for track and field, plyometrics were originally developed as a shock method of training. Verkhoshansky believed that in order for athletes to develop a higher level of muscle performance, they needed to be presented with a stimulus that was unique and different from their usual training methods.

Plyometric exercises have been described as activities that involve maximal effort, such as high-intensity depth jumps.[2,6,7] On the other hand, plyometric exercises have also been described as any movement that involves the stretch-shortening cycle, whether that movement requires maximal or submaximal effort.[8,9] Fred Wilt, an American track and field coach from the University of Iowa, was credited with coining the term *plyometric*. Based on its roots, the word seemed to aptly describe

Selected text on pages 13-20 adapted, by permission, from T.L. Chmielewski, G.D. Myer, D. Kauffman, and S.M. Tillman, 2006, "Plyometric exercise in the rehabilitation of athletes: Physiological responses and clinical application," *Journal of Orthopaedic & Sports Physical Therapy* 36(5): 308-319. © Orthopaedic Section and the Sports Physical Therapy Section of the American Physical Therapy Association.

exercises consisting of hops, jumps, and bounds used largely by track and field athletes to improve performance in their events.

The terms *plyometrics* and *stretch-shortening cycle* are used synonymously by some authors;[10] whereas others use the term *stretch-shortening cycle* instead of *plyometric* to differentiate from the literal translation of the Greek word *pliometric* (plio = more, plythein = increase, metric = measure), meaning "to increase the measurement."[2,11] The use of terminology often seems to differ by field of study. In the physiology literature, the term *stretch-shortening cycle* is used to describe activities such as running, jumping, or throwing.[2,12] However, in the rehabilitation and conditioning literature, the term *plyometric* is used to describe these activities when they are part of training designed to capitalize on the SSC for maximizing force production or enhancing performance.[2,13]

The term *amortization* has been a source of confusion when used to describe plyometric activity. Amortization means a "gradual extinction, extinguishing, or deadening."[2,14] In reference to a depth jump, amortization has been described in various ways—as the time from initial ground contact to reversal of motion,[1] as the time from initial ground contact to takeoff (entire stretch-shortening cycle),[2,15] and as the transition between muscle lengthening and shortening.[8,16,17] In this book, we use the term *amortization* to describe the transition between eccentric and concentric actions of antagonistic muscle groups, which is synonymous with the coupling phase.

The focus and application of plyometric training have evolved in recent years. In athletic conditioning programs, plyometric exercises are now often performed at a submaximal level and are directed at the achievement of proper biomechanical technique[2,18,19,20] and injury prevention in sport.[21,22] Training in this manner has been effective in reducing lower-extremity injuries as well as improving performance.[21,22,23,24,25] Plyometric training has also crossed over into the rehabilitation field.[2] Recently published rehabilitation protocols include plyometric exercise as a means for improving function and facilitating a return to sport.[2,8,9,26,27,28,29,30]

In this book, plyometric exercise is defined as activities that involve and capitalize on the mechanisms of the SSC to increase the efficiency of force production at a joint or to increase performance. Simply stated, plyometrics are defined as exercises that enable a muscle to reach maximum strength in as short a time as possible. This speed-strength ability is known as power. Although most coaches and athletes know that power is the name of the game, few understand the mechanics necessary to develop it. To understand plyometrics, a person must be familiar with the important points of muscle physiology. These are reviewed in the next section, which will serve to demonstrate the simple yet complex way in which plyometric training relates to better performance.

Ever since athletes started using plyometric training in the development of their athletic ability, researchers have put a great deal of effort into trying to verify the effectiveness and safety of plyometrics. As might be expected, the results of these studies are mixed. Athletes of various sports and equally varied levels of conditioning have been compared to untrained athletes under all sorts of variables and conditions. The point that is missed in this research is that athletic development follows its own time curve. A 6-, 12-, or 24-week testing period can in no way reflect the longitudinal development that will occur throughout an athlete's overall career. For some athletes, this time span may be a single season; for others, it may be up to 30 years of highly competitive activity. Therefore, plyometric training should be considered in the context of the athlete's age, skill level, injury history, and numerous other variables that make up his athletic development. In this way, through applied research, practitioners can learn to establish realistic expectations.

PHYSIOLOGY OF PLYOMETRIC EXERCISE

The physiological research supporting the effectiveness of plyometrics, or the SSC of muscle tissue, has been reviewed by many authors. Most cite the importance of two factors: (1) the serial elastic components of muscle, which include the tendons and the crossbridging characteristics of the actin and myosin that make up the muscle fibers; and (2) the sensors in the muscle spindles (proprioceptors) that play the role of presetting muscle tension and relaying sensory input related to rapid muscle stretching for activation of the stretch reflex.

Muscle elasticity is an important factor in understanding how the SSC can produce more power than a simple concentric muscle action. The muscles can briefly store the tension developed by rapid stretching so that they possess a sort of potential elastic energy. For an analogy, consider a rubber band—whenever you stretch it, the rubber band has the potential for a rapid return to its original length.

The stretch reflex is another mechanism that is integral to the stretch-shortening cycle. A common example of the stretch reflex is the knee jerk experienced when the quadriceps tendon is tapped with a rubber mallet. The tapping causes the quadriceps tendon to stretch. That stretching is sensed by the quadriceps muscle, which contracts in response.

The stretch, or myotatic, reflex responds to the rate at which a muscle is stretched and is among the fastest reflexes in the human body. The reason for this is the direct connection from sensory receptors in the muscle to cells in the spinal cord and back to the muscle fibers responsible for action. Other reflexes are slower than the stretch reflex because they must be transmitted through several channels (interneurons) and to the central nervous system (brain) before a reaction is elicited. Because of the minimal delay in the stretch reflex, muscle undergoes action faster during an SSC than in any other method of action. A voluntary or thought-out response to a muscle stretch would occur too late to be of use to an athlete in jumping, running, or throwing.

Besides response time, the strength of the response is also a consideration when determining how plyometrics relates to sport performance. Although the response time of the stretch reflex remains about the same even after training, training will change the strength of the response in terms of muscle action. As a muscle is stretched or lengthened, the potential for greater concentric force after the stretch can be incrementally increased with increases in the speed of stretching the muscle. The resultant contraction of a rapidly stretched muscle is a more forceful movement for overcoming the inertia of an object, whether it is the individual's own body weight (as in running or jumping) or an external object (e.g., a shot put, a blocking bag, an opponent).

PHASES OF PLYOMETRIC EXERCISES

The delineation of plyometric exercise into phases is another area of confusion in the literature. Plyometric exercise has been described as biphasic, consisting of phases for eccentric and concentric muscle action,[2,11] or triphasic, with an additional phase for the transition between the eccentric and concentric phases.[9,31] One author has further divided plyometric exercise into five phases by adding momentum phases at the beginning and end of the triphasic description.[2,6]

In this book, we use a triphasic description of the movement. The terminology used for the phases may be *loading, coupling,* and *unloading;* or it may be *eccentric, isometric,* and *concentric* actions. The following sections describe the physiological responses that occur during each phase of a plyometric exercise. Figures 2.1 through 2.3 present the phases of plyometric exercises for the lower body, the upper body, and the trunk.

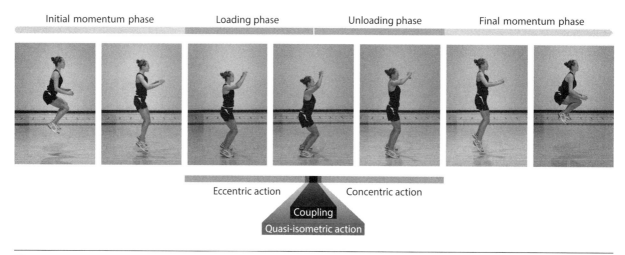

Figure 2.1   Phases of a lower-extremity plyometric exercise.

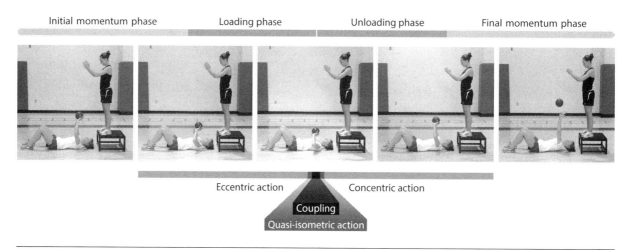

Figure 2.2   Phases of an upper-extremity plyometric exercise.

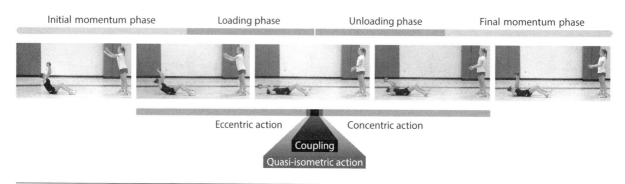

Figure 2.3   Phases of a plyometric exercise for the trunk.

Loading Phase

The initial phase of a plyometric movement, which involves rapid muscle lengthening, is called the loading phase. This phase has also been labeled with many other terms—including the *eccentric, deceleration, yielding, countermovement,* or *cocking* phase—and the terminology often varies depending on the primary plyometric movement the authors are describing.[2,4,15,31,32,33,34] In our definition, the loading phase of a plyometric exercise occurs when the muscle-tendon units of the prime movers and synergistic muscle groups are stretched as a result of kinetic energy or loading applied to the joint.[2] The kinetic energy may be derived from the preceding action, such as flight from a preceding jump (refer to figure 2.1), or from an external source such as an approaching medicine ball (refer to figures 2.2 and 2.3). It may also be derived from a countermovement—that is, the concentric action of the antagonistic muscle group (see figure 2.4).[2]

Stretching of the muscle-tendon unit during the loading phase elicits the stretch-shortening cycle, which results in enhanced force production and performance when compared to the absence of stretch.[3,4] The loading phase begins when the muscle-tendon units begin to perform work to resist gravity or the preceding movement; this is described as negative work in the resistance training literature.[2,12] Termination of the loading phase has been variably described, but in general during a jumping plyometric exercise, it is at the point at which the center of mass reaches its lowest position and the velocity of the center of mass reduces to zero.

The stretch of active muscle during the loading phase can elicit increased force output via three related mechanisms associated with the stretch-shortening cycle: muscle potentiation, the stretch reflex, and the series elastic components.[2,35,36] Muscle potentiation is an alteration of the muscle contractile properties, causing a slight lengthening of the muscle sarcomere and thus increasing actin and myosin proximity (figure 2.5). Increased proximity leads to increased crossbridge formation, which induces higher force production.[2,36]

Figure 2.4 The countermovement squat jump, which includes *(a)* a deep knee bend before *(b)* the jump, is an example of a plyometric exercise with the initial momentum being created by the antagonistic muscle groups.

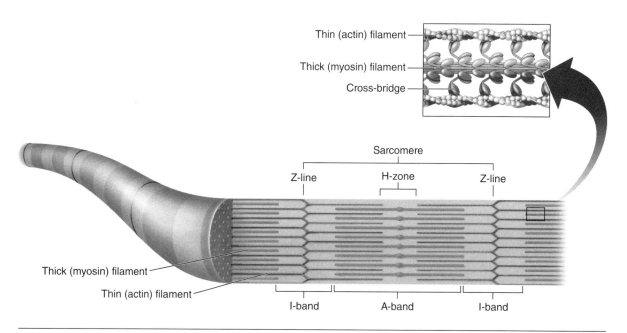

Figure 2.5 A muscle fiber, showing actin and myosin.

The second mechanism of increased force production may be gained via the stretch reflex. Interestingly, the stretch reflex mechanism may not be elicited simultaneously in all muscles that are stretched during a plyometric activity; rather, the muscle response depends on the number of joints that are crossed and the specific activity that is being performed.[2] For example, during stretch-shortening activities, reflex muscle activity is apparent in the soleus (figure 2.6), which crosses only one joint (monoarticular);[37] however, the reflex muscle activity is inconsistent for the gastrocnemius, which crosses two joints (biarticular) and is a synergist to the soleus at the ankle.[2,38,39] Differences in reflex muscle activity between mono- and biarticular muscles may be explained by differences in the changes in muscle length during loading. Without muscle fascicle lengthening, muscle spindles may not be stimulated, which may be related to the inconsistent reflex muscle activity in muscles crossing multiple joints during plyometric activities. Monoarticular muscles may benefit more than biarticular muscles from the force augmentation gained from the stretch reflex for enhanced work output.[2]

A third mechanism associated with the SSC is the storage of elastic potential energy in the series elastic components.[2,40] The series elastic components (actin and myosin filaments within the muscle and the tendon) are stretched when the joint is loaded;[41] however, the tendon has been found to be the main contributor to length changes in muscle-tendon units[40,41] and the storage of elastic potential energy.[2,41,42] The Golgi tendon organ, a sensory receptor that lies in the tendon, is stimulated by the stretch of the tendon.[43] Sensory information from the Golgi tendon organ synapses onto an interneuron in the spinal cord, and inhibitory feedback is sent to the contracting muscle (figure 2.7).[44]

Superficial dissection

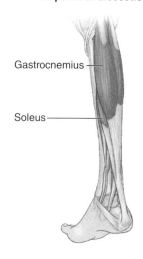

Figure 2.6 Soleus and gastrocnemius muscles.

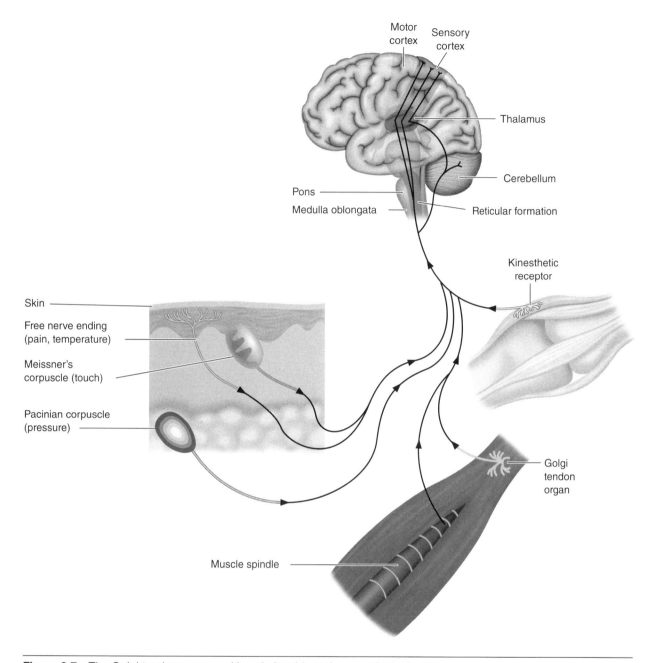

Figure 2.7 The Golgi tendon organ and its relationship to the neurological system.

It was previously thought that the inhibitory feedback allowed the Golgi tendon organ to function as a means of protecting muscle from excess tension[44,45] and could interfere with the forces generated during plyometric exercise.[8,30,31] However, this hypothesis has been challenged[44,45] because the Golgi tendon organ can respond to submaximal forces;[43] in addition, excitatory reflexes have been initiated by the Golgi tendon organ during locomotion and therefore may actually aid in force generation during plyometric exercise.[2,46] Ultimately, the storage of elastic potential energy can initiate a slingshot effect and support the transference of positive work that begins during the coupling phase of the plyometric movement.

Coupling Phase

The transition between the loading phase (negative work) and unloading phase (positive work) of a plyometric exercise may be described as the coupling phase (refer to figures 2.1 through 2.3). This phase is commonly referred to as the amortization phase[8,30] and has also been called the transmission phase.[47] The coupling phase is the definitive phase of plyometric exercise that ultimately determines the synergistic effects gained from the SSC.[6] If the transition between the loading and unloading phase is not continuous and rapid, delayed and disjointed coupling will occur, and the gained energy will be dissipated and lost as heat.[2]

With long delays in the amortization phase or pauses in movement, the activity will no longer be considered plyometric because the benefits of the stretch-shortening cycle will be lost.[2] In fact, measurable decreases in stored elastic energy occur in coupling phases that last over 25 milliseconds.[48,49] The average duration of the coupling phase for countermovement jumps has been calculated to be 23 milliseconds, and the ideal coupling time may be less than 15 milliseconds.[6,36] Training movements that include a pause or a delayed amortization phase may have muscle-strengthening benefits; however, when using plyometric exercises with the goal of increased power and force production, athletes should avoid having a visible pause in joint movement during the SSC.[6]

Unloading Phase

This final phase of plyometric activity has also been called the rebound, shortening, push-off, or propulsion phase.[2,6,50,51] The unloading phase of a plyometric exercise occurs immediately after the coupling phase and involves shortening of the muscle-tendon unit.[2,12,52,53] When isolated to a single lower-extremity joint, the unloading phase has been defined as beginning when the curve of the joint angle reverses direction and ending when the ground reaction force goes to zero[36]—or beginning when the muscle-tendon unit begins to shorten and ending at toe-off.[54] In the biphasic analysis of plyometric jumps reported in the literature, the unloading phase begins at the start of upward movement of the center of mass, and it ends when the toes are no longer in contact with the ground.[51]

The unloading phase is often considered the payoff or resultant phase, because this portion of the plyometric activity is when the mechanisms elicited during the loading phase contribute to increased efficiency of force production.[2] The improved efficiency and force generation are gained from the summation of storage and reuse of elastic energy,[12,55,56] muscle potentiation,[3,36,57] and the contribution of the myotatic stretch reflex.[2,58]

ANATOMY OF AN ATHLETE'S MOVEMENT

As our understanding of functional anatomy and athletic movement has increased, an interesting phenomenon has been observed. When athletes move their body in more anatomically efficient ways, this not only decreases the risk of injury but also improves performance. Therefore, to understand optimal movement mechanics, coaches must appreciate the complex role of the musculoskeletal system in absorbing and developing force. Plyometric training can be used for the analysis of sport movement. In addition, plyometric training gives coaches the opportunity to provide feedback that will help athletes achieve functional movement patterns that are more anatomically efficient.

When analyzing the most basic jump, a review of the anatomy of the jump is essential—from the prime movers down to the intrinsic muscles of the feet. Gone are the days of high-level athletes sitting on machines and cranking out tremendous numbers of repetitions with no attention to biomechanical or functional detail. When an athlete is performing an exercise during training, the exercise must serve the purpose of improving performance in the athlete's chosen sport. Plyometric exercise takes this idea to the next level by adding power and timing to movements that are essential for optimal sport performance.

To analyze movement based on plyometric activity, a coach should focus on seven key muscle groups; the coach should also be aware that a variety of other muscles play a role in plyometric exercise (figure 2.8). The following seven muscle groups are essential as prime movers and stabilizers during the development of speed and power in the lower extremities:

1. **Gluteal muscle group.** The muscles in the gluteal group are the largest, most capable muscles in the human body. They possess the greatest potential for power development. When athletes can develop greater forces with these muscles, this results in higher forces being driven into the ground and returned to the body. As a result, greater force is provided for lengthening the stride, driving the body off the ground, and overcoming the inertia of the body when the athlete is initiating movement. Athletes can develop strength in this muscle group by using various forms of squatting that require the thigh to exceed a parallel position to the ground.

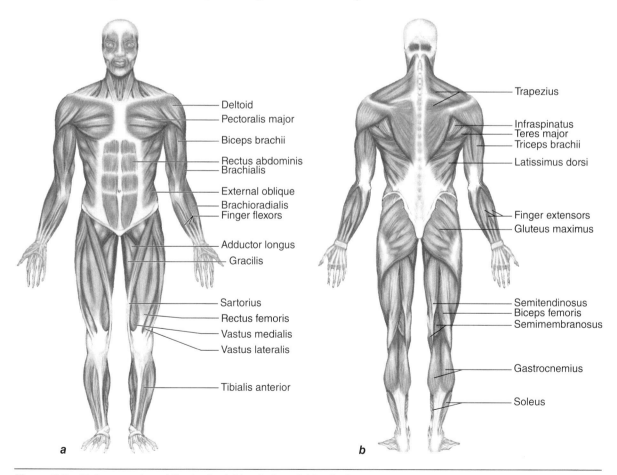

Figure 2.8   Major muscles of the body: *(a)* front view; *(b)* back view.

2. **Hip flexor group.** By virtue of its size and cross section, the hip flexor group has the second most potential for powerful movement. These muscles provide knee drive or lift in all jumping and running events. Their development is imperative in producing the forward drive of the body during running.

3. **Quadriceps muscle group.** The quadriceps have multiple roles that are essential. These muscles are dynamic shock absorbers in running. Without the ability of the quadriceps to develop eccentric strength, running and jumping would be virtually impossible. As an extensor of the leg and a stabilizer of the knee, these muscles are extraordinarily important in running and jumping.

4. **Hamstring muscle group.** The hamstrings are important in various roles. These muscles serve as a posterior stabilizer and a flexor of the knee while also being an extensor of the hip; thus, the hamstrings aid the gluteus group in providing forward drive to the body.

5. **Gastrocnemius.** The gastrocnemius has multiple roles in its position as the posterior support to the knee joint in the lower extremity. It provides ankle plantar flexion, which is the end of the kinetic chain when it comes to pushing off the ground. Not only does this muscle have a role at the knee in flexing the joint, but it is also extremely important in allowing the ankle to develop force into the ground.

6. **Anterior tibialis.** The gastrocnemius' counterpart is the anterior tibialis. Often overlooked, this muscle is extremely important in stabilizing the ankle. The anterior tibialis even helps to pull the body forward over the foot when the foot is in contact with the ground. This muscle allows the athlete to lock the ankle so that when the foot makes contact with the ground, the ankle and foot become a rigid lever from which to more effectively transmit forces when running or jumping.

7. **Abdominal muscles.** The abdominal muscles are the anterior core of the body. They are essential to connecting the top half of the body with the bottom half. This is important because as the muscles in the lower extremities are contracting and pulling, they will have an effect on the upper body. The trunk and abdominal muscles hold the cylinder of the body together and form a major platform against which the lower-extremity muscles can efficiently do their job.

Each muscle group must be accounted for in strength training as part of the preparation for plyometric training. The listed muscles are basically in opposition to each other (on opposite sides of the body), which emphasizes the need for properly designed strength programs that provide balance in strength and flexibility. Only after using this type of strength program will athletes be able to perform plyometric training effectively and gain the desired increases in performance.

The following muscles can be described as role players in plyometric training:

1. Spinal erector muscle group
2. Latissimus dorsi (lats)
3. Trapezius (traps)
4. Scapular stabilizers
5. Rotator cuff muscles
6. Deltoids
7. Biceps
8. Triceps

Although these muscles may not seem to have much of an obvious role in plyometric training for the lower extremities, they actually do. The first three muscle groups (spinal erectors, latissimus dorsi, and trapezius) have a direct connection via tendon or fascia to the pelvis. Think about tucking your shirt into your pants. If you shove it way in there, you will have difficulty bending over. These muscles are postural muscles that support the spine and hold the body erect. They are part of the many muscles that contribute to trunk stability.

The rotator cuff and scapular stabilizers play a huge role in plyometrics for the upper extremities. Weakness in these muscle groups can be devastating in the performance of throwing, supporting the body weight on the hands, or projecting force through the arms when striking an object (such as in boxing or martial arts). In addition, the arms make an important contribution during the act of jumping from the ground. Balance in strength and power is essential to good performances involving the upper extremities.

The triad of smaller muscles in the arms and shoulders are also involved in the development of strength and power during specific activities. The deltoids, biceps, and triceps form a group that has important roles in shoulder and elbow function and stability. Strength in these muscles improves the performance of a multitude of activities, including plyometric drills.

To give you a sense of the anatomical analysis necessary, let's look at a double-leg vertical jump (see figure 2.1). The mechanics and execution of the countermovement, which sets up or precedes the actual liftoff, require the body's center of gravity to drop rapidly in a way that is similar to the landing technique of a depth jump. The loading needed to develop momentum for the countermovement can be gained from a rapid counterstep before initiation or from dropping from a box (e.g., depth jump). The latissimus dorsi muscles act to forcefully pull the arms down while assisting in the extension of the lumbar spine. The squatting motion occurs with the leg muscles eccentrically loading, preparing to rapidly uncoil. This springlike mechanism develops tension (stored energy) in the glutes, quadriceps, hamstrings, and gastrocnemius muscles. Think of the body acting like a spring being compressed at this point. The abdominal muscles contract isometrically to maintain stability over the pelvis (hips), thus aiding in the transfer of energy from the legs up the torso.

Next, a brief amortization phase takes place. Split-second isometric actions occur at this point—the ultimate goal of plyometric training is minimizing the time spent in this transition. The rapid transition from countermovement to concentric action maximizes the amount of energy gained from the eccentric loading during the countermovement.

Finally, the athlete explodes upward as if the spring were suddenly decompressed! The stored energy gained from the rapid descent is now ready to be displayed. The biceps, deltoids, and trapezius explosively contract to fire the arms upward. Again, the abdominal muscles are used to hold the pelvis stable and transfer energy up the chain. The glutes fire to extend the hips, and the hamstrings aid in this extension. The quadriceps muscle group forcefully extends the knee joint, and the gastrocnemius plantar flexes or extends the ankle, aiding in toe-off. The gastrocnemius uses the elastic properties of the Achilles tendon to create an efficient force transfer at toe-off, which in turn contributes to the explosion of the jump.

These key points can assist coaches and athletes in determining the proper technique:

- Maintain an even distribution of body weight over the entire foot as well as between the right and left sides of the body.

- Flex all three joints of the lower extremity. This ready position allows the athlete to maximally utilize the musculature of the thighs and glutes during the vertical propulsion phase.
- Tilt the trunk slightly forward and pull the arms to a position behind the midline of the body.

Coaches should monitor stability at the knee joint. Common errors in technique include the knee diving out over the toes or collapsing to the inside (creating the genu valgus or knock-knee position).

CENTER OF GRAVITY AND MOVEMENT

The body's center of gravity plays a key role in stability and movement. The center of gravity represents a balance point, a location in the body about which all its particles are evenly distributed. It is an abstract point that moves when the body segments are moved relative to one another. The center of gravity is not even confined to the body. In the case of a pike position, it is possible for the center of gravity to actually be outside of the body. The center of gravity is most stable, or in balance, when the body is directly over the base of support, which is usually formed by the position of the feet relative to the ground surface. The wider the base, the lower the body's center of gravity in the standing position, and the more stable the individual.

The standing center of gravity, in a practical sense, is somewhere in the vicinity of the belly button. The center of gravity will differ among individuals according to how their body mass is distributed. A person with more mass or weight distributed through the legs will tend to have a lower center of gravity than a person with thinner legs. Having a standing center of gravity that is higher is a distinct advantage to an athlete participating in the high jump. This is why coaches would want to recruit tall athletes to participate in this particular event. The higher the standing center of gravity, the less the athletes have to work to get their body into the air and ultimately over a specific bar height. Shorter athletes must be very gifted in terms of muscle development and fiber types in order to have the explosive capability to reach elite-level heights in the high jump.

Regardless of the height of the center of gravity, athletes must be able to move quickly laterally and change directions easily. With these skills, the athlete can allow the center of gravity to move out away from the feet and then quickly recover. Moving the center of gravity out from over the feet results in a position of instability, forcing the athlete to react quickly to recover his position or he will topple to the ground.

The concept of the inverted funnel (first described by John Frappier) is based on the fact that athletic movements often require the individual to move the feet out from under the body's center of gravity and then recover the position quickly in order to regain balance and stability. The Frappier footwork drills (see chapter 9) were designed to teach the athlete to maintain the center of gravity in a relatively constant position while the feet rapidly work out from under it in all directions. The result is improved kinesthetic awareness, or that sense of where the body is in relation to the environment. Note that these movements are largely submaximal plyometric drills. Subsequent chapters will provide feedback cueing and plyometric techniques that coaches can use to help athletes optimize center of gravity and trunk control in plyometric activities.

SUMMARY

- For an exercise to be truly plyometric, it must be a movement preceded by an eccentric action. This results not only in stimulating the proprioceptors that are sensitive to a rapid stretch, but also in loading the serial elastic components (the tendons and crossbridges between muscle fibers) with a tension force from which they can rebound.

- The key to using the potential kinetic energy is the initiation of the unloading phase with the briefest amortization times. Brief ground contact yields greater forces at takeoff.

- Many movements in sport activity take place when the feet move out from under the athlete's center of mass and then quickly recover. The inverted funnel principle takes this into account and is used in planning and executing many movement drills.

How Plyometrics Works

This chapter provides an overview to help coaches and athletes understand the keys to optimizing power development through plyometric exercise. The quest for optimal power training has led to the development and use of various training methods. Traditionally, heavy resistance training techniques have been used to improve strength and, subsequently, performance. These techniques have typically involved using weights of 80 to 95 percent of one-repetition maximum (1RM) and performing one to four repetitions. More current strategies combine a variety of training modalities—including plyometrics and dynamic weightlifting—to enhance explosive power. (The integration of training techniques is further detailed in chapter 10.)

When it comes to training, the relationship between strength and power is often complex. In general, as the resistance goes up, the speed of the movement will go down. When athletes perform lifts at maximal effort, the speed of the movement is often very slow. As the overall resistance is reduced, the speed of force development increases, and power will also show increases. Because power production is the key determinant of success in sport, athletes need to use training techniques that are focused on transitioning the strength gained from heavy (but slow) resistance training to high-velocity movements. Plyometric training done with rapid force absorption (e.g., landing from a jump) and force generation (push-off of a jump) is critical to help the athlete convert strength into power.

The research has indicated that heavy lifting with external resistance and plyometrics as individual methods of training can effectively improve power output. This has led people to think that by combining both systems the athlete might show even greater improvements. And this has proven to be the case, particularly in the area of specific skills such as vertical jumping. The next question was whether lifting for maximal power output, as opposed to maximum strength, could be of benefit to the athlete.

RESISTANCE TRAINING FOR POWER

For resistance training to be focused on increasing power, the lifts must be made more dynamic in nature. A form of squatting known as the jump squat is an example of this type of exercise. In this type of exercise, the athlete uses a load of approximately 30 to 60 percent of 1RM. The exercise involves using all of the basic components of muscle contraction that are necessary to prepare the athlete for higher-intensity plyometric exercises. The goal is to use a resistive load that maximizes the mechanical power output of the exercise. The 5-5-5 squat (see figure 3.1) embodies this principle.

5-5-5 SQUAT

This drill can be done with body weight or up to 60 percent of 1RM in the form of a medicine ball or barbell. The athlete assumes a start position with the feet shoulder-width apart, the toes turned slightly out, the abdominal muscles tight, and the spine in slight extension (figure 3.1a). The weight (if used) is on the shoulders behind the neck. The athlete performs five controlled squats, lowering to a position with the thighs parallel to the floor (figure 3.1b). The movement should include a stop or isometric catch position at the bottom. On the ascent, the athlete returns to the standing position, focusing on accelerating during the ascent (figure 3.1c). A useful tempo for this first movement is 6-1-2, or 6-second descent, 1-second pause at the bottom, and 2-second return to the standing posture. Next, the athlete drops into the squat position five times rapidly. The quick squat is performed at a much faster rate and a very different tempo—2-0-2. The athlete drops quickly, comes to a quick stop at the bottom, and then performs a rapid ascent. The legs should fully extend, but the feet should not leave the ground. Finally, the athlete drops into the squat position and explodes vertically five times in a row. The feet should leave the ground after each repetition. The tempo is very explosive—2-0-1. The athlete must keep the weight in contact with the shoulders while jumping because letting the weight come away from the shoulders may result in injury.

Figure 3.1 5-5-5 squat: *(a)* start, *(b)* squat, and *(c)* explosion.

Extensive research has demonstrated that maximal strength levels can be improved by using lighter weights followed by doing highly accelerated movements in both the upper and lower extremities. In the East European literature, this type of training is described as one form of complex training. (Another form involves using heavy weights and quickly freeing yourself from the resistance by dropping or releasing the weight, described as contrast training.) Using maximal power training and plyometrics in an integrated fashion can lead to rapid increases in power, although the intensity of this type of training would be too stressful for long-term training (greater than a 12-week cycle). However, it can be applied for short periods of training, and it is often used in the later stages of the preparation (off-season) cycle of a periodization training scheme. (See chapter 8 for more information about cycles or periodization training.) This type of training can often help to sharpen or refine the body's ability to develop force rapidly, resulting in the athlete being able to develop greater impulse forces—which are essential in jumping, running, and throwing.

RESEARCH ON DEPTH JUMPS

Many researchers have been fascinated with studying the depth jump. This maximal-effort plyometric training, or shock training, was first introduced to Russian athletes in order to help them develop explosive speed and strength.[1] Research on the shock method of training examined drop jumps from heights of up to 10 feet (3 m), which pushed the limits of safety and sanity; this research also demonstrated how the East Europeans were willing to test the high end of the intensity spectrum in order to seek gains using plyometric techniques.[2,3] Fortunately, we now have research that demonstrates the limits and diminishing returns to help guide us with intensity recommendations. Specifically, this early Soviet research helped to establish that depth jumps were an effective means of increasing athletes' speed and strength capabilities.

Dr. Yuri Verkhoshansky's training programs were based on resistance training and drills that emphasized various forms of jumping. The Soviet Olympic success in track and field caused the world to take notice. It wasn't long before the rest of the world began to use the same drills and exercises, which became known in the United States as plyometrics. As a coach, Verkhoshansky relied on evidence-based research (performed by many others) to make training decisions. His writings detailing his training programs became revered by track coaches all over the world.

Verkhoshansky proclaimed 0.8 meters as the ideal height to drop from when trying to achieve maximum speed in switching from the eccentric to the concentric phase of the stretch-shortening cycle; he proclaimed 1.1 meters as ideal for developing maximal dynamic strength. He also recommended no more than 40 jumps in a single workout—to be performed no more than twice a week. Recovery between sets was facilitated by light jogging and calisthenics. Today, plyometric training is much less rigid in its application and can be modified to teach movement skills with submaximal efforts; in addition, plyometric training is not only considered safe for athletic development, but it is also now used to reduce injury risk in children and elite athletes.[4,5,6,7,8,9]

A later publication by Verkhoshansky and Tatyan[10] comparing three groups of athletes showed that depth jumps were more effective than weight training, the jump-and-reach, or horizontal hops for developing speed and strength capabilities. This shows the specificity of many plyometric exercises. Depth jumps are most useful in the development of vertical velocity from the ground, which ultimately determines how high one can jump. Other researchers—such as Adams,[11] Bosco and Komi,[12] and Asmussen and Bonde-Peterson[13]—have conducted studies seeking the optimal height for depth jumps. Over a dozen studies conducted in the United States and Europe have only served to confuse the issue. Research conducted in the United States since the late 1970s has shown that depth jumps generally increase an athlete's ability to jump higher (vertically) in test situations. Any conflicts in the research about the effects of depth jumps are probably due to the many experimental designs that have been used. The research results have served to emphasize the point that depth jumps are not a panacea for all training ills. Athletes need a well-rounded training program that emphasizes the skills they need for their sport.

Determining the Proper Height for a Depth Jump

In practical terms, the task of determining the proper height for a depth jump centers on the athlete's ability to achieve maximal elevation of the body's center of gravity after performing a depth jump. If the height is too great for the strength of the legs, then the legs spend too much time absorbing the impact of the landing. As a result, the legs cannot reverse the eccentric loading quickly enough to take advantage of the serial elastic component of muscle and the stretch reflex phenomenon. The result is a jump that is dependent on strength and devoid of power. In this case, the athlete will spend a long time on the ground.

Coach and athlete should work to find the proper height—one that lets the athlete maximize the height jumped and also achieve the shortest amortization phase. A recent study supports this contention because it found that as drop jump height increased there was a subsequent increase in quadriceps activation.[4] However, when the study participant dropped from 60 centimeters (about 2 feet), the ground contact time increased during the takeoff phase. In addition, the highest drop heights increased the peak vertical ground reaction force and resulted in a straighter knee when landing. The study authors argued that the altered muscular activation and movement patterns of the knee at the highest depth jump height diminished the effectiveness of plyometric training and increased the potential risk for knee injury.

The following procedure outlines one method described by many authors for determining maximum height for the depth jump:

1. The athlete is measured as accurately as possible for a standing jump-and-reach. (For the standing jump-and-reach, suspend an object overhead or mark a target on a wall. The athlete stands with feet shoulder-width apart then squats slightly and explodes up, reaching for the object or target. The athlete should not step before jumping.)

2. The athlete performs a depth jump from a box at a height of 24 inches (61 cm) for males or 18 inches (46 cm) for females, reaching as high as he or she can after takeoff, trying to attain the same height as measured for the standing jump-and-reach in step 1. (If the athlete cannot attain this height, see the note at the end of this procedure.)

3. If the athlete successfully executes this task, the athlete may move to a higher box. The box height should be increased in 6-inch (15 cm) increments.

4. Repeat steps 2 and 3 until the athlete fails to reach the standing jump-and-reach height. The previous box height then becomes the athlete's starting point for this drill.

Note: If the athlete cannot reach the standing jump-and-reach height from a 24- or 18-inch box, the height of the box should be lowered, or depth jumping should be abandoned for a while in favor of strength development. If the athlete cannot rebound from a basic height of 24 or 18 inches, the athlete probably does not have the musculoskeletal readiness for depth jumping.

Recent efforts have examined the differences between training with the depth jump (DJ) versus the countermovement jump (CMJ).[14,15,16] The mechanical distinction between these two activities is that the CMJ is simply flexing the hips, knees, and ankles, allowing for a rapid descent of the body's center of gravity before using concentric muscle activity to jump vertically. This is exactly what is performed when a person does a jump-and-reach test. The DJ, on the other hand, requires the use of body weight to eccentrically load the muscles via a vertical drop from a prescribed height. This activity requires the athlete to time the drop and be mentally prepared to reverse the descent (eccentric to concentric muscle action) at the time the stimulus is perceived (when the feet make contact with the ground). Prior data indicate that the athletes trained with plyometric exercise such as the DJ (stretch-shortening movement) improved more in both peak power and vertical jump height than any of the other groups.

There is no doubt that motor learning is a major factor in an athlete's ability to effectively use the depth jump in a training program. To achieve maximum results, athletes must learn and adhere to factors related to timing and positioning throughout the training program. This is why the coaching of technique in the performance of these exercises is so important. Young, Pryor, and Wilson[17] found that instructions given to subjects play a significant role in the type of jumping ability that the subjects develop. Three groups were instructed to emphasize different aspects of the vertical jump, such as overall height achieved, time spent on the ground, or both maximum height and minimum ground contact. A fourth group stressed training with the countermovement type jump.

The study showed that when athletes received different instructions (verbal cues) and feedback, they developed clear differences in the characteristics of the jump. When the objective of the jump was absolute height, regardless of time spent on the ground, depth jumps and countermovement jumps were similar. However, when contact time was the focus of the task, the technique for the depth jump was considerably altered and resulted in wide differences in the outcomes of the tests. Because the absolute jump heights between DJ and CMJ demonstrate a big difference when ground contact time is reduced, this shows the importance of training as specifically as possible for the sport task. For example, if the sport requires a jump initiated from a static squat position (e.g., volleyball block), athletes should train with prolonged stance times and CMJ techniques to optimize specific transfer of training. However, if optimal athletic performance requires rapid loading and jumping (e.g., volleyball attack swing), the athletes may get the most benefit from DJ training.

The relative simplicity of performing the depth jump has made it an easy task to study. Investigators have tried to relate depth jumps to improvements in start speed, acceleration, and absolute speed in running and jumping; but they have tended to ignore the more elusive role of horizontal jump training (standing jumps, multiple jumps, and bounding). Today, the depth jump is not only one of the most investigated movements related to sport performance, but it is also commonly used in the assessment of athletes' risk of injury.[18] However, because running and jumping involve both horizontal and vertical components, it makes sense that both horizontal and vertical jump training would contribute to improvements in both activities.

MECHANICS OF VERTICAL JUMPING

Vertical jumping is a component of most sport activities. People often take it for granted that an athlete instinctually knows how to jump vertically. In actuality, jumping vertically is a skill that can and should be taught to athletes. If we examine the event a little more closely, we find that the jump is preceded by a countermovement in which the center of gravity drops rapidly. This is seen as a flexing of the hips, knees, and ankles of the athlete. The trunk tilts slightly forward, and the arms are pulled to a position behind the midline of the body.

Before the vertical movement of the body, a rapid extension of the hips, knees, and ankles takes place, which is largely the result of force developed by the arms and legs. The arms should be brought forward rapidly and allowed to travel to a position above and in front of the shoulders. The quick bend of the knees to lower the center of gravity is accompanied by moving the arms into a position where the shoulders are extended and the arms are behind the body. This position of the arms allows the athlete to develop force that is directed into the ground as the arms come forward.

The arms can contribute to the development of force into the ground only while they are swinging down toward the ground. The force put into the ground is then recovered as the arms move past the midline and into a position in front of the shoulders. The athlete can imagine that he just compressed a spring by moving into the squat position with the legs and swinging the arms down rapidly; then as he starts to extend the legs and as the arms move past the midline of the body, the pressure on the spring is released, and it follows its natural path—namely, up! Therefore, athletes must get the arms as far back and as straight as possible for maximum force development.

The more the arms bend at the elbow, the faster they will come through, but the less they will contribute to overall force development. A practical view of this is to compare the arm swing of elite triple jumpers with that of elite high jumpers. Longer levers develop more force; shorter levers move more rapidly. Whereas maximum force is important for the triple jumper, high jumpers using the flop technique must rely more on arm speed to effectively carry out their technique.

Research by Everett Harman, PhD, et al.[19] at the U.S. Army Research Institute of Environmental Medicine has shown that the countermovement (literally, a stretch reflex) is crucial to development of force and can contribute up to 6 percent of the total jump height. The arms can increase the overall jump height attained by as much as 21 percent. The researchers concluded that the arms developed their positive effect by exerting downward force on the body as they swung through in the early phase of the jump; the arms also kept the body in a position where the quadriceps and gluteus muscles could exert force over a longer period of time. Another conclusion was that because the countermovement did not contribute that significantly to jump height, many sport situations may not require a large countermovement in order for the athlete to be effective. If speed of movement and reaction time are more crucial, such as in a volleyball block, the athlete may be just as effective by simply starting the jump with the knees less bent. In other words, if an athlete does not need to attain maximum height, a small countermovement will clearly be the more effective technique.

Because of the arms' large contribution to overall jump height, resistance training exercises that strengthen these areas should be included in all jump training programs. Here are some of the exercises that are important in the development of the arms for jumping:

- Reverse pull-down
- Triceps dip
- Shoulder swing with dumbbells
- Straight-arm pull-down
- Seated row
- Backward medicine ball throw
- Underhand medicine ball throw

USING MUSCLE PHYSIOLOGY TO OPTIMIZE PLYOMETRIC TRAINING

Based on the prior examples and results of study investigations, it is clear that subtle changes to plyometric techniques can have a large impact on power output and sport-related performance in tasks that involve the stretch-shortening cycle. In most sport skills, eccentric (lengthening) muscle actions are rapidly followed by concentric (shortening) actions. For example, whenever a long jumper makes contact with the takeoff board, the jumper's body absorbs the shock of landing by executing slight flexion of the hip, knee, and ankle; this is followed by a rapid extension of the takeoff foot and leg as the jumper leaves the board.

Think about the basketball player who drives for the slam dunk. As the player takes the last step toward the basket, the supporting leg must take the full body weight and stop the horizontal inertia of the run-up. This loads the leg by rapidly forcing its muscles to stretch and undergo a rapid eccentric action. Nerve receptors firing information to the muscle then cause a concentric action. These muscle responses occur with no conscious thought on the part of the player; however, without these responses, the knee would buckle, and the player would collapse to the floor. Another way of thinking about these muscle actions is to think back to the earlier example of a spring. In the case of the basketball player, the run-up puts pressure on the takeoff leg, compressing the coils of the spring. The energy stored within the spring is then released as the athlete leaves the floor.

The amortization phase is crucial to distinguishing the average athlete from the elite athlete. Successful execution of this timing phase is the result of training and motor learning from plyometric drills. All individuals have a genetic limitation in speed and power; however, they all have a window of opportunity to maximize their abilities if taught and trained properly. Even small differences can lead to magnificent outcomes if they are executed at the proper time.

Studies examining great jumpers, sprinters, or other athletes who rely on the speed and strength of their muscles show that these elite athletes do not spend much time on the ground during sport maneuvers. They have learned that energy is stored during the eccentric phase of muscle action and is partially recovered during the concentric action. However, the potential energy developed in this process can be lost (in the form of heat) if the eccentric action is not immediately followed by a concentric action.

Plyometric activities terminate with a momentum phase, during which the body segments are propelled as a result of the forces summated during the unloading phase (e.g., flight of a jump or passive follow-through after ball release) and captured during the coupling phase.[2] Ultimately, the performance achieved during the momentum phase, such as the height of a jump, is increased compared to the same activity being performed without benefit of the stretch-shortening cycle.[20] The degree of performance enhancement during the momentum phase depends on the magnitude of the forces[21,22,23] and the quickness of the movement[20] during the plyometric activity. In particular, higher forces are associated with a shorter coupling phase[24] and with greater energy stored in the series elastic component.[23]

Performance is also a result of the total duration of contact (loading through unloading phases); as the contact duration becomes shorter, higher forces and joint moments are generated,[25] and the tendon contribution to work is increased.[2,26] As mentioned, this coupling of the eccentric-concentric action should be quick and should begin and end within hundredths of a second. Typically, great high jumpers are on the ground for a mere 0.12 seconds!

An entire system of exercise—plyometrics—has arisen just to address the development of a shorter amortization phase. And, perhaps surprisingly, the length of the amortization phase largely depends on learning. Although strength and innate speed are important, an athlete can shorten the amortization phase by applying learning and skill training to a base of strength development.

CRITERIA FOR INITIATING PLYOMETRIC EXERCISE

Plyometric exercises, even at low intensities, can expose joints to substantial forces and movement speeds;[27] these exercises are not appropriate for an athlete who does not maintain sufficient neuromuscular control to generate and attenuate high-impulse joint loads. Before initiating dynamic lower-extremity plyometric exercise, athletes should first be able to demonstrate a body weight squat with good posture and limited forward trunk lean while maintaining neutral knee alignment; otherwise, these functional deficits are likely to be exacerbated when plyometric exercise is implemented (because of the high forces). Furthermore, the athlete must have full range of motion and an adequate base level of strength, endurance, and neuromuscular control in order to properly perform plyometric exercise without developing or reinforcing bad techniques.

Guidelines for initiating plyometric exercise are poorly developed. Most of the criteria have been established using older literature based on high-intensity exercise (shock training) and is grounded in opinion rather than research. For example, some have suggested that plyometric exercise should be initiated only after achieving minimum strength levels. For the lower extremity, the specified strength levels include the ability to perform a full squat with free weights of 1.5 to 2.5 times body weight or to squat 60 percent of body mass five times within 5 seconds; for the upper extremity, the strength levels include the ability to perform a bench press with free weights equal to body mass or to perform five hand-clap push-ups.[28] These guidelines may exclude a majority of female athletes and many younger athletes from participating in plyometric exercise, even though these same athletes would be allowed to participate in competitive sports whose activities induce ground reaction forces five to seven times body mass.[29,30]

Although validated guidelines are currently unavailable for the initiation of plyometric exercise, empirical evidence suggests that plyometric exercise may be initiated when athletes can tolerate moderate loading during traditional resistance training exercise and can perform functional movement patterns with proper form. Coaches often develop general rules for what they consider minimal standards in leg strength for lower-body plyometrics. A good rule is that novice but physically mature high school athletes should be able to perform a back squat three times with resistance equal to their body weight. At that point, the athletes can safely execute moderate-level plyometric activities. When athletes attain these milestones, plyometric exercise is typically implemented in the training program in combination with an integrative neuromuscular training program (see chapter 10).

◀ SUMMARY ▶

- Performance is enhanced as a result of training with plyometric exercises, and it is optimized when the activity imparts higher forces and faster speeds of movement.

- The amortization phase is a key determinant in whether performance will be enhanced from the stretch-shortening cycle.

- Prolonged contact times should be avoided because they will limit the benefits achieved from plyometric training. In addition, prolonged contact times may be indicative of excessive intensity during the loading (eccentric) phase.

- When the transition between the loading and unloading phases is not continuous, the effects of the SSC will be lost.

P A R T

II

CONSIDERATIONS

Plyometric Training and Young Athletes

As more children and adolescents begin to participate in sports and conditioning activities in schools and private programs (select or club sports)—sometimes without consideration for cumulative workload—coaches and teachers need to have age-appropriate guidelines to help ensure that plyometric training will enhance athletic performance and reduce the risk of sport-related injury in young athletes.[1] In this chapter, we review the scientific evidence on strength and conditioning practices for youth. We also provide age-appropriate recommendations for integrating various plyometric activities into a well-designed program that is safe, effective, and enjoyable. The cornerstone of plyometric training for young athletes is age-appropriate education and instruction by qualified professionals who understand the physical and psychosocial uniqueness of children and adolescents.[1]

TRAINABILITY

Previously, people have had concerns regarding the safety and efficacy of strength and plyometric training for youth;[2] however, a growing body of evidence indicates that regular participation in well-designed, sensibly progressed, and properly instructed training programs that include resistance and plyometric training can offer measurable value (health and fitness) for children and adolescents.[3,4,5,6,7] This is particularly important for aspiring young athletes. Young people are often ill-prepared for the physical and psychological demands of sport practice and competition because of the decline in physical activity among children and adolescents during their free time.[8,9]

Recent studies have investigated the trainability of youth when using plyometric and resistance training protocols that include appropriate intensity and volume of training; these studies have demonstrated that children and adolescents show significant improvements in selected performance measures when following progressive training programs.[10,11,12,13,14,15,16,17,18] The literature often notes that great athletes usually learn how to perform complex skills early in life. Plyometric training is a foundation of training that helps the youngster learn how to perform the basic components of these complex skills. The observable benefits of resistance, plyometric, and speed training are now known to be greater than those attributable to normal growth and development in children and adolescents. It is difficult to imagine how a young child could grow to become an Olympic ice skater and build the skills and quality of movement necessary to perform at this level without establishing these qualities at a young age. A child may miss that opportunity if she does not learn the motor skills of hopping, skipping, running, and throwing—and if she is never exposed to this type of training.

In addition to improving muscular strength and power, regular participation in a progressive resistance, plyometric, and speed training program has the potential to positively influence several measurable indexes of health-related and skill-related fitness and can reduce the risk of sport-related injury.[3,4,6,19] Moreover, regular participation in a plyometric strength and conditioning program with qualified instruction can provide an opportunity for aspiring young athletes to learn proper exercise technique, gain confidence in their ability to be physically active, and receive basic education on several issues—program design, safety concerns, and healthy lifestyle choices such as proper nutrition and adequate sleep.[1]

RISKS AND CONCERNS

If appropriately supervised and sensibly progressed, resistance and plyometric training programs can be safe, effective, and enjoyable for children and adolescents.[3,4,20,21] However, because unsupervised and poorly designed training programs can be injurious, qualified professionals should supervise training sessions and design exercise programs that are consistent with the needs, interests, and abilities of all participants. Without qualified supervision and instruction, youth are more likely to attempt to lift weights that exceed their abilities or to perform an excessive number of repetitions with improper exercise technique.[22,23,24]

Though few research studies have focused specifically on measures to prevent training-related injuries in young athletes who participate in plyometric activities, the best course of action is to engage qualified professionals who understand youth training guidelines. These professionals should have a philosophy about training that is consistent with the needs, interests, and abilities of children and adolescents; and they should provide supervision and instruction. Regardless of the age and experience of the participants, the focus of youth resistance and plyometric training programs should be on the development of correct exercise technique, proper movement mechanics, the safe use of exercise equipment, and proper weight room etiquette.[1]

EDUCATION AND INSTRUCTION

Proper education and instruction are paramount for safe, effective, and enjoyable plyometric training. Age-appropriate education and qualified instruction are required in order to successfully integrate various components related to the mastery of fundamental movements, exercise variation, exercise progression, and structured recovery. These components are discussed in turn in the sections that follow.

A growing number of school-age youth are exposed to strength and conditioning activities in physical education classes, recreational activities, and sport training programs; therefore, the importance of qualified and enthusiastic instruction that is consistent with individual needs, goals, and abilities should not be underestimated.[1] Children and adolescents who participate in plyometric training programs should be knowledgeable about the potential risks and concerns associated with exercise equipment (e.g., boxes, medicine balls, resistance equipment). They should be aware of the potential risk of injury if they do not follow established training guidelines and safety procedures. Ultimately, education and instruction will determine the levels of success that can be achieved within each component of a plyometric training program.[1]

Mastery of Fundamental Movements

Although there is no minimum age for participation in resistance and plyometric training programs, all participants must be able to follow coaching instructions and undergo the stress of a training program. In general, a child who is deemed ready for structured sport participation (about 7 or 8 years old) would typically be ready for some type of resistance training.[3] However, regardless of the starting age, all youth should receive safety instructions on appropriate use of plyometric equipment and the risks associated with dropping from excessive heights. This is particularly important in schools and recreation centers because untrained youth tend to overestimate their physical abilities and this may increase their risk of injury.[1,25] Qualified instruction enhances participant safety and enjoyment of the training experience; in addition, direct supervision of youth during resistance and plyometric training can improve program adherence and optimize strength gains.[26]

To reduce the occurrence of nonaccidental injuries in children and adolescents, an emphasis should be placed on the development of proper fundamental movement skills and gradual progression of plyometric training programs.[1] If a young athlete does not master fundamental movement skills at less intense levels, deficits displayed during the exercise will likely be amplified as training intensity is increased over time. Qualified instructors should give continuous and immediate feedback to every participant during and after each exercise session. This will improve the athlete's awareness of proper movement mechanics. It should also reduce the likelihood of undesirable or potentially injurious body positions and enhance the performance gains achieved through plyometric training.

The use of mirrors and video equipment can help young athletes involved in plyometric training become aware of poor biomechanics that have the potential to be injurious.[27,28] Visual and verbal feedback can help young athletes to match their perceived performance of technique with their actual technique. Other modifiable risk factors that have been associated with injuries in youth resistance training include supervision, environmental factors, equipment storage and use, exercise prescription, and exercise technique.[29]

A wide variety of strengthening and plyometric training programs have been shown to be safe and effective for children and adolescents.[7,19,30,31,32,33,34] Although weight machines, free weights (e.g., barbells and dumbbells), and medicine balls can certainly be beneficial in a global program for youth, the development of strength and conditioning techniques can be initiated without the addition of external resistance.[35] For example, progressive resistance, plyometric, and speed training can be initiated using only body weight as resistance. Although some body weight exercises such as the squat may be challenging for young lifters who lack flexibility and core strength, the fundamental movement should be mastered before the exercise is performed with external resistance.[1]

Qualified instructors who focus on proper exercise technique, correct movement mechanics, and a sensible number of repetitions can increase the likelihood of success. For example, during the squat exercise, some inexperienced young lifters have difficulty maintaining normal lordotic posture (neutral spine alignment that avoids excessive arching), and they often demonstrate excessive forward tibial and trunk progression.[35] Instructors should correct these technical flaws by providing feedback and coaching cues, demonstrating proper exercise technique, and providing continuous feedback on movement mechanics during each phase of progression.[1]

Young athletes who want to begin plyometric training must be able to develop proper techniques using fundamental movement skills. One of the most basic and important movement techniques used when teaching plyometrics to children is the squat exercise. Performing the squat correctly is critical for advancing to higher demand plyometric activities by developing hip hinge and postural control and by developing prime movers used in jumping and landing. The following is a progression designed to help young athletes master the squat movement.

FUNDAMENTAL MOVEMENT PROGRESSION: SQUAT

Phase I Ball Squat

The athlete performs a squat with the aid of a Swiss ball. The athlete is encouraged to shift the body weight backward, using the support of the Swiss ball to complete the exercise (figure 4.1). The athlete's feet are positioned far enough from the ball that the knee cannot pass over the ankle when the athlete is at the deepest squat position. Once the exercise is initiated, the athlete should avoid locking the knees into extension.

Figure 4.1 Ball squat: *(a)* start; *(b)* finish.

Phase II **Box Touch Squat**

A box is placed behind the athlete, and the athlete starts with feet shoulder-width apart (figure 4.2). The athlete performs a squat down to the height of the box, softly touches the box without resting, and then ascends up to the initial starting position. This progression of the squat exercise is used to help athletes gauge appropriate squat depth and give them confidence when performing the exercise. Instructors should position the box far enough away so that the athlete extends behind herself to touch the box. The athlete must avoid excessive forward positioning of the knee over the ankle when performing this exercise.

Figure 4.2 Box touch squat: *(a)* start and *(b)* finish.

Phase III **Overhead Broomstick Squat**

The athlete starts with feet shoulder-width apart and raises the arms overhead, holding a long stick (figure 4.3). The athlete performs a squat down until the thighs are parallel. Once the thighs are parallel to the floor, the athlete, without resting, ascends to the initial starting position. Athletes should keep the arms and the stick behind the head through the entire squat movement.

Figure 4.3 Overhead broomstick squat: *(a)* start and *(b)* finish.

Phase IV Assisted Single-Leg Squat

For this exercise, the athlete stands on a single leg and slowly squats, attempting to squat until the thigh is parallel and then ascends back to the starting position (figure 4.4). Band assistance is often required to aid the athlete in performing the exercise correctly with weight shifted to the heels. This exercise improves unilateral strength and control during squatting movements. The single-leg squat exercise can be used to progress the intensity without the addition of external weights. This initiation of unilateral activities also helps to decrease asymmetries in strength and performance that are indicative of leg dominance in young athletes.

Figure 4.4 Assisted single-leg squat: *(a)* start and *(b)* finish.

(Phase V) Box Drop-Off With Deep Hold

Three versions of this drill are useful, including forward, lateral, and rotational versions. For all three versions, the athlete stands on a box about 8 to 10 inches (20 to 25 cm) tall. In the forward version, the athlete drops down straight off the box, landing with both feet simultaneously in the deep hold position (figure 4.5). For the lateral version, the athlete drops down laterally from the box, landing with both feet simultaneously in the deep hold position (figure 4.6). For the rotational version, the athlete rotates 90 degrees while dropping down from a box, landing with both feet simultaneously in the deep hold position (figure 4.7).

Figure 4.5   Forward box drop-off with deep hold: *(a)* start, *(b)* drop, *(c)* landing, and *(d)* deep hold.

Figure 4.6   Lateral box drop-off with deep hold: *(a)* start, *(b)* drop, *(c)* landing, and *(d)* deep hold.

Figure 4.7   Rotational box drop-off with deep hold: *(a)* start, *(b)* drop and start rotation, *(c)* rotate and prepare for landing, and *(d)* deep hold.

(Phase VI) Squat Jump

The athlete begins in the athletic position with feet flat on the floor pointing straight ahead (figure 4.8). The athlete drops into deep knee, hip, and ankle flexion; touches the floor or as close to the heels as possible; and then takes off into a maximum vertical jump. The athlete jumps straight up vertically and reaches as high as possible. On landing, the athlete immediately returns to the starting position and repeats the initial jump. The athlete repeats the sequence for the allotted time or until technique begins to deteriorate.

Teach the athlete to jump straight up vertically, reaching as high overhead as possible. Encourage the athlete to land on the same spot on the floor and to maintain upright posture when regaining the deep-squat position. Do not allow the athlete to bend forward at the waist to reach the floor. The athlete should keep the eyes up, keep the feet and knees pointed straight ahead, and have the arms to the outside of the legs.

Figure 4.8 Squat jump: *(a)* start, *(b)* flexion, *(c)* jump, and *(d)* landing.

Exercise Variation

Although a potentially limitless number of program components and exercises can be used to enhance muscular strength and power (work/time), instructors need to select exercises that are appropriate for the participants' body size, fitness level, and experience with exercise technique.[1] There is no single mode of exercise that is the most effective or safest method for every young athlete who is starting resistance or plyometric training, but body weight training is particularly beneficial for young beginners. This type of training enables athletes to develop fundamental motor skills that will benefit them as they progress into more intense training programs. Body weight exercises are effective in helping young athletes master technique because there are no external objects to distract or affect the movement technique.

Training exercises that progress to free weights and medicine balls may provide a unique opportunity for young athletes to achieve desirable muscle adaptations that can increase muscle power, improve core stabilization, and enhance balance. Although additional research is needed, the integration of various resistance training methods may optimize training adaptations and reduce the likelihood of plateaus in performance.[33,35]

Although the isolated effects of core training (e.g., pelvis, abdominal, trunk, and hip training) on measures of performance are difficult to evaluate with the existing literature, a recent systematic review indicated that core stability training provides marginal benefits to athletic performance.[36] However, the effects of this core-focused neuromuscular training are likely substantial and complement plyometric training.[37] For example, core strengthening combined with balance training can improve dynamic balance and stability.[38,39] Increased dynamic balance may help provide the athlete with a dynamically stable core that can be better prepared to respond to the high forces generated at the distal body parts during plyometric training for athletic competition.[7,19,40] Young athletes can safely and effectively strengthen their core musculature without the aid of external resistance.[35]

Although many factors (e.g., age, fitness level, exercise choice, progression of training loads) should be considered when designing and progressing core training programs, the importance of strength and conditioning for enhancing core strength should not be overlooked. Insufficient strength, muscular endurance, or stability in the lower back may be associated with current or future lower back pain in adolescents;[41,42] therefore, progressive core strengthening exercises should be integrated into all youth resistance and plyometric training programs as a prophylactic intervention to potentially reduce the prevalence or severity of sport-related injuries to the lower back. The global effects of core training may be best attained through the integration of functional balance and core strengthening into a young athlete's training program.[1]

As with all forms of training, plyometric activities should begin with movements that an athlete can perform with proper technique and should progress only if the desired movement can be performed with adequate dynamic postural control.[1] Plyometric training should be progressed by carefully manipulating the exercise, intensity, volume, and rest interval between sets. The decision on which program variables to manipulate at which time is based on an athlete's performance and training goals, as well as consideration of other activities (e.g., sport practice and competition) that are part of the weekly program.

Core Movement Progression

The following training protocol combines core and plyometric neuromuscular training, and it can be instituted with young athletes to target enhanced performance related to trunk and hip control.[31] Five exercise phases are used for progressions designed to improve the athlete's ability to control the trunk and improve core stability during dynamic activities. The exercises in each phase progressively increase the intensity of the exercise techniques. End-stage progressions incorporate lateral trunk perturbations that force the athlete to decelerate and control the trunk in the coronal plane in order to successfully execute the prescribed technique.

CORE MOVEMENT PROGRESSION: PELVIC BRIDGE

Phase I Pelvic Bridge

The athlete lies supine with the hips and knees flexed and with the feet planted on the ground (figure 4.9). The athlete then extends the hips and elevates the trunk off the ground to execute a pelvic bridge. This position should be held for 3 seconds before starting the next repetition. The exercise is used to establish a movement pattern that involves moving the hips through gluteus recruitment.

Figure 4.9   Pelvic bridge: *(a)* start and *(b)* finish.

Phase II **Pelvic Bridge on BOSU**

The athlete lies supine with the hips and knees flexed and with the feet planted on the flat side of the BOSU (figure 4.10). The athlete then extends the hips and elevates the trunk off the ground to execute a pelvic bridge. This position should be held for 3 seconds before starting the next repetition.

Figure 4.10   Pelvic bridge on BOSU: *(a)* start and *(b)* finish.

Phase III **Single-Leg Pelvic Bridge on BOSU**

The athlete lies supine with the hips flexed. The athlete flexes the knee of one leg, plants the foot of that leg on the flat side of the BOSU, and extends the other leg (figure 4.11). The athlete then extends the hips and elevates the trunk off the ground to execute a pelvic bridge. This position should be held for 3 seconds before starting the next repetition.

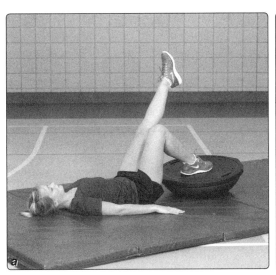

Figure 4.11   Single-leg pelvic bridge on BOSU: *(a)* start and *(b)* finish.

Phase IV   Single-Leg Pelvic Bridge on BOSU With Abduction and Rotation

The athlete lies supine with the hips flexed. The athlete flexes the knee of one leg, plants the foot of that leg on the flat side of the BOSU, and extends the other leg (figure 4.12). The athlete then extends the hips and elevates the trunk off the ground to execute a pelvic bridge. To further challenge strength, balance, and trunk control, the athlete holds the bridge position while abducting and externally rotating the extended leg. The athlete then returns to the bridge position with the leg fully extended upright before returning to the start position. When performing this exercise, the athlete should be reminded to keep the pelvis level and not let it roll when the leg gets out to the side.

Figure 4.12   Single-leg pelvic bridge on BOSU with abduction and rotation: *(a)* start, *(b)* bridge, *(c)* abduction, and *(d)* rotation.

Phase V **Single-Leg Pelvic Bridge on Bench**

The athlete assumes a supine position with the shoulders laid across a weight bench or plyometric box and with the hips flexed. The knee of one leg is flexed, and the foot or heel of that leg is planted on the flat side of a weight bench or chair. The other leg should be fully extended (figure 4.13). The athlete then extends the hips and elevates the trunk away from the ground to execute a pelvic bridge while thrusting the nonstance leg in the air toward the ceiling. This position should be held for 3 seconds before starting the next repetition.

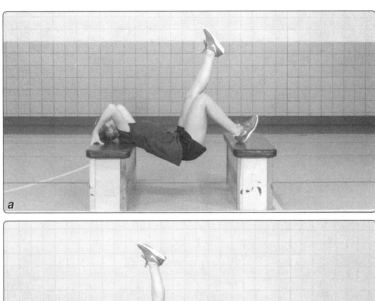

Figure 4.13   Single-leg pelvic bridge on bench: *(a)* start and *(b)* finish.

Strength and Plyometric Movement Progressions

The integration of resistance training with plyometric training may provide additional benefits.[1] A study showed that subjects who performed a combined plyometric and squat training program made greater gains in the vertical jump than subjects who trained with squats or plyometrics alone.[43] In support of these observations, others reported that plyometrics and resistance training had combined effects that were greater than those achieved when each type of training was performed alone.[1,44] Thus, as with core stability training, resistance training exercises likely complement the performance gains that can be achieved with plyometric training.

STRENGTH MOVEMENT PROGRESSION: WALKING LUNGE*

Phase I Front Lunge

The athlete begins in a standing position (figure 4.14) and then steps forward. The step should be exaggerated in length to the point that the front leg is positioned with the knee flexed to 90 degrees and the lower leg is completely vertical (note that the knee should remain over or behind the toe of the supporting foot). The back leg should be as straight as possible and the torso upright. Emphasis should be placed on getting the hips as low as possible while maintaining the described body position. The exercise is completed by driving off the front leg and returning to the original position.

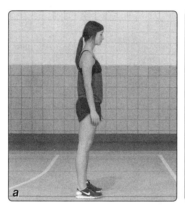

Figure 4.14 Front lunge: *(a)* start and *(b)* lunge.

Phase II Walking Lunge

The athlete performs a lunge, and instead of returning to the start position, the athlete steps through with the back leg and proceeds forward with a lunge on the opposite leg (figure 4.15). Encourage the athlete to step the front foot out far enough so that the knee does not advance beyond the ankle during the exercise. An alternative coaching method is to instruct the athlete to attempt to maintain a constant low center of gravity while progressing through each lunge. This increases the intensity of the exercise and mimics motions that are frequently used in sports.

Figure 4.15 Walking lunge: *(a)* start, *(b)* lunge, *(c)* step through, and *(d)* lunge on the other side.

*Adapted from *Clinics in Sports Medicine* 27(3) G.D. Myer, D.A. Chu, J.L. Brent, and T.E. Hewett, "Trunk and hip control neuromuscular training for the prevention of knee joint injury." 425–448, 2008, with permission from Elsevier.

Phase III Walking Lunge Unilaterally Weighted

The athlete starts in a standing position and holds a weight plate or dumbbell on one side (figure 4.16). The athlete performs a walking lunge, stepping with the leg opposite the arm with the weight, and continues through the rest of the walking lunge while holding the plate in the same hand. Encourage the athlete to lunge the front foot far enough out so that the knee does not advance beyond the ankle during the exercise. This exercise is then repeated with the weight plate or dumbbell in the opposite hand.

Figure 4.16 Walking lunge unilaterally weighted: *(a)* start, *(b)* lunge, *(c)* step through, and *(d)* lunge on the other side.

Phase IV Walking Lunge With Weight Crossover

The athlete starts in a standing position and holds a weight with both hands in front of the chest (figure 4.17). The athlete performs a walking lunge while holding the weight. On each lunge, the athlete twists the torso so the weight is to the side of the body—on the same side as the leg that is in front. During the steps, the athlete's torso should face forward, and the weight should be to the front. Encourage the athlete to lunge the front foot far enough out so that the knee does not advance beyond the ankle during the exercise.

Figure 4.17 Walking lunge with weight crossover: *(a)* start, *(b)* lunge with torso twisting, *(c)* step through, and *(d)* lunge with torso twisting to the other side.

Phase V Walking Lunge With Unilateral Shoulder Press

The athlete starts in a standing position, holding a dumbbell at head height. The shoulder and elbow on that arm should be positioned close to right angles. The athlete performs a lunge (figure 4.18). The athlete should maintain the position of the dumbbell through the step before and during the lunge. Then, instead of going directly into the next lunge, the athlete steps the back leg forward to bring the feet together and presses the dumbbell overhead. The athlete then continues by stepping forward with the other leg, lunging, stepping out of the lunge, stepping the legs together, and completing another shoulder press. The weight should move up and down with the same tempo and direction (upward or downward) as the lunge. Encourage the athlete to lunge the front foot far enough out so that the knee does not advance beyond the ankle during the exercise.

Figure 4.18 Walking lunge with unilateral shoulder press: *(a)* lunge, *(b)* step through, *(c)* shoulder press, and *(d)* lunge on other leg.

PLYOMETRIC MOVEMENT PROGRESSION: TUCK JUMP

Phase I   Single Tuck Jump With Soft Landing

The athlete starts with feet shoulder-width apart (figure 4.19). The athlete initiates a vertical jump with a slight crouch downward while extending the arms behind the body. The athlete then swings the arms forward while simultaneously jumping straight up and pulls the knees up as high as possible. At the highest point of the jump, the athlete should be positioned in the air with the thighs parallel to the ground. The athlete should land softly, using a toe to midfoot rocker landing. The athlete should not continue this jump if he or she cannot control the high landing force or cannot keep the knees aligned during landing. If the athlete is unable to raise the knees to the proper height, the athlete may try grasping the knees and then bringing the thighs to horizontal.

Figure 4.19   Single tuck jump with soft landing: *(a)* start, *(b)* crouch, *(c)* tuck, and *(d)* landing.

Phase II   Double Tuck Jump

This exercise is similar to the single tuck jump but with an additional jump performed immediately after the first jump (figure 4.20). The athlete should focus on maintaining good form and minimizing time on the ground between jumps.

Figure 4.20   Double tuck jump: *(a)* first tuck jump, *(b)* landing, *(c)* second tuck jump, and *(d)* second landing.

Phase III   Repeated Tuck Jump

The athlete starts in the athletic position with feet shoulder-width apart. The athlete initiates a vertical jump with a slight crouch downward while extending the arms behind (figure 4.21). The athlete then swings the arms forward while simultaneously jumping straight up and pulling the knees up as high as possible. At the highest point of the jump, the athlete should be positioned in the air with the thighs parallel to the ground. After landing, the athlete should immediately begin the next tuck jump. Initially, the athlete can be given a goal of four to six repeated jumps with perfect technique. As the athlete masters the movement, the number of repetitions can be increased.

Figure 4.21   Repeated tuck jump: *(a)* crouch, *(b)* tuck, *(c)* landing, and *(d)* second tuck.

Phase IV Side-to-Side Barrier Tuck Jump

The athlete starts in the athletic position with feet shoulder-width apart, positioned to the side of a barrier or line. The athlete initiates a vertical jump over the barrier or line with a slight crouch downward while extending the arms behind the body. The athlete then swings the arms forward while simultaneously jumping up and pulling the knees up as high as possible and over the barrier or line (figure 4.22). At the highest point of the jump, the athlete should be positioned in the air with the thighs parallel to the ground. When landing, the athlete should immediately begin the next tuck jump back to the other side of the barrier or line.

Figure 4.22   Side-to-side barrier tuck jump: *(a)* tuck jump over line, *(b)* landing on one side, *(c)* tuck jump back over line, and *(d)* landing on other side.

Phase V Side-to-Side Barrier Tuck Jump With Reaction

The athlete starts in the athletic position with feet shoulder-width apart, positioned next to a barrier or line. The athlete initiates a vertical jump with a slight crouch downward while extending the arms behind the body (figure 4.23). The athlete then swings the arms forward while simultaneously jumping straight up and pulling the knees up as high as possible. At the highest point of the jump, the athlete should be positioned in the air with the thighs parallel to the ground. When landing, the athlete should immediately begin the next tuck jump. When prompted, the athlete initiates a tuck jump to the other side of the barrier or line without breaking rhythm. The athlete remains on this side of the barrier or line, repeating tuck jumps, until prompted to again move to the other side of the barrier or line.

Figure 4.23 Side-to-side barrier tuck jump with reaction: *(a)* tuck jump to side as prompted, *(b)* landing, *(c)* tuck jump on same side, *(d)* landing.

Stability and Agility Movement Progressions

A growing body of evidence indicates that plyometric exercises may be safely initiated if athletes begin with less intense exercises and learn how to perform functional movement patterns with proper form.[1] Of note, youth can benefit from technique training and feedback during plyometric exercises even without prior participation in a resistance training program provided the exercises are consistent with individual abilities and training experience.

The step progression that follows can be used as a movement pattern check before the initiation of lower-extremity plyometric exercises. Once young athletes have mastered stability progressions, agility and movement progressions can be integrated into their programs.[1]

STABILITY MOVEMENT PROGRESSION: SINGLE-LEG MOVEMENT PATTERNS*

Phase I Step and Hold

The athlete starts in the standing position with feet together. The athlete begins the movement by taking a quick step forward (figure 4.24) and continues by balancing in a deep hold position on the leg stepped onto.

Figure 4.24 Step and hold: *(a)* beginning of step, *(b)* step, and *(c)* hold.

*Adapted from *Clinics in Sports Medicine* 27(3) G.D. Myer, D.A. Chu, J.L. Brent, and T.E. Hewett, "Trunk and hip control neuromuscular training for the prevention of knee joint injury." 425–448, 2008, with permission from Elsevier.

Phase II Jump and Hold

The athlete begins this exercise in the athletic position (figure 4.25). The athlete jumps forward, landing and balancing on one leg in a deep hold position.

Figure 4.25 Jump and hold: *(a)* start, *(b)* jump, and *(c)* hold.

Phase III Hop and Hold

The athlete starts in a balanced position on one foot (figure 4.26). Then the athlete hops forward, landing on one leg and balancing in a deep hold position.

Figure 4.26 Hop and hold: *(a)* start, *(b)* hop, and *(c)* hold.

Phase IV Hop, Hop, and Hold

The athlete starts in the standing position with feet together. The athlete quickly hops forward twice; after the second hop, the athlete lands and balances on one leg in a deep hold position (figure 4.27).

Figure 4.27 Hop, hop, and hold: *(a)* second hop, *(b)* landing on one leg, *(c)* hold.

Phase V Crossover Hop, Hop, Hop, and Hold

The athlete starts in a balanced position on a single foot. The athlete hops forward quickly three times while alternating legs (figure 4.28); after the third hop, the athlete lands and balances on one leg in a deep hold position.

Figure 4.28 Crossover hop, hop, hop, and hold: *(a)* third hop, *(b)* preparing to land, *(c)* landing, *(d)* hold.

AGILITY MOVEMENT PROGRESSION: LATERAL AGILITY

Phase I **Lateral Hop, Hop, and Hold Opposite Leg With Barriers**

The athlete starts in a balanced position on one foot; three barriers are located to the side of the leg that is off the ground (figure 4.29). The athlete hops laterally over each barrier and then hops to the other foot in a deep hold position and maintains this position for 3 seconds. The athlete repeats the same movement in the opposite direction on the same leg. The maneuver is performed in both directions on both legs.

Figure 4.29 Lateral hop, hop, and hold opposite leg with barriers: *(a)* start, *(b)* hop and landing, *(c)* hop and landing, and *(d)* hop to other leg and hold.

Phase II Lateral Hop, Hop, and Hold Opposite Leg With Four Barriers

The athlete starts in a balanced position on one foot; four barriers are located to the side of the leg that is off the ground. The athlete hops laterally over each of the first two barriers and takes the final two barriers with one hop, landing on the other leg and holding position. The hold position should be held stable for 3 seconds. The same movement is repeated back in the opposite direction with the same leg. The maneuver is performed in both directions on both legs.

Phase III Dynamic Lateral Hopping With Four Barriers

The athlete starts in a balanced position on one foot; four barriers are located to the side of the leg that is off the ground. The athlete hops laterally over each of the first two barriers and takes the final two barriers with a single jump to the other leg. As soon as that foot contacts the ground, the athlete immediately reverses direction to repeat the movement, hopping individually over the first two barriers (landing on the opposite leg from the first pass) and over the final two with a single jump to the original starting support foot. The maneuver is performed on both legs.

Phase IV Lateral Hop, 90-Degree Hop, and Hold With Barriers

The athlete starts in a balanced position on one foot; barriers are located to the side of the leg that is off the ground (figure 4.30). The athlete hops laterally over the first barrier, then immediately hops into a maximum-effort 90-degree hop over the second barrier and holds on both feet. The hold position should be held stable for 3 seconds. The maneuver is performed in both directions on both legs.

Figure 4.30 Lateral hop, 90-degree hop, and hold with barriers: *(a)* starting position, *(b)* first hop, *(c)* hop with 90-degree turn, and *(d)* hold.

Phase V Lateral Hop, Hop 90 Degrees Opposite to Sprint With Barriers

The athlete starts in a balanced position on one foot; two barriers are located to the side of the leg that is off the ground. The athlete faces forward and hops laterally over the first two barriers and immediately hops into a maximum-effort 90-degree hop and sprint (e.g., 5-10 yards) maneuver. The maneuver is performed on both legs.

Progressive Exercises

Progressive exercises are a critical component of plyometric training protocols.[45] Five or more progressive exercise phases can be used to facilitate progressions designed to improve the athletes' ability to master fundamental movements while enhancing core stability. End-stage progressions can incorporate unexpected disruptions (e.g., ball toss or push) that require the athlete to react, decelerate, and control the trunk in order to successfully execute the prescribed technique.[1]

Exercises selected for the initial phases of the presented progressions have been adapted from previous literature that has reported reductions in injury risk or risk factors.[46,47,48,49] The elimination of all risk of sport-related injuries during maximized performance is an unrealistic goal; however, evidence indicates that multifaceted plyometric programs that include progressive resistance, plyometric, and speed training are not only safe activities for young athletes, but may also reduce injuries and enhance performance during sport practice and competition.[50,51,52,53] Including progressive resistance, plyometric, and speed training in both a preseason and in-season program may provide optimal benefits related to injury prevention.[51,52]

The importance of proper exercise technique must be emphasized and reinforced throughout plyometric training periods. Most young athletes who begin this type of program will have little if any prior exposure to resistance training techniques.[1] Therefore, youth should be encouraged to progress gradually, embrace self-improvement, and feel good about their ability to perform advanced movements with proper technique. The use of workout logs can help athletes monitor progress, remember coaching cues, and focus their efforts on their own goals.[1]

Volume and Recovery Guidelines

When implementing plyometric training to enhance performance in youth, the suggested approach is to integrate resistance, plyometric, and speed training into a progressive conditioning program in which the volume and intensity of training periodically change throughout the year. The systematic structuring of program variables—along with individual effort, qualified instruction, and adequate recovery—will determine the outcomes associated with the resistance, power, and speed training.

In general, the volume (i.e., repetitions and sets) of a particular plyometric activity is increased first to ensure that the athlete has appropriate neuromuscular control before increasing the intensity or frequency of training. Young athletes should be given adequate time to recover between sets in order to maintain a high level of performance; however, studies have shown that recommendations regarding rest intervals for adults may not be consistent with the needs and abilities of children and adolescents because of differences related to growth and maturation in response to physical exertion.[54,55] Thus, a shorter rest interval between sets (about 1 to 2 minutes) may suffice for children and adolescents when performing this type of training.[1]

The importance of adequate recovery between training sessions is sometimes overlooked in youth conditioning programs; these programs often seem to be primarily focused on rest between sets or on the allotted time for protocol completion. For plyometric training programs, instructors should remember that training athletes of any age involves balancing the demands of training with the need for recovery, which are both required for adaptation. This is particularly important for youth who play multiple sports and engage in additional conditioning outside of their sport practices.[1]

The total work performed within an exercise session (total sets and repetitions) is the volume of exercise. Too often, nonplyometric programs base volume solely on one particular variable or component of training and do not take into account the cumulative workload from competition, practice, and other conditioning efforts.[1] For example, guidelines for volume prescription related to a single plyometric training bout based on experience level suggest that adult athletes with novice experience should employ a training volume with 80 to 100 foot contacts per session while adult athletes with more experience can use 120 to 140 foot contacts per session.[56] Other guidelines for trained adult athletes suggest that up to 400 contacts is considered appropriate if the exercise is low intensity and that a maximum of 200 contacts is appropriate if the exercise is high-intensity exercise.[57] These volume recommendations are difficult to use because they consider only an isolated variable, not to mention ignoring the influence of other confounding variables such as sport training, sport competition, and recreational free play.[1] The prevalence of adult-only recommendations and the need to consider multiple variables make it difficult to determine proper volume guidelines for youth.

Thus, other training factors, most notably technical performance and fatigue response, need to be considered along with experience level and intensity of exercise when determining a young athlete's training volume. In addition, activities that occur outside of the plyometric training programs (e.g., exercises performed with other fitness trainers or sport coaches) should be considered when evaluating a young athlete's overall training exposure. In short, young athletes are not miniature adults, and strength and conditioning exercises need to be carefully prescribed in order to avoid overtraining and injury.[32,33,35,58]

The prescribed exercises, sets, and repetitions for a plyometric exercise program should serve as an attainable goal for the athlete, but these variables should also be modified as needed. The initial volume should be low so that the athlete can learn how to perform the exercise with proper technique. Volume (or resistance, when applicable) should be increased after the athlete can properly perform the exercise at the prescribed volume and intensity.[1] The professional who supervises the athletes should be skilled in recognizing proper technique for a given exercise and should provide constructive feedback when appropriate. Once the athlete becomes proficient with all exercises within a progression phase, he can advance to the next successive phase.[1]

Also, young athletes should participate periodically in less intense training exercise (LITE) in order to reinforce learning of specific movement patterns.[59] Because recovery is an integral part of all training programs, high-intensity or high-volume training sessions should be balanced with LITE sessions as well as other recovery strategies to help maximize training adaptations while minimizing the risk of overtraining.[59,60]

Although children and adolescents should be encouraged to engage in 60 minutes or more of physical activity daily,[61] high-intensity training should be performed only two or three times per week on nonconsecutive days; this will allow time for recovery between training sessions.[3] Some young athletes may participate in strength and conditioning activities more than three days per week; however, factors such as the training volume, training intensity, exercise selection, and nutritional intake should be considered, because these factors may influence an athlete's ability to recover from and adapt to the training program.

As training programs become more advanced, and sessions become more frequent, the importance of reinforcing proper exercise technique should not be overlooked.[1] Moreover, youth coaches should be aware of the symptoms of overtraining (e.g., muscle soreness that lingers for several days, decreases in performance, and lack of desire to train) and should realize that some children with relatively immature musculoskeletal systems may not be able to tolerate the same amount of exercise that most of their teammates can tolerate. Of potential relevance, recent data indicate that participation in organized sport activities does not inevitably ensure at least 60 minutes of moderate to vigorous physical activity during practice sessions.[62,63] Plyometric training may also provide coaches with a supplemental mechanism to ensure that youth gain the health effects of an active lifestyle.[1]

◀ SUMMARY ▶

- For youth, comprehensive plyometric training programs that integrate all fitness components can enhance athletic performance, improve movement biomechanics, and reduce the risk of sport-related injury.

- Plyometric training programs for youth may be most beneficial if qualified professionals first focus on basic training guidelines, the proper use of equipment, and safe training procedures. At the same time, the professionals should be encouraging the young athletes to embrace self-improvement and positive awareness about their ability to perform plyometric training activities.

- Once fundamental skills and abilities are developed, young athletes can begin to participate in resistance and plyometric training programs using the appropriate intensity and volume of training to optimize training adaptations.

- To design appropriate training for young athletes, coaches and instructors must have an understanding of the physical and psychosocial uniqueness of childhood and adolescence. Plyometric training that is sensibly progressed over time and consistent with individual needs, goals, and abilities can be part of a safe and health-oriented approach to lifelong physical activity.

Plyometric and Neuromuscular Training for Female Athletes

The myth that females must train differently than males still exists in some circles. But there is no reason why female athletes cannot perform plyometrics with the same degree of skill, proficiency, and intensity as males. To do so, however, females must establish a similar strength base. Female athletes who have not engaged in a proper strength training program may not possess the requisite entry-level abilities.

In addition, female athletes may be susceptible to developing neuromuscular deficits that increase their risk of ACL injury. The good news is that plyometric training has been shown to be an effective tool in correcting neuromuscular deficits and preventing injuries in female athletes.[1,2,3] The coach and the athlete are responsible for upgrading the athlete's strength development before the athlete attempts plyometric training.

In this chapter, we review previously published reports that outline a novel theory regarding the mechanisms related to increased risk of ACL injury in female athletes.[4,5] We also synthesize the prior descriptions of the underlying mechanisms that lead to increased risk for injury; in addition, we review techniques for plyometric and supporting resistance training that can be used to reduce the risk of injury while enhancing performance in athletes.[4,5]

INJURY RISKS

Despite the many scientific advances in the treatment of ACL injury, the rate of occurrence for osteoarthritis (OA) is 10 times greater for individuals who have had an ACL injury,[6] regardless of the treatment strategy (nonsurgical management versus surgical treatment).[7] ACL injury during youth can cause personal and professional impairment for athletes, along with a high economic cost for both athletes and institutions.[8] Aside from financial costs and almost certain OA, young athletes must also consider the potential loss of entire seasons of sport participation, loss of scholarship funding, lowered academic performance,[9] and long-term disability.[10] Therefore, the prevention of ACL injury is a major concern in sports medicine.[11]

Most ACL tears occur in the absence of player-to-player (body-to-body) contact.[8] The most common playing scenarios leading to a noncontact ACL injury include performing change-of-direction or cutting maneuvers combined with deceleration, landing from a jump in or near full extension, and pivoting with the knee near full extension and a planted foot.[8,12] The most common body position during injury in

Selected text and all tables on pages 67-72 adapted from *Clinics in Sports Medicine* 27(3), G.D. Myer, D.A. Chu, J.L. Brent, and T.E. Hewett, "Trunk and hip control neuromuscular training for the prevention of knee joint injury," 425-448, 2008, with permission from Elsevier.

young athletes occurs during a deceleration task—this position involves high-knee internal extension torque (with or without a visual perturbation) combined with dynamic valgus (knock-knee position), the body weight shifted over to the injured leg, and a flat foot on the playing surface.[8,12]

Anatomical Risk Factors

There is no definitive evidence that any anatomical risk factors are directly correlated with an increased rate of ACL injury with respect to age and gender.[8,12] Moreover, because anatomy is difficult to modify, the potential for injury prevention based on anatomical factors is relatively small. However, some anatomical considerations should be taken into account in order to understand the biomechanics that may lead to an ACL tear.

Neuromuscular Risk Factors

The known linkage between lower-limb biomechanics and injury risk led to the development of neuromuscular and plyometric training programs designed to prevent injury.[13,14,15,16,17,18,19] The most effective training protocols for injury prevention have primarily used plyometric exercises to bring about positive biomechanical adaptations that reduce the risk of injury.[2,15,16,20] The effectiveness of these programs appears to be most evident when they are implemented with younger athletes and maintained throughout adolescence.[21] Most important, current research indicates that plyometric training can be useful in identifying and targeting deficits that increase the risk of injury and hamper performance.[22] Young female athletes, who may not be exposed to plyometric and technique training until their adult years, appear to be the most responsive to neuromuscular and plyometric training for improving performance and reducing deficit-related injury risk.[19]

BIOMECHANICS RELATED TO INCREASED RISK OF ACL INJURY SPECIFIC TO FEMALE ATHLETES

Reduced neuromuscular control of the lower extremity during sport movements causes excessive out-of-plane (side-to-side and rotation) knee loads during plyometric activities; this increases the risk of ACL injury in female athletes.[14] Specifically, young female athletes who land in a knock-knee position during jump-landing tasks are at high risk for ACL injury.[14] The tendency to land in a knock-knee position during plyometric activities and sport performance is most common in females and is highly related to their risk of knee injury.[23,24,25,26,27,28,29,30,31,32,33,34,35]

When implementing plyometric training programs specifically targeted to females, coaches or instructors need to understand the biomechanics that put these athletes at risk. They must also understand the potential contributors to these abnormal landing techniques so that targeted technique training can be successful.[5]

GROWTH AND CORE RISK MECHANISMS

Although knee injuries can occur in the preadolescent athlete, differences among boys are evident in children before their growth spurt.[36,37,38] In contrast, during maturation, a young girl's risk of knee injury peaks at about age 16;[39] furthermore, after their growth spurt, teenage girls have higher rates of knee sprains than males do, and without the implementation of plyometric training, this unfortunate trend continues into maturity.[40]

When adolescents are growing the fastest, the tibia and femur grow at relatively the same rates in both sexes.[41] This growth of the two longest levers (tibia and femur) in the human body quickly initiates increases in overall body height (increased height of the center of mass), making the ability to control the trunk during plyometric activities more difficult.[5] Compounding this difficulty, a growing athlete is subject to rapid increases in weight; this weight gain, in combination with the growth of long bones at the knee, initiates greater forces on the knee joints. These forces at the knee are much less manageable. Young girls who do not adapt naturally or who are not trained with plyometric training will not have adequate ability to balance and dampen during high-velocity landing maneuvers that put them at increased risk of injury.[28,42,43] The prevailing theory is that the onset of maturational changes that influence increased demand on the neuromuscular control system—in the absence of increases in strength and recruitment of the musculature at the hip gained from proper plyometric training—will lead to reduced core stability or control of trunk motion during plyometric tasks.[44] This maturational reduction in relative core stability underlies the tendency to demonstrate biomechanics with a high injury risk, especially knock-kneed landings.[5]

As previously reported, there is a strong linkage between an athlete's core stability, her hip strength and power, and her ability to modulate high loads during plyometric activities.[5] Plyometric training during maturation may help young females learn to pre-activate in order to counterbalance trunk motion with their trunk and hip stabilizers and ultimately regulate lower-extremity postures that are related to injury.[5,45,46,47] If the athlete doesn't have the ability to adequately activate the trunk and hip stabilizers, increased lateral trunk positions will incite high forces that push the knees together.[48] Landing and jumping with a knock-knee technique will reduce performance during plyometric training and during sport activity. A female athlete with decreased core stability and muscular synergism of the trunk and hip stabilizers will further succumb to reduced sport performance during power activities and will increase the risk of injury.[5,49,50]

TARGETED NEUROMUSCULAR TRAINING FOR THE TRUNK

The protocol presented in tables 5.1 through 5.5 provides a neuromuscular training regimen that can be used with female athletes in order to target deficits in trunk and hip control that reduce performance and increase injury risk.[4] Five exercise progressions are presented that provide the plyometric and strength work that will improve the athletes' ability to control their trunk during plyometrics and will help them develop the core stability needed to achieve success in sport.[4] The exercises in each table will progressively increase the intensity of the exercise techniques. End-stage progressions incorporate lateral trunk perturbations that force the athlete to decelerate and to control the trunk in the lateral planes in order to successfully execute the prescribed technique. The specified sets and repetitions are only soft guidelines that lead to an attainable goal for the athlete. The progressions should be considered an important additive to plyometric training programs for young females. These progressions will help athletes develop the hip and trunk control needed for success in more advanced plyometric training protocols.

Table 5.1 Progression 1

Exercise	Time	Reps	Sets	
Lateral jump and hold		8		
Step and hold		8	R	L
BOSU (round) superman		10		
BOSU (round) double-knee hold	20 sec			
Single-leg lateral Airex hop and hold		4	R	L
Single tuck jump with soft landing		10		
Front lunge		10	R	L
Lunge jump	10 sec		R	L
Pelvic bridge on BOSU		10		
Single-leg 90-degree hop and hold		8	R	L
BOSU (round) lateral crunch		10	R	L
Box double crunch		15		
Swiss ball back hyperextension		15		

Table 5.2 Progression 2

Exercise	Time	Reps	Sets	
Lateral jump	10 sec			
Jump with single-leg hold		8	R	L
BOSU (round) toe touch swimmers		10	R	L
BOSU (round) single-knee hold	20 sec		R	L
Single-leg lateral BOSU (round) hop and hold		8	R	L
Double tuck jump		6		
Walking lunge		10		
Scissor jump	10 sec			
Single-leg pelvic bridge on BOSU		10	R	L
Single-leg 90-degree Airex hop and hold		8	R	L
Box lateral crunch		10	R	L
Box swivel double crunch		15	R	L
Swiss ball back hyperextension with ball reach		15		

Table 5.3   Progression 3

Exercise	Time	Reps	Sets	
Lateral hop and hold		8	R	L
Hop and hold		8	R	L
Prone bridge (elbows and knees) with hip extension and opposite-shoulder flexion		10		
Swiss ball bilateral kneel	20 sec			
Single-leg lateral BOSU (round) hop and hold with ball catch		4	R	L
Repeated tuck jump	10 sec			
Walking lunge unilaterally weighted		10	R	L
Lunge jump unilaterally weighted	10 sec		R	L
BOSU (flat) single-leg pelvic bridge with ball hold		10	R	L
Single-leg 90-degree Airex hop and hold with reaction and ball catch		6	R	L
BOSU (round) lateral crunch with ball catch		8	R	L
BOSU (round) swivel ball touch (feet up)		15		
Swiss ball hyperextension with back fly		15		

Table 5.4 Progression 4

Exercise	Time	Reps	Sets	
Lateral hop	10 sec		R	L
Hop, hop, and hold		8	R	L
Prone bridge (elbows and toes) hip extension		10	R	L
Swiss ball bilateral kneel with partner perturbations	20 sec			
Single-leg four-way BOSU (round) hop and hold		3 cycles	R	L
Side-to-side barrier tuck jump	10 sec			
Walking lunge with weight plate crossover		10	R	L
Scissor jump unilaterally weighted	10 sec		R	L
Supine Swiss ball hamstring curl		10		
Single-leg 180-degree Airex hop and hold		8	R	L
Swiss ball lateral crunch		15	R	L
BOSU (round) double crunch		15		
Swiss ball hyperextension with ball reach (lateral)		15	R	L

Table 5.5 Progression 5

Exercise	Time	Reps	Sets	
X-hop		6 cycles	R	L
Crossover hop, hop, hop, and hold		8	R	L
Prone bridge (elbows and toes) with hip extension and opposite-shoulder flexion		10	R	L
Swiss ball bilateral kneel with lateral ball catch	20 sec			
Single-leg four-way BOSU (round) hop and hold with ball catch		3 cycles	R	L
Side-to-side barrier tuck jump with reaction	10 sec			
Walking lunge with unilateral shoulder press		10	R	L
Scissor jump with ball swivel	10 sec		R	L
Swivel Russian hamstring curl		10		
Single-leg 180-degree Airex hop and hold with reaction and ball catch		8	R	L
Swiss ball lateral crunch with ball catch		8	R	L
BOSU (round) swivel double crunch		15	R	L
Swiss ball hyperextension with lateral ball catch		15		

All of the exercises selected for the trunk-focused protocol are adapted from previous epidemiological or interventional investigations that have reported reductions in ACL injury risk or risk factors.[1,4,51,52,53] The protocol progressions were also developed from previous biomechanical investigations that reported reductions in knee abduction load in female athletes who followed these training protocols.[15,17,18,19] The novelty to this training approach is that the protocol will incorporate exercises that perturb the trunk, helping female athletes improve control of the trunk, improve core stability, and decrease the mechanisms that induce the knock-kneed landing that puts athletes at risk for injury.[4] Pilot studies that used the proposed trunk protocol indicate that female athletes can gain increased standing hip recruitment to help modulate the detrimental effects of a weak core musculature.[54] As noted, this program should be considered an important supplement to plyometric training programs for growing female athletes.[4]

◖ SUMMARY ◗

- Dynamic neuromuscular and plyometric training appears to reduce ACL injuries in adolescent and mature female athletes.

- A preemptive approach that institutes early interventional training may also reduce the peak rate of ACL injuries that occurs near age 16 in young girls.

- Specifically, neuromuscular training that focuses on trunk control instituted just before pubertal development may provide the most effective interventional approach and may alleviate high-risk biomechanics in female athletes.

Plyometric Training for Injury Rehabilitation

Given that healthy limbs often have difficulty sustaining the impact placed on the body during practice and competition, injured athletes returning to activity need to have some means of ensuring a safe and complete return. Physical therapists and other rehabilitation specialists are beginning to recognize the importance of eccentric strength in rehabilitating musculoskeletal injuries. Research has shown that eccentric strength development is crucial to the return of injured athletes to their sports.

Eccentric strength is a precursor to success in plyometrics. Before an injured athlete can return to plyometric training in the end stages of his rehabilitation, the athlete must complete a period of training that focuses on the development of stability and eccentric strength in the lower extremities. Resistance training that isolates a single joint (open kinetic chain activities) and relegates it to performing single-plane movements will not rehabilitate the athlete sufficiently to enable him to return to activity. Simply put, you do not play the game sitting in a chair.

Closed kinetic chain activities—which require the athlete to use the lower extremities in functional multiplanar movement patterns involving the foot, ankle, knee, and hip—have risen to the top of the list of effective rehabilitation exercises. Plyometric training also falls into the realm of closed kinetic chain activities. Ultimately, for rehabilitation, the goals of the functional and plyometric training are to strengthen major muscle groups through the complete range of motion and to provide adequate muscular power so the athlete can progress to more advanced plyometric components.[1]

Plyometric drills and skill activities can serve as functional tests to determine an injured athlete's readiness for return to play. The environment of competition places tremendous mental and physical stress on participants, and if an athlete is not sure of his physical ability, this puts him at risk of a disastrous performance—or worse, reinjury.

GUIDELINES FOR REHABILITATION

An athlete who is unable to tolerate plyometric activities during rehabilitation will be even less able to tolerate a return to sport participation. In addition, recent injury prevention programs focused on the lower extremities often include plyometric exercise; these programs provide evidence that plyometric training not only supports

Selected text on pages 73-77 adapted, by permission, from T.L. Chmielewski, G.D. Myer, D. Kauffman, and S.M. Tillman, 2006, "Plyometric exercise in the rehabilitation of athletes: Physiological responses and clinical application," *Journal of Orthopaedic & Sports Physical Therapy* 36(5): 308-319. © Orthopaedic Section and the Sports Physical Therapy Section of the American Physical Therapy Association.

progression back to sport but also provides prophylactic effects that help prevent injury[2,3,4,5,6,7] and likely reduce the chances of reinjury. Nevertheless, in rehabilitation settings, plyometric exercise should be used cautiously to avert adverse reactions, such as increased pain or joint swelling, which will ultimately slow the athlete's progression back to sport.

Guidelines for plyometric training variables and the criteria for initiating plyometric exercise have been developed for uninjured athletes, who primarily perform high-intensity plyometric exercise; however, these guidelines do not address training variables specific to injured athletes. These variables are often the most important consideration in the rehabilitation setting. Therefore, rehabilitation specialists must consider and carefully manipulate all relevant training variables—including frequency, intensity, volume, recovery, and progression—when implementing plyometric exercise as part of a rehabilitation program. (See chapter 8 for more information on frequency, volume, and recovery outside of the rehabilitation setting.) They should also include metabolic variables, such as tissue healing time, tissue response (e.g., swelling and pain), and learning of technical performance skills. Each of these variables is examined further in the following sections. By judiciously implementing all of these variables, rehabilitation specialists will help patients avoid the delayed-onset muscle soreness that is often associated with high-intensity eccentric exercise or novel exercise.[2,8]

Frequency

The frequency of exercise is how often an exercise is performed within a training cycle. High-intensity plyometric exercises are often incorporated on a twice-per-week training cycle for a healthy population;[9] this allows 48 to 72 hours of rest for full recovery between plyometric sessions.[2,10] When initiating end-stage rehabilitation plyometrics, athletes may begin with a single workout of low-intensity exercises on a weekly basis to ensure proper learning and recovery between bouts. Because so much learning occurs during this phase, athletes need time to absorb information and prepare themselves between workouts. The frequency curve should experience a sharp rise as long as parameters such as pain, swelling, and ability to execute remain under control. Two times per week is a commonly used frequency in rehabilitation. Because plyometric exercise is often initiated at a low intensity in rehabilitation, athletes may tolerate more frequent bouts (up to three times per week) without joint irritation or significant muscle soreness.[2]

Intensity

Intensity is the effort required to perform the exercise and is associated with loading force.[2] Anything that increases the stretch load (kinetic energy) will increase the intensity of the plyometric activity (e.g., increasing the mass of a medicine ball or increasing drop height).[11] Intensity and frequency are often inversely proportional in training programs. As the intensity of the plyometric exercise increases from low intensity to high intensity, the frequency typically decreases to allow for proper recovery between bouts.[2]

The appropriate intensity for plyometric exercise is primarily associated with the ability of the healing tissue to handle external loads and the ability of the athlete in rehabilitation to perform an activity with the desired technical performance. Similar to other forms of training (e.g., resistance training and plyometrics for uninjured athletes), the intensity of plyometric exercise used in rehabilitation should follow a gradual progression from low- to high-intensity activities in order to help the athlete avoid adverse responses.[2]

A technique used by rehabilitation specialists to decrease the intensity of a lower-extremity plyometric exercise is to initiate it on equipment that unloads the body weight. The intensity can then be progressed for this plyometric movement by having the athlete perform full body weight exercise against gravity. Progressing to increased heights for jumps or box drops or adding distance for jumps and bounding—with the ultimate goal of progressing to single-extremity exercise—can help resolve deficits during rehabilitation of a unilateral injury.

In addition, athletes in rehabilitation can help reduce impact loads on the joints by performing plyometric activities on gymnastics mats. Keep in mind that this may cause a prolonged amortization phase, reducing the overall effect of plyometric training; thus, athletes in rehabilitation eventually need to progress to more rigid and sport-specific surfaces that promote the adaptations and improved quality of movement.[2]

Upper-extremity plyometric exercise can also be initiated at a lower intensity level by reducing the effects of gravity (e.g., using wall push-ups instead of floor push-ups) or by using lighter (1- to 2-pound) medicine balls.[2] Likewise, intensity of upper-extremity plyometric exercises can be increased by using heavier resistance. This can be done by moving the body or ball (up to 30 pounds) through greater distances, by increasing the speed of movement, or by progressing from double-arm to single-arm activities.[2]

Volume

The most important variable to control during rehabilitation is volume. The volume of exercise is most often defined by the number of contacts made, either with the ground or some object (e.g., a ball). These recommendations are usually based solely on one particular variable.[2] Rehabilitation specialists must be sure to consider other variables, including the exercise intensity, the athlete's technical performance of the plyometric movement, the athlete's response to the activity, and the athlete's experience level.[2] An example would be to tailor rehab programs for the shoulder to the number of anticipated contacts an athlete might have during his competition (i.e., a pitcher might be expected to throw 100 to 120 pitches in nine innings). Eventually, the volume should approximate that as a goal.

Progression of volume should occur only when the athlete has perfected the technique and can maintain it through the current volume—and when the athlete experiences no adverse joint responses. In general, athletes must demonstrate tolerance of a low-intensity and high-volume activity before progressing to a higher-intensity and low-volume activity.[9] In addition, any plyometric training occurring outside the clinical setting not under the direction of the rehabilitation specialist (e.g., drills performed with a team athletic trainer) should be considered, and the volume should be adjusted accordingly. Throughout the transition from injury recovery to full sport integration, the athlete, coaches, and trainers should be in constant communication with clinicians (physicians, physical therapists, and athletic trainers) to ensure that the progression of exercises is appropriate.

Recovery

Recovery is defined as the rest time between repetitions, sets, and sessions of plyometric exercise. The work-to-rest ratio for a plyometric exercise depends on the intensity of the exercise and the energy system used. In high-intensity plyometric exercise, a work-to-rest ratio of 1:5 to 1:10 is recommended to ensure that the athlete gets enough rest for proper execution of the exercise.[10] For example, when performing a drop vertical jump at maximum effort, athletes may rest for 5 to 10 seconds between repetitions. In rehabilitation, the intensity of plyometric exercises is typically lower, and exercises are done in quick succession with smaller work-to-rest ratios (e.g., 1:1 or 1:2).[12] An example of this would be line jumps performed for 10 seconds followed by 10 to 20 seconds of rest.[2]

In general, 48 to 72 hours of rest is ideal recovery between plyometric training sessions.[10] Recovery time between sessions is also dependent on the presence of delayed-onset muscle soreness. If an athlete experiences excessive delayed-onset muscle soreness after plyometric exercise, the soreness will be most pronounced 24 to 48 hours after the exercise bout and will be reduced within 96 hours.[13,14]

Progression

Like all other forms of rehabilitation exercise, plyometric activities should start at the most demanding level that the athlete can tolerate and should progress only when the athlete can complete the activities with proper form and without any increase in symptoms. As described previously, plyometric exercise is progressed by carefully manipulating the frequency, intensity, volume, and recovery, just as it is for uninjured athletes. Deciding which variable to manipulate at which time is based on the athlete's experience, empirical evidence, and most important, the athlete's response. The volume (sets and repetitions) of a particular plyometric activity should be increased first. This ensures that the athlete has gained appropriate neuromuscular control and endurance before increasing the intensity or frequency of the exercise or decreasing the recovery time.

Adverse responses, such as joint pain or joint swelling, should slow or limit the progression of plyometric exercise.[15] In such cases, the recovery period should be prolonged until the impairment has completely resolved. When the plyometric exercises are reinitiated, the volume or intensity of the exercises should be reduced to the level used before the progression. If an athlete experiences joint pain or joint swelling after exercise but the symptoms resolve before the next rehabilitation visit or after a warm-up, then the program should not be progressed but rather maintained and monitored for reoccurrence of symptoms.[15] Prior literature suggests that an athlete should tolerate two or three sessions at a specific intensity and volume without any adverse responses before being allowed to progress.[2]

Technique

A major focus when using plyometric exercise in rehabilitation is to assist the athlete with skill reacquisition and the establishment of biomechanically safe and proper techniques that will allow the athlete to achieve optimal performance. Rehabilitation specialists should focus on addressing any underlying technical deficits that may stem from the injury or that were related to the cause of the initial injury.[16,17] If an athlete is allowed to perform plyometric exercise maneuvers improperly during training, then improper techniques will be reinforced.

During the initial implementation of plyometric exercise, rehabilitation specialists should give continuous and immediate verbal feedback to the athlete both during and after each exercise bout; this will increase the athlete's awareness of proper form and technique as well as undesirable and potentially dangerous positions.[18] In addition, visual feedback should be provided through the use of video or by having the athlete perform exercises in front of a mirror.[19] The rehabilitation specialist should be skilled in recognizing the desired technique for a given exercise and should encourage the athlete to maintain perfect technique for as long as possible. If the athlete fatigues to a point at which technique degrades and a sharp decline in proficiency is displayed, the activity should be stopped. The athlete's goal should be to increase the volume or intensity of plyometric exercises while maintaining proper form.

GUIDELINES FOR PREPARING FOR RETURN TO SPORT

Before an athlete returns to sport after injury rehabilitation, we recommend that the rehabilitation specialist assess the athlete's lower-extremity plyometric techniques.[1,20] Specifically, the specialist should assess the athlete's performance of a depth jump and cutting tasks in order to identify residual lower-extremity deficits (side-to-side asymmetries when loading or knock-knee position when landing) that may be related to the initial injury.[21] These deficits are often determined by field testing one extremity versus another. Single or bilateral leg tests measuring for distance or frequency of jumps per unit of time are common forms of evaluation. Mechanical devices such as switch mats that record ground contact times can play a major role in determining if athletes are close to the level they were at before being injured. These devices can also be crucial in providing objective data that indicate a level of difference between limbs.

DEPTH JUMP TEST

The athlete is instructed to drop (not jump) off a 12-inch (30.5 cm) box (figure 6.1). During the depth jump, the coach or trainer evaluates the athlete for limb deficits and asymmetry.

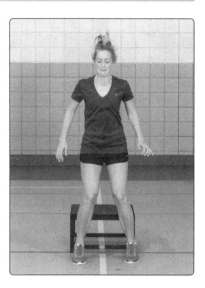

Figure 6.1 Depth jump test.

CUTTING TEST

Plyometric cutting activities with technique patterns should be targeted for correction before the athlete returns to sport. Clinicians and coaches should provide active feedback to the athlete, encouraging him to perform reactive training with limited knock knees.

Assessment of Agility

After the rehabilitation of injury, athletes should be assessed through agility testing and single-leg hop tests, and they should be evaluated with the tuck jump assessment tool. The modified agility T-test (MAT test) is focused on identifying side-to-side deficits in multiplanar cutting and agility tasks. The single hop, crossover hop, and triple hop for distance can identify strength and power deficits in athletes after ACL surgery. The tuck jump assessment tool, which is fully detailed in chapter 7, can be used to identify deficits during jumping and landing movements.

MODIFIED AGILITY T-TEST (MAT TEST)*

Set up cones 1, 2, and 3 in a line with 15 feet (4.5 m) between each end cone and the middle cone. Place a fourth cone (cone 4) 15 feet to the side of the middle cone to create a T shape (figure 6.2). The start and finish lines for the test are 15 feet from cones 3 and 1 respectively and in line with the cone at the bottom of the T. On the coach's or trainer's signal, the athlete runs from the start line past cone 3, side shuffles past cone 2, backpedals past cone 4, runs forward past cone 2, shuffles past cone 1, and backpedals through the finish line. Timing is stopped as soon as the athlete crosses the finish line. The athlete should repeat the test in the opposite direction by starting from the finish line and repeating the pattern. The goal of this test is for the athlete to attain greater than 10 percent asymmetry in the time taken to complete the task.

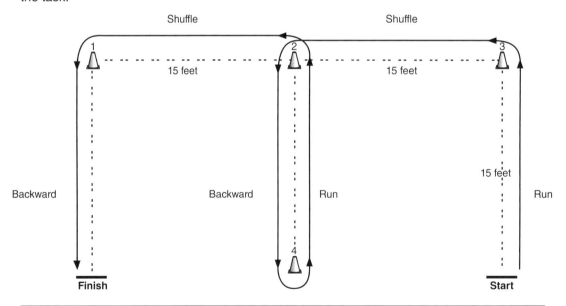

Figure 6.2 Setup for the modified agility T-test (MAT).

*Adapted, by permission, from G.D. Myer, M.V. Paterno, K.R. Ford, C.E. Quatman, and T.E. Hewett, 2006, "Rehabilitation after anterior cruciate ligament reconstruction: Criteria-based progression through the return-to-sport phase," *Journal of Orthopaedic & Sports Physical Therapy* 36(6): 385-402. © Orthopaedic Section and the Sports Physical Therapy Section of the American Physical Therapy Association.

SINGLE-LEG HOP DISTANCE TESTS

The athlete should complete three single-leg hop tests for distance (figure 6.3):

- For the single-leg single hop, the athlete stands balancing on one leg, hops as far as possible straight forward, and lands maintaining balance on the single leg.

- For the single-leg crossover hop, the athlete begins on a single leg next to a straight line marked on the floor. The athlete hops forward over the line, then forward and back over the line to the original side, and then forward and back over the line to the starting side. On each hop, the athlete should cover the largest distance possible while still maintaining balance and control.

- For the single-leg triple hop, the athlete starts on one leg and then hops forward three times in a straight line. The athlete hops as far as possible each time while maintaining balance and control.

The athlete repeats each test on the other leg. Before returning to sport, athletes should be able to jump on their repaired leg at least 90 percent of the distance that they can hop on their uninjured leg. Athletes should be assessed visually for any knee alignments that are out of plane or that push the knee inward.

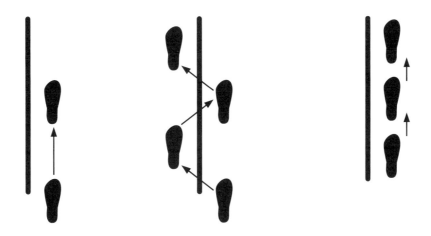

Figure 6.3 Footwork patterns for the *(a)* single-leg single hop, *(b)* single-leg crossover hop, and *(c)* single-leg triple hop.

Final Evaluation

Side-to-side differences in performance between limbs or other deficits during athletic tasks may be potential risk factors for reinjury or secondary injury; therefore, these deficits should be minimized before an athlete returns to sport.[1,20,22] All stages of the return-to-sport rehabilitation program should attempt to minimize these asymmetries, not only with strength but with athletic maneuvers.[23,24]

Once athletes meet acceptable measures during these tests, they should be prepared to leave therapy and begin reintegration into their respective sport training and conditioning programs. However, we do not suggest that this is the time for unrestricted full participation in competitive events; rather, these athletes can resume practice activities and begin to prepare themselves for competitive play. The return to sport after a lower-extremity injury can be a high-risk period in which athletes may reinjure themselves.[23,24]

◀ SUMMARY ▶

- Eccentric strength development is important for all athletes and particularly for injured athletes.

- Before an injured athlete is reintegrated back into sport, plyometric testing should be completed to evaluate residual deficits and limb asymmetries.

- Plyometrics are a key transition tool for ensuring that techniques achieved during rehabilitation can be matched to sport performance.

- Plyometrics are the key to specificity of training in the end stages of rehabilitation. These exercises come closer to simulating actual performance on the field than any machine or weight training exercise. The use of plyometrics often means the difference between success and failure when an athlete returns to the field.

APPLICATIONS

Strength and Power Assessment for Plyometric Training

Plyometric training was initially thought of as an exercise program to be used to develop power and speed in elite athletes. Therefore, the concept of a strength base was a high priority. Athletes need to possess a high level of lower-extremity strength in order to endure these high-quality efforts of maximal force production and great intensities. Thus, athletes should be assessed both for their technical performance and their readiness to participate in this type of activity.

Yuri Verkhoshansky, the national high jump coach of the old Soviet Union, stated that in order to endure high-intensity plyometric training, an athlete had to have the ability to squat 2.5 times his body weight.[1] If that rule applied today, few athletes in the United States would qualify to engage in plyometric training programs. Young male athletes (13 years old) might be able to do 75 percent of their body weight, and only a few would ever reach their body weight. Few if any female athletes would reach their body weight.

When an athlete performs a simple drop (depth) jump from a height of 24 inches (61 cm), it is possible that he will hit the ground with a force equal to five times his body weight. That amount of force is greater than the amount required to shatter the bones of the lower extremities. This does not actually happen because the impact forces of hitting the ground are absorbed and distributed throughout the body by the soft-tissue structures (muscles, tendons, and ligaments) of the body. That is why it is so important for athletes to build muscular strength. Muscular strength allows the body to effectively absorb and dissipate these impact forces without harming the soft tissue and joints.

Poor strength in the lower extremities results in loss of stability when landing, and high-impact forces are *excessively* absorbed by the passive restraints of the body. Early fatigue also becomes a problem for athletes without adequate development of lower-extremity strength. These factors will result in the deterioration of performance during exercise and will cause the athlete to approach overuse levels much more rapidly, thus subjecting the athlete to possible injury.

ATHLETE EVALUATION

Various strength requirements for allowing an athlete to begin high-intensity programs have been proposed, but Verkhoshansky's 2.5 times body weight does not seem feasible or necessary for all athletes. Prudence and common sense are required when determining whether an athlete is ready to begin a plyometric training program. Certain criteria make sense when judging the readiness of an athlete to undertake this type of training. Keep in mind that the criteria for implementing plyometric training should not be viewed as hard-and-fast rules because several factors need to be considered.

First, the chronological age of the individual athlete affects the criteria. If the athlete is preadolescent, then ballistic power-producing exercises may not be the priority. Youngsters in this age group need to focus on body control and strength development against light resistances in order to improve tensile strength of muscle, tendons, and ligaments. They need to develop spatial awareness and proper movement patterns. For further information on this topic, refer to the American College of Sports Medicine's (ACSM) Position Paper on Plyometric Training for Children and Adolescents (December 2001) by Donald A. Chu and Avery D. Faigenbaum or a more recent book titled *Progressive Plyometrics for Kids* (Healthy Learning, 2006) by Donald A. Chu, Avery D. Faigenbaum, and Jeff E. Falkel.[2]

Along with age, gender is a major factor to consider. It is well established that young females have a much higher incidence of injuries to the anterior cruciate ligament (ACL) of the knee. Two major contributing factors are the manner in which the quadriceps, hamstring, and gluteus muscle groups interact and the ability of these muscle groups to maintain proper knee alignment during plyometric tasks. In males, the posterior chain muscle group may more effectively prevent forward translation of the tibia and more neutral knee alignment than in females.[3] Also the different firing sequence in some females can be changed with the application of appropriate plyometric training exercises.[4]

The athlete's history of injury is another crucial factor in the implementation of plyometric training. If an athlete has never sustained serious injury to the ankle, knee, or hip, then fewer limits will need to be placed on the athlete's training. However, if an athlete has had surgeries to repair ligament damage, osteoarthritis, or involvement of joint surfaces, then stricter rules on intensity and quantity of exercises must be considered.

Another consideration is the athlete's history of training. If the athlete is a novice, this represents a much different situation than if the athlete has participated in prior training programs that involved explosive movements (e.g., dance and gymnastics). For novice athletes, the assessments and exercise selections should begin with basic levels and should be progressed until appropriate intensities are found for a given athlete.[5]

TESTING AND ASSESSMENT METHODS

Testing (data collection) and assessment (comparing the gathered data in order to establish performance standards) of an athlete before and after training periods, or cycles, are vital for measuring improvement and providing direction and motivation. Test results can often be compared to national or international databases that will give some idea of where the individual ranks against his peers.

Plyometric training should be a means of helping athletes improve their self-image and achieve self-realization. Athletes should be concerned with competing against themselves and should be encouraged to do as well as they can in training and in testing. Testing should be done both before and after training modules to let athletes rate themselves against their own accomplishments as well as against established norms. For athletes in individual events, such as track and field or swimming, the ultimate posttest is the competition itself—even more so during the championship season. That is when all the time and effort spent in preparation, planning, and performance can culminate in that moment of synthesis known as peaking.

A variety of methods are available for assessing an athlete's physical abilities. These are usually performance tests known as *field tests*. They are simple to administer and require very little in the way of equipment; usually, just a tape measure, a stopwatch or other timing device, and perhaps a weighted object (such as a Plyoball or medicine ball) that can be thrown for distance will suffice. We recommend limiting the number of tests to four or five. This amount of testing is sufficient to gauge the athlete's status and yet not fatigue the athlete, which might skew the results and also make the athlete more susceptible to injury. The test results will often expose weaknesses or deficiencies in the athlete. These results should become the basis for program development, helping determine the types, intensities, and quantities of exercise that the athlete is subjected to.

Standard tests of physical fitness—such as the 300-yard shuttle, the standing vertical jump, and the standing long jump—are good for gathering baseline data. Scores from these or similar tests should be recorded for future reference. More advanced athletes can be tested on skills such as the standing triple jump, the single-leg hop over 25 meters, and the 90-second box drill.

Screening for High-Risk Athletes

Laboratory-based screening tools have been used to demonstrate that altered neuromuscular strategies or decreased neuromuscular control during the execution of sport movements—as evidenced by abnormal lower-limb joint mechanics (motions and loads) during plyometric tasks—may underlie the increased risk of injury in athletes.[6,7,8,9,10,11] Abnormal mechanics measured during landing are indicative of athletes who are at high injury risk.[7]

Calculation of injury risk factors during plyometric activities has been performed in laboratories using inverse dynamics. This process requires laboratory-based three-dimensional kinematic and kinetic measurement techniques that are very complex.[12] Unfortunately, biomechanical laboratories with costly and labor-intensive measurement tools are required for these measurements. This restricts the potential for coaches on the field to perform athletes' risk assessments during training sessions. For this reason, current research is focused on developing real-time field tests that can be used to test and, more important, train athletes in ways that maximize performance and reduce injury risk factors.[12]

TUCK JUMP ASSESSMENT (TJA) TOOL

The tuck jump exercise is useful for identifying technical flaws in the lower extremity during a plyometric activity.[13] The tuck jump requires a high level of effort from the athlete. Because of this, the test may readily identify potential deficits, especially during the first few repetitions. In addition, the tuck jump exercise may be used to assess improvement in lower-extremity biomechanics as the athlete progresses through her training.[12,13,14]

Figures 7.1 and 7.2 demonstrate the desired technical performance of the tuck jump exercise. To perform the tuck jump assessment, the athlete starts in the athletic position with the feet at least shoulder-width apart and preferably 35 centimeters (13.8 in.) apart (figures 7.1*a* and 7.2*a*). The athlete initiates a tuck jump by performing a slight crouch downward while extending the arms behind the body (figures 7.1*b* and 7.2*b*). Then the athlete swings the arms forward while simultaneously jumping straight up and pulling the knees up as high as possible. At the highest point of the jump, the athlete should pull the thighs to a position parallel to the ground (figures

Figure 7.1 Front view of the desired execution of a tuck jump.

Figure 7.2 Side view of the desired execution of a tuck jump.

7.1c and 7.2c). The athlete should land softly, using a toe to midfoot rocker landing, and should land in the same footprint with each jump (figures 7.1d and 7.2d). After landing, the athlete immediately begins the next tuck jump.

Figure 7.3 provides a technique assessment tool that can be used to score deficits during a sequence of jumping and landing movements. Coaches can use this tool to monitor an athlete's performance of the tuck jump before, during, and after training. Specifically, the athlete performs repeated tuck jumps for 10 seconds, which allows the coach to visually grade the outlined criteria. If a sharp decline in technique occurs during the allotted time frame, the test should be stopped. To further improve accuracy of the assessment, a standard 2D camera in the frontal and sagittal planes may be used to assist the coach.

Using the assessment tally sheet, the coach rates the athlete's technique areas and checks for any of the deficiencies that can limit optimum sport performance. The deficits can be tallied for the final assessment score. Indicators of flawed technique

TJ Assessment Tally Sheet

Knee and thigh motion	Pre	Mid	Post	Comments
1. Lower-extremity valgus is present at landing (photo a).				
2. Thighs do not reach parallel at peak of jump (photo b).				
3. Thighs are not equal from side to side during flight (photo c).				
Foot position during landing				
4. Foot placement is not shoulder-width apart (photo d).				
5. Foot placement is not parallel from front to back (photo e).				
6. Timing of foot contact is not equal (photo f).				
7. Excessive contact noise is heard on landing.				
Plyometric technique				
8. Athlete pauses between jumps.				
9. Technique declines before 10 seconds.				
10. Athlete does not land in same footprint as start (excessive in-flight movement).				
Totals				

Figure 7.3   TJ assessment tally sheet.

Reprinted, by permission, from G.D. Myer, K.R. Ford, and T.E. Hewett, 2008, "Tuck jump assessment for reducing anterior cruciate ligament injury risk," *Athletic Therapy Today* 13(5): 39-44.

should be noted for each athlete and should be the focus of feedback during subsequent training sessions. The athlete's baseline performance can be compared to repeated assessments performed at the midpoint and conclusion of training protocols in order to objectively track improvement in jumping and landing technique. To aid coaches and trainers in the identification of deficits that can reduce performance and potentially increase the risk of injury, the assessment criteria can be grouped into four general categories: ligament dominance, quadriceps dominance, leg dominance, and trunk dominance and core dysfunction. These categories are detailed in the following sections.

Ligament Dominance

Ligament dominance is defined as an imbalance between the neuromuscular and ligamentous control of dynamic stability at the knee joint.[13] This imbalance in the control of knee joint stability is demonstrated by an inability to control frontal-plane motion of the lower extremity during landing and cutting. External valgus load (visually seen as a knock-kneed position) is the lab-based kinetic measure that is predictive of future injury and likely contributes to the stress on an ACL during injury; it is visually associated with a knock-knee position during dynamic tasks.[12]

Figure 7.4 shows a ligament-dominant athlete who lacks sufficient frontal-plane control of the lower extremity during performance of the tuck jump.[12] The athlete demonstrates lower-extremity valgus at landing, which can be seen by the athlete's knock-kneed position while in contact with the ground. Figure 7.5 provides another example of ligament dominance. In this case, the athlete is unable to maintain a foot placement that is shoulder-width apart during landing. This deficit can involve the feet being too close together or too far apart. This athlete's ligament-dominant landing mechanics may be driven from a lack of frontal-plane control (increased knock-knee position) at the hip. Both types of ligament dominance may be improved with targeted training for the trunk and hip.[4,12,13,15,16,17]

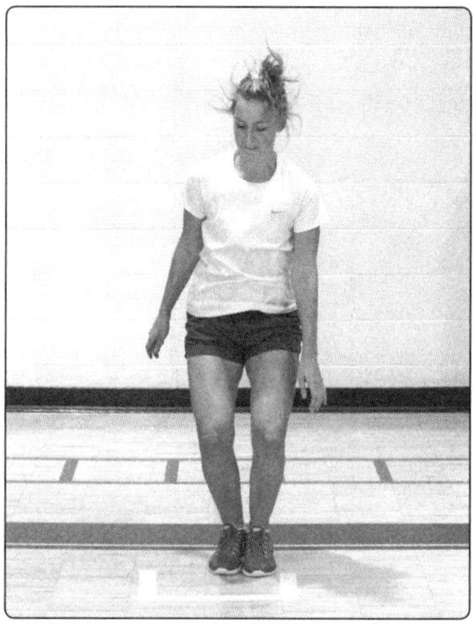

Figure 7.4 Lower-extremity valgus at landing.

Figure 7.5 Foot placement not shoulder-width apart.

Quadriceps Dominance

Quadriceps dominance is defined as an imbalance in strength, recruitment, and coordination between the knee extensors and knee flexors.[12,13] Landing with the knee at nearly full extension is a common mechanism of knee injury.[18] Decreased hamstring strength relative to the quadriceps is implicated as a potential mechanism for increased lower-extremity injuries[3,19,20,21,22] and potentially ACL injury risk in female athletes.[13] Joint stability through cocontraction of the hamstrings and quadriceps may be necessary when the joint experiences high quadriceps activation or when the passive structures are compromised.[23,24] Withrow and colleagues reported that increased hamstring force during the flexion phase of simulated jump landings greatly decreased relative strain on the ACL.[25]

Another proposed theory related to neuromuscular imbalances and increased risk of ACL injury in females is the relatively low knee flexor recruitment (compared to extensor recruitment) that may be reflective of a closed-chain dynamic hamstrings–quadriceps peak torque output.[26,27] For example, hamstring activation can decrease the load on the passive restraints of the knee,[28] increase the compression force of the knee joint, and stabilize the knee from external varus or valgus loads.[29]

An athlete who lands with small knee flexion angles and a flat foot position demonstrates characteristics of a quadriceps-dominant athlete and will likely demonstrate excessive contact noise at landing. If this noise criterion is identified with the tuck jump assessment (figure 7.3), the deficit should be targeted with posterior chain and deep knee flexion exercises.[3,4,6,13,30]

Leg Dominance

Leg dominance is defined as an imbalance in strength, coordination, and control between the two lower extremities.[12,13] Coaches should be cognizant during their risk assessment that side-to-side imbalances in neuromuscular strength, flexibility, and coordination can be important predictors of increased injury risk.[7,22,31] Specific to ACL injury risk in female athletes, leg-to-leg differences in dynamic valgus measures were observed in injured females but not uninjured females. Side-to-side differences in knee load were 6.4 times greater in ACL-injured females versus uninjured females. Female athletes tend to demonstrate side-to-side differences in visually evident maximum angles of knee valgus (knock-knee position) during a box drop vertical jump.[10] In addition, after injury, female athletes often demonstrate leg-to-leg deficits that increase their risk of subsequent injury.[32,33]

Clinical examination of post-surgical knee patients of all types shows a specific set of characteristics on initial evaluation. These characteristics reinforce the presence of side-to-side deficits and may be used to mark progress in further reevaluations of the athlete. Post-surgical patients will tend to shy away from the surgically-repaired limb when asked to perform a squat maneuver, even with mere body weight, and will always take a shorter step on the surgically-repaired limb when asked to perform a lunge maneuver. These tendencies may be noted and used to mark progress toward the return to play of the athlete.

Leg dominance or residual injury deficits may be evident in the tuck jump assessment in three ways. First, the thighs may not be equal side to side during flight (figure 7.6). Side dominance is often visible when an athlete has one thigh that does not achieve the same height as the contralateral thigh. Second, foot placement may not be parallel from front to back (figure 7.7). Often, an athlete drops one foot behind the other while on the ground to help minimize forces on a weaker limb. Third, the timing of foot contact may not be equal (figure 7.8).[12] Similar to not placing the feet

Figure 7.6 Thighs not equal side to side during flight.

Figure 7.7 Foot placement not parallel from front to back.

Figure 7.8 Timing of foot contact not equal.

parallel, the athlete may change the timing of the foot contacts to protect a weaker limb. Athletes identified with leg-to-leg deficit should use integrated training that combines both plyometric and dynamic stabilization to improve leg-to-leg symmetry during dynamic tasks.[6,30]

Trunk Dominance and Core Dysfunction

Trunk dominance and core dysfunction may be defined as an imbalance between the inertial demands of the trunk and the control and coordination of the core to control those demands.[12] Hewett and Myer have developed a concept of trunk and lower-extremity function that identifies the body's core as a critical modulator of lower-extremity alignments and loads during dynamic tasks.[34] The trunk and hip stabilizers may pre-activate to counterbalance trunk motion and regulate lower-extremity postures.[34,35,36,37] Reduced pre-activation of the trunk and hip stabilizers may allow increased lateral trunk positions that can increase knee valgus loads.[34,38]

Decreased core stability and muscular synergism of the trunk and hip stabilizers may affect performance in power activities and may increase the incidence of injury secondary to lack of control of the center of mass, especially in female athletes.[32,33,39,40] One study reported that factors related to core stability predicted the risk of knee injuries in female athletes but not in male athletes.[41] Thus, the current evidence indicates that compromised function of the trunk and hip stabilizers, as they relate to core neuromuscular control, may underlie the mechanisms of increased risk of ACL injury in female athletes.[7,41,42,43]

Core dysfunction imbalance may be evident in the athlete's tuck jump in several ways. The thighs may not reach parallel to the floor at the peak of the jump (figure 7.9). This deficit is typically a product of the athlete's inability to create enough power to achieve a height at which the legs can become properly tucked. The athlete may also pause between jumps, or the athlete may not land in the same footprint (figure 7.10).[12] Many times an athlete tends to move or drift around the jumping

Figure 7.9 Thighs not parallel to the floor at the peak of the jump.

Figure 7.10 Landings not in the same footprint as the takeoff.

area because of a lack of full body or core control. When this deficit is present, the coach should be careful in determining the cause so that training can be properly applied. Athletes identified with any of these deficits should perform trunk and hip training in order to improve core control.[15,16]

Technique Perfection

The tuck jump assessment tool can be used to help athletes improve high-risk techniques performed during an exercise that requires a high level of effort from the athlete. As suggested earlier, an athlete may place most of her cognitive efforts solely on the performance of this difficult jump and still demonstrate many technical flaws that are indicative of increased risk for injury. However, the athlete can improve her neuromuscular control and biomechanics during this jump and maintain control during the entire jump-landing sequence; she may gain dynamic neuromuscular control of the lower extremity and create a learned skill that can be transferred to competitive play. Empirical evidence from our laboratory indicates that athletes who do not improve their scores, or who demonstrate six or more flawed techniques, should be targeted for further technique training.

Pilot work in our laboratory indicated that the intra-rater reliability was high $R = 0.84$ (range 0.72 to 0.97). These data indicate that the tuck jump assessment is most useful when a coach is reassessing athletes to determine changes in technical performance of the tuck jump exercise.[44,45]

Use of the field-based assessment and training tool may guide the application of appropriate interventions that will have greater potential to reduce injury risk. Targeted correction of high risk factors for injury is important for optimal biomechanics of athletic movements that maximize sport performance—and ultimately, for the reduction of the incidence of knee ligament injury in female athletes.[12,46,47]

◀ SUMMARY ▶

- Although various recommendations have been outlined regarding how to determine an athlete's readiness for plyometric training, prudence and common sense are key in deciding when to have an athlete begin a plyometric training program.

- Assessment of technique is the PRIMARY determinant of whether an athlete is ready to progress to more intense exercises.

- Plyometric exercises such as the tuck jump can be used to assess and address (with plyometric training) technical deficits that may increase the risk of injury.

Introduction of a Plyometric Training Program

In the previous chapter, we outlined the criteria for judging the readiness of an athlete to undertake a plyometric training program and the need to address injury risk factors. This chapter provides key points to keep in mind when designing a program and considerations to examine when initiating a plyometric training program with athletes. The most important consideration in implementing and administering a plyometric training program is the athlete. Age, experience, training background, and athletic maturity are all important criteria in establishing and modifying plyometric training for the evolving needs of the athlete.

CONSIDERATIONS FOR PROGRAM DESIGN

A basic plyometric program might be intended for the novice or the young athlete. It should follow the rules of safety and the considerations set forth in chapter 4. If the program is intended for the more advanced athlete, the same rules apply, but the requirements for a strength base become higher because exercises become more complex and more intense. The following considerations affect the design of training programs at any level.

Movement Skills

Coaches should teach beginners the concepts behind plyometric activities, including the importance of eccentric versus concentric strength. They should stress the importance of the stretch-shortening cycle (the countermovement of the legs) in the athlete's ability to start quickly. Initial activities should be of lower intensity and preparatory in nature. The coach must be aware of the progression needed in both intensity and skill requirements.

The athlete's feet should be nearly flat in all landings. The ball of the foot may touch first, but the rest of the foot should also make contact. Landings should be reversed quickly; the object is to spend minimal time on the ground. For the arms to develop force into the ground (in order to compress the spring), the elbows must be swung behind the midline of the body and then brought forward rapidly. Follow-through occurs at the end of the concentric arm action at liftoff. This movement is usually taught as a simultaneous double-arm swing.

Age

Attention span is a major consideration in starting youngsters in plyometric training programs. Children will always run and jump as a part of play. But adults tend to take this element of play (also known as fun!) out of training programs by rigidly applying specific regimens with set rules.

Elementary school children can successfully do plyometric training as long as the coach does not call it plyometrics. Children of this age need images to relate to, such as animals in the forest jumping over streams and logs. They can visualize and cognitively grasp the ease and skill with which a deer bounds through the woods. If movement patterns are placed in the proper context, children can attempt to express them in a plyometric fashion. In fact, hopscotch is a great early plyometric drill!

Young athletes can benefit more from direct training as they approach pubescence. They can begin to relate more to sport situations and see the correlation between what the coach asks them to do and their development in their sport. Plyometrics for this group should always begin as gross motor activities of low intensity. Plyometric activities should be introduced into warm-ups and then added to sport-specific drills.

As athletes approach the stage of individualization, they can begin to look at developing off-season and preseason training programs as preparation for performance. For most athletes, this will be when they reach high school, although in certain activities (ice skating, gymnastics, swimming, diving, dance, and track and field) the coach and the athlete may need to begin developing training cycles that use regimented plyometrics at an earlier age. This also depends on the athlete's level of competition.

Training Level

Two considerations regarding training level are important when structuring a plyometric training program: the intensity level of the exercise and the experience of the athlete. Plyometric training should be a progression of exercises and skilled movements that are considered to be elementary, intermediate, and advanced in scope. The activities should focus on improving the ballistic and reactive skills of the exerciser and should be considered physically stressful. Drills should be evaluated for intensity before they are incorporated into a workout. Examples of low-, moderate-, and high-intensity drills may be found in chapter 9. Categorizing exercises by intensity helps both in choosing starting points for exercise and in developing program progression.

Another factor in program design is the training experience of the athlete. The exercise must be geared to the individual. An athlete who is barely past pubescence and is relatively unskilled should be considered a beginner. Beginners should be placed in a complementary resistance training program and should progress slowly and deliberately into a program of low-intensity plyometrics. Low-intensity plyometrics may include skipping drills, 8-inch (20 cm) cone hops, and box drills from 6 to 12 inches (15 to 30 cm).

High school competitors who have been exposed to weight training programs can benefit from moderately intense plyometrics. And accomplished, mature, college-level athletes with strong weight training backgrounds should be able to perform ballistic-reactive exercises of high intensity with no undue problems. Once an athlete has been classified as beginner, intermediate, or advanced, the coach and athlete can begin to plan a program.

Time Frame or Cycle

After the athlete has been evaluated and assessed, it is time to consider the program design points for a plyometric training program. One of the most difficult tasks for the coach of a good high school athlete is finding the appropriate time to insert a training program. The best athletes are almost always multiple-sport athletes. They play one sport in the fall, have two weeks until they move to the winter sport, and face the same situation as they move to spring activities.

Research has shown that physical development is best accomplished over a 4- to 6-week period. The theory of periodization is one in which an athlete's training year is divided into cycles or blocks of time with specific training goals. After each cycle, an attempt is made to reassess whether or not the expected development has occurred.

Plyometric training, because of its ability to improve explosiveness and reactivity of muscles, needs to be properly brought into the overall training program of the athlete. It should be used after the athlete completes a strength phase and should be gradually introduced to the athlete before the actual competitive season. Some athletes, such as jumpers in track and field, will continue to do plyometric training throughout the season, backing off just before the championship event or season. Other athletes, such as professional basketball players, would be foolish to attempt high levels of plyometric training during their season because of the tremendous workload during their competitive season.

The coach needs to determine the most opportune time to impose these types of activities. With the advent of year-round competitive sports—such as traveling soccer, basketball, and volleyball programs—many young athletes are going to miss a crucial aspect of their development. Although playing the game may result in some physical development, the soft-tissue system that is influenced by maturity and exposure to training stimulus may stagnate. An athlete may never reach his full potential if the opportunity to physically develop is not acknowledged.

It is in the best interest of all athletes to use off-court or off-field training not only for physical improvement but also for recovery. The body reacts best when it is exposed to a variety of different stimuli. This has long been shown to be an essential part of the general adaptation syndrome described by Hans Selye, a biologist and endocrinologist, to explain how animals react to stress. The stress can be mental or physical as long as the body experiences a new stress or a more intense stress than usual (e.g., lifting heavier loads or performing new forms of jumping). The first reaction of the body is one of alarm because the stress is a shock to the body. This initial phase lasts several days to several weeks, and the body may undergo muscle soreness, decrements in performance, or other changes.

Next, the body goes through the resistance phase. The body adapts to the stimulus and returns to normal function, demonstrating that it can withstand the stress. The athlete relies on neurological adaptations (learning), and the muscle tissue adapts through various biochemical, structural, and mechanical adjustments that lead to increased performance. A persistent stimulus that is beyond the tolerance level of the athlete and that continues for long periods of time can lead to a third phase known as the exhaustion phase, which is associated with overtraining.

Specific to plyometric training, program design that exposes athletes to a variety of maneuvers in a variety of scenarios will provide the greatest opportunity for adaptation. Diverse exercise selection will optimize the potential for the general adaptation syndrome to occur so that the training will be most beneficial to athletic performance.

All of the program design considerations must be kept in mind when developing a plyometric program that will benefit athletes. Specific attention to these details, which may seem minor, will ultimately help determine the types of exercises chosen, the level of intensity for the exercises, the proper number of repetitions, and how frequently the athlete performs them. Sport-specific program design is explained in-depth in chapter 11.

PLYOMETRIC TRAINING EQUIPMENT

Plyometric training is quite versatile. It can be performed indoors or out. Some basic requirements are important, however. One requirement is adequate space that is free of obstructions. Gym floors, large weight rooms, and outdoor fields are all suitable environments as long as the landing surface is appropriate. A yielding landing surface with some give to prevent jarring the lower extremities with excessive force is also essential. Resilite wrestling mats, spring-loaded gymnastics floors, and grass or synthetic playing fields are all possibilities for landing surfaces.

A significant advantage to plyometric training is that it requires so little prefabricated equipment. The following represents the ultimate list of needed items.

Cones. Plastic cones ranging in height from 8 to 24 inches (20 to 61 cm) serve as barriers for athletes to jump over. The flexibility of cones makes them less likely to cause injuries if landed on.

Boxes. These need to be specially constructed, but they are far from complex in their design. A variety of boxes are needed, and they should be constructed of 3/4-inch plywood or a similar flexible yet durable wood. To make nonslip landing surfaces, attach treads like those used on stairways, mix sand into the paint used to cover the boxes, or glue carpeting or rubberized flooring to the landing surfaces. In schools, physical education and athletic departments can often collaborate with industrial arts departments to build plyometric boxes. This is cost effective and can promote camaraderie between departments as students see their products being put to use. Some manufacturers are producing boxes made of various forms of plastic and wood with built-in adjustments for height.

Boxes should range in height from 6 to 24 inches (15 to 61 cm). Elite athletes with strong weight training backgrounds can use heights up to 42 inches (107 cm). The boxes also need adequate landing (top) surfaces of at least 18 by 24 inches (46 by 61 cm).

Numerous variations of the plyometric box have been developed over the years:

- Adjustable boxes can be altered to accommodate the varying abilities of athletes.

- Storage boxes can double as containers. If one side is left open, the box needs to be constructed very sturdily on the remaining sides.

- Special-effects boxes are built to provide a special type of exercise stimulus. The most common of these is an angle box, which emphasizes the small muscles of the ankle and lower leg. The angle box is used to prevent ankle injuries by teaching athletes how to land on irregular surfaces. It is also useful in the rehabilitation of ankle and knee injuries.

Hurdles. Most school physical education programs own hurdles. Hurdles, which are adjustable for degree of difficulty, do represent a hazard because of their rigid construction; therefore, they should be used only by experienced plyometric exercisers. Collapsible hurdles are available and are ideal for training athletes at any level.

Barriers. Foam barriers are manufactured for gymnastics and tumbling. Barriers can also be constructed by scoring Styrofoam sheets on one side and then folding them to form pliable triangular obstacles. Barriers can also be formed simply by balancing a wooden dowel (1/2-inch [1.3 cm] diameter and 3 feet [91 cm] long) on top of two cones.

Steps. Stairways, bleachers, and stadium steps are all usable for plyometric training; but a coach must be sure to inspect them carefully to make sure they are safe for jumping before sending athletes bouncing up them. Concrete steps are undesirable for jumping because they are unyielding surfaces.

Weighted objects. Medicine balls and other objects are useful for upper-body exercises and in combination with lower-extremity training. They should be easily gripped, durable, and of varying weights to accommodate all strength levels.

BEST WARM-UP DRILLS

One of the basic tenets of all exercise programs is that major efforts of training should be preceded by lower-level activities. These warm-up activities can take various forms and can be general or specific in nature. The exercises of choice when using plyometric drills should be specific or related to the larger efforts. These warm-up drills are not classified as true plyometrics because they require less voluntary effort, focus, and concentration to complete. However, they are used to develop fundamental movement skills and raise the body's core temperature; therefore, they help prevent injury and are helpful in establishing motor patterns that will directly carry over to speed development and jumping ability.

Let's take a look at some of the activities that fit into the category of warm-up or submaximal plyometrics. Keep in mind that all of these drills are performed not as conditioning drills, but as skill enhancement drills aimed at teaching or rehearsing certain motor patterns. Therefore, they are performed over distances of 10 to 20 meters (or yards) with a relatively long recovery between exercises. A good general rule to use in this situation is to have the athlete perform the drill in one direction and walk back in the other. This allows adequate recovery as well as mental rehearsal for the next repetition.

Usually 8 to 12 exercises are considered an adequate amount of movement to elevate the core temperature of the body and form an adequate warm-up. Each exercise may be performed 2 to 4 times depending on the athletes' execution and learning. With a group of athletes, a coach can make administering the warm-up easier by placing individuals in groups according to ability and need for instruction.

Marching Drills

These drills are intended to mimic running movements. They are designed to break down the act of running into its component parts. This allows the coach to stress parts such as posture, joint angles, range of motion, foot placement, and other biomechanical features that are often overlooked when athletes are simply asked to perform the whole activity. Several Canadian track and field coaches (Mach, McFarlane, Biancani) were early proponents of the use of these types of drills to enhance proper hip, thigh, and leg actions in preparation for and during running.

Jogging Drills

Many variations of jogging can be used to emphasize speed development because this activity can be easily modified to be plyometric in nature. The simple act of jogging on the toes with special emphasis on achieving quick ground reaction by not letting the heel touch the ground can be a mini-plyometric activity. Jogging with the legs straight and limiting knee flexion can teach the athlete to expect a sharp impact when performing maximal-effort plyometric drills.

Ankling is a specific jogging drill that involves using the elastic component of the calf musculature to improve speed of foot movement and decrease contact time with the ground during sprinting. The athlete uses a straight leg and keeps the ankle relatively rigid. The athlete moves forward with a straight leg and lands on the first third of a slightly plantar-flexed foot. At contact, the athlete quickly responds to the ground by pushing down against the ground surface and bringing the foot through at about the level of the other ankle (also known as stepping over the ankle). This movement is continued for the length of the prescribed distance.

Special effects can be achieved by using drills such as butt-kickers, which emphasize knee flexion and closing the angle of the knee by bringing the heel to the buttocks; these can be extremely useful when the athletes begin to work on the recovery phase of sprinting. This movement teaches athletes economy of movement and that the shortest lever they have to swing forward will speed up their ability to cycle or turn over the legs during running. Heel recovery is an essential ingredient in absolute speed development. This drill also is an excellent rehabilitation drill for assessing dynamic knee flexion range of motion. If the athlete does not have full and equal knee flexion in both legs when running at all-out speeds, the knee with less range will not swing through at the same speed nor will it fully extend upon landing. Therefore the stride on that side will be slightly shorter. In essence, the athlete will be running with a limp that can throw off the entire running mechanics and put the athlete at risk for a running injury involving the opposite leg or same side quadriceps/hamstrings complex.

Skipping Drills

Synchronization of limb movements is basic to normal motor development. So-called reciprocal movements occur between the legs and arms in running. Generally, efficient running requires a runner to move his left arm forward as the right leg comes forward, then switch limb movements to the opposite side of the body as he continues to move forward. This reciprocal motion is fundamental to the development of the athlete. Skipping drills require an exaggerated form of this reciprocal motion, which is often lost if not practiced. Because of the need to perform reciprocal limb movements and the emphasis on quick takeoff and landing during skipping, this activity is ideal as a submaximal plyometric activity that can be used to warm up athletes and prepare them for more complex skills.

Various forms of skipping are used to achieve explosive movements initiated by the calf–ankle complex, including the following:

- In **straight-line skipping,** the athlete initiates forward movement by quickly rising onto the toes of both feet and assuming a slight (10-degree) forward lean, then rapidly lifting the thigh to a position parallel to the ground. The ankle is dorsiflexed, pulled into the neutral position, and held while the foot is being lowered to the ground. The most important detail of this type of drill is that the foot, knee, and hip are in a single line or plane of movement. As the knee is being lifted into the up position, the opposite foot is extending to raise the athlete onto the toes of the opposite side; this drives the athlete's body up so that it briefly clears the ground surface. As soon as the leg and thigh hit parallel, a reversal of motion takes place; the leg extends, and the foot makes contact with the ground. The same action occurs on the opposite side. Keep in mind that the arms should be flexed to 90 degrees and will move forward in a reciprocal manner (opposite arm, opposite foot).

- **Single-leg skipping** is not only a drill but an assessment tool as well. In this movement, the action that occurs is the same as in straight-line skipping, but only one leg is allowed to drive up to parallel. This results in a small hop on the opposite side of the body. The athlete brings the thigh to parallel with enough force to lift the body off the ground. As the leg drops, the athlete prepares to repeat the motion on the same leg, using the arm on the opposite side to help propel himself up and forward. Because this motion requires the isolation of right versus left, it will allow for the assessment of each leg regarding speed of movement, strength to bring the thigh to parallel, and endurance and repeatability of each leg.

- **Skipping with a pop-off** is the same motion as in straight-line skipping, but the motion on the opposite side is exaggerated to emphasize complete ankle plantar flexion, and the lift or pop off the ground is greater. Maximal controlled height should be achieved with both legs for the prescribed distance.

Footwork Drills

As mentioned in chapter 2, submaximal footwork drills developed and presented by John Frappier (1995) in his Acceleration Training program are useful supplements to plyometric conditioning programs. However, these drills require hip movement and quick changes of direction that can also make them useful as warm-up drills. Drills such as shuttle drills, multidirectional side-shuffle drills, and drop-step drills are continuations of these simple and brief footwork movements that rely largely on the ankle complex for propulsion—and they all fit under this heading.

Lunging Drills

These drills are taken from the basic exercise movement known as the lunge. When used as submaximal drills, these exercises can take many forms, such as forward, side, crossover, disassociated multidirectional, reverse, and walking lunges. They can (and should always) be used as preparation before doing long amplitude jumps. These drills can be extremely useful in developing basic strength in the upper hip and thigh areas when used with simple body weight.

The following alternative movement drills include those movements not previously classified. Each activity is aimed at achieving a special effect in a specific area of the body.

Backward Running

Hamstring and hip extension are never to be overlooked in the development of the athlete and in the prevention of injuries. Backward running has a particular way of strengthening the hamstrings in preparation for the tremendous eccentric forces applied to this area when running straight ahead. Many practitioners of rehabilitation advocate backpedaling as an important rehabilitation exercise for the athlete after injury to the knee and hamstring areas. These exercises work particularly well if there is a small incline (3 to 5 degrees) available near the training field. They are best done outdoors, and the technique is crucial. When one thinks of backpedaling, one tends to think of the defensive back in football. The athlete uses a posture in which the hips are lowered, flexion of the trunk and knees occurs, and there is a slight forward lean. The backward steps are short and compact, and the center of gravity remains over the base of support as much as possible. The arms work reciprocally to the legs, and the elbows are usually kept close to the body while rotation occurs at the shoulders. The forward lean is exaggerated when going up an incline, which puts even more stress on the hamstring muscle group.

Athletes may also use an alternative posture that involves flexing the hip and knee on one side, picking that foot up, and reaching it back to cover as much distance as possible with each stride. This is sometimes referred to as backward skipping because there is a time lag as the leg extends back in an attempt to cover the ground. The opposite foot may briefly leave the ground during this motion; thus, the idea of skipping comes into play.

Carioca

This movement is probably as familiar to football coaches as the three-point stance. It has long been used to improve hip rotation and foot placement. The upper body is held relatively stationary as the player travels down a line by moving sideways; one knee and foot are lifted to a position in which the knee is in front of the opposite hip (crossed over). On dropping the foot to the ground, the athlete switches the feet from a crossover position to a reversed position (placed behind the opposite leg) in rapid fashion. Some coaches and athletes prefer the idea of really emphasizing the knee lift in front of the thigh, even to a point of exaggerating this so that the knee comes above the waist. Although not necessary, this technique may reinforce acceleration of the lead knee during this type of movement.

DISASSOCIATION DRILLS

Disassociation drills refer to functional exercises that require body balance and trunk stability simultaneously. Generally, the movements force the upper body to work in one direction while the legs do something else. Many versions of this type of exercise exist, but the following simple progression of exercises can be particularly useful.

The first version of the exercise (figure 8.1) is performed by starting on two feet and then lifting one thigh forward at the hip. The athlete holds a Plyoball with the arms extended at a 90-degree angle to the torso. The athlete then rotates the arms to the side and attempts to achieve 90 degrees of trunk rotation.

In the second version of the exercise (figure 8.2), the athlete begins in the same starting position with the Plyoball. The athlete executes a lunge movement by stepping forward with the lead leg and rotates the arms to the same side until a 90-degree rotation of the shoulders is achieved. The athlete then pushes back off the lead leg and returns to the starting position.

The third version of the exercise requires the athlete to perform a walking lunge (figure 8.3). The athlete rotates the ball toward the side of the leg that moves into the lead position. The athlete moves over the desired distance, moving the ball back and forth.

Figure 8.1 Leg lift and shoulder rotation: *(a)* start and *(b)* execution positions.

Figure 8.2 Lunge and shoulder rotation: *(a)* start and *(b)* execution positions.

Figure 8.3 Walking lunge with shoulder rotation: *(a)* on one side and *(b)* on the opposite side.

TRAINING CONSIDERATIONS

Plyometric training can be structured to individuals or to groups. Individual training requires exercisers to perform every task to the best of their ability and according to their level of development. It focuses on responsibility, concentration, and follow-through to complete the training session. Group achievement can be structured to encompass—in addition to physical skills—social skills such as communication, cooperation, trust, and immediate and long-term feedback in goal setting and achievement. Both individual and group sessions should take place in an environment that is positive in nature and emphasizes individual development.

Several considerations must be taken into account in implementing a plyometric training program, whether for an individual or a group. Coaches should rely on their own common sense and experience. Programs must be prudently planned and administered. One of the major tasks is to conduct a needs analysis, taking into account the athlete's sport and the specific movements that the athlete must perform to participate effectively. Other issues to consider include the athlete's age, experience, and athletic maturity.

The responsibility in initiating a plyometric program is enormous. The best coaches do not always win with their athletes, but they do make training an enjoyable, organized, and progressive activity that ultimately leads the athlete to higher levels of performance.

Intensity

Intensity is the effort involved in performing a given task. In weightlifting, intensity is controlled by the amount of weight lifted. In plyometrics, intensity is controlled by the type of exercise performed. Plyometric movements range from simple tasks to highly complex and stressful exercises. Starting out with skipping is much less stressful than alternate bounding. Double-leg hops are less intense than single-leg bounds.

The intensity of plyometric exercises can be increased by adding light weights (in certain cases), by raising the platform height for depth jumps, or simply by aiming at covering a greater distance in longitudinal jumps. Other writers have rated the intensity of various plyometric exercises from low to very intense. The exercises in chapter 9 are rated low to high. Any attempt to classify exercises by intensity is imperfect at best, but the guidelines provided here should help coaches in their program design. Figure 8.4 depicts the scale of intensity for jump training exercises.

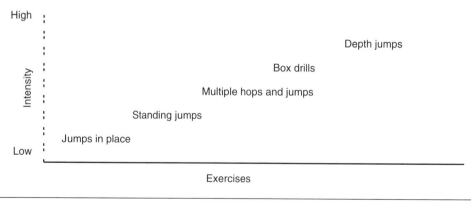

Figure 8.4 Intensity scale for jump training exercises.

Volume

Volume is the total work performed in a single workout session or cycle. In the case of plyometric training, volume is often measured by counting foot contacts. For example, an activity such as the standing triple jump, which is composed of three parts, counts as three foot contacts. Foot contacts provide a means of prescribing and monitoring exercise volume. Low-intensity exercises used during warm-ups are generally not included in the number of foot contacts when computing volume. Thus, warm-ups should stay low in intensity and progressive in nature so they do not overextend the athlete.

The actual number of jumps to be implemented in any program depends on many variables. Remember that this is a theoretical program design, and your particular situation might call for variation. Refer to the information on intensity, frequency, volume, and recovery earlier in this chapter. The key guiding concepts are prudence and simplicity.

Some variables are related to whether an athlete is involved in complementary resistance or weight training. An athlete without prior experience generally should not perform plyometric and resistance training on the same day. If it is necessary to do so, the number of foot contacts should be reduced by 60 percent from the normal prescription for the training level of the athlete. An experienced athlete who wishes to combine plyometrics and resistance training should do plyometrics first; this will allow for maximal response from muscles that are not fatigued by prior exertions. Plyometrics and weight training can also be effectively combined by advanced or elite athletes in complex training (see chapter 10).

Another concern regarding plyometric training is the timing of the athletic season. In the off-season or preseason, training should progress toward more intense exercises. To supplement in-season training, conditioning levels should be maintained using exercises of low to moderate intensity.

Prudence in prescribing and performing plyometric exercise has to do with when and how much training is done. A hard, skill-oriented sport practice should not be followed by a high-volume, high-intensity plyometric workout. More will be accomplished by using warm-up and low-intensity plyometric work to allow for recovery. An even better plan would be devoting a single training day to plyometrics in order to provide variety and allow physiological and mental recovery from skill practice.

The recommended volume of specific jumps in any one session will vary with intensity and progression goals. Table 8.1 shows sample exercise volumes for beginning,

Table 8.1   Number of Foot Contacts by Season for Jump Training

| | LEVEL | | | |
	Beginning	Intermediate	Advanced	Intensity
Off-season	60-100	100-150	150-250	Low-moderate
Preseason	100-250	150-300	150-450	Moderate-high
In-season		Depends on sport		Moderate
Championship season		Recovery only		Moderate-high

intermediate, and advanced workouts. In a single workout in an off-season cycle, a beginner could do 60 to 100 foot contacts of low-intensity exercises. The intermediate exerciser might be able to do 100 to 150 foot contacts of low-intensity exercises and another 100 of moderate-intensity exercises in the same cycle. Advanced exercisers might be capable of 150 to 250 foot contacts of low- to moderate-intensity exercises in this cycle.

The volume of bounding (exaggerated running) activities is best measured by distance. In the early phases of conditioning, a reasonable distance is 30 meters (or yards) per repetition. As the season progresses and the abilities of the athletes improve, the distance may be progressively increased to 100 meters per repetition.

Frequency

Frequency is the number of times an exercise is performed (repetitions) as well as the number of times exercise sessions take place during a training cycle. Research on frequency in plyometrics is obscure. There seems to be no conclusive evidence that one frequency pattern is the best means of increasing performance. Practical experience and some European writings have led us to believe that 48 to 72 hours of rest is necessary for full recovery before the next exercise stimulus, although the intensity of the exercises has to be considered. Skipping performed as a plyometric exercise is not as stressful as bounding and will not require the same amount of recovery time. If the athlete does not get enough recovery, muscle fatigue will prevent the athlete from being able to respond to the exercise stimuli (ground contact, distance, height) with maximal, high-quality efforts. The overall result is less efficient training for athletic development, along with possible overuse and injury.

Various methods are used for establishing frequency in plyometric training. Some coaches prefer to use a variety of programs to schedule the preparation cycle (see table 8.2). Using the principle of 48 to 72 hours of recovery for lower-extremity training, one can easily see the many program variations that can be developed. Running programs can also be integrated into the training cycle along with or replacing weight training on certain days; however, weight training should be a priority, particularly for rapidly developing athletes (high school age), because the athletes

Table 8.2 Samples of Frequency for Off-Season or Preseason Plyometric Training

	Program 1	Program 2	Program 3
Monday	Weight training	Plyometrics (lower extremities)	Plyometrics (lower extremities)
Tuesday	Plyometrics (lower extremities)	Weight training	Plyometrics (upper extremities—medicine ball)
Wednesday	Weight training	Plyometrics (upper extremities—medicine ball)	Running program
Thursday	Plyometrics (lower extremities)	Weight training	Plyometrics (lower extremities)
Friday	Weight training	Plyometrics (lower extremities)	Rest

need to develop and maintain the strength base necessary to carry out a successful plyometric training program.

Because of the stressful nature of plyometrics and the emphasis on quality of work, plyometric exercises should be performed before any other exercise programs. They can be integrated into weight training (this combination, called complex training, is described in chapter 10) at a later cycle in the training year if desired, or they might make up the entire workout. This is quite conceivable, in fact, if the athlete is involved in track and field, where the plyometric training might be very specific to the event or to skill development.

Recovery

Recovery is a key variable in determining whether plyometrics will succeed in developing power or muscular endurance. For power training, longer recovery periods (45 to 60 seconds) between sets or groupings of multiple events, such as a set of 10 rim jumps, allow maximum recovery between efforts. As described in chapter 6, a work-to-rest ratio of 1:5 to 1:10 is required to ensure proper execution and intensity of the exercise. Thus, if a single set of exercises takes 10 seconds to complete, 50 to 100 seconds of recovery should be allowed.

Remember, plyometric training is an anaerobic activity. Shorter recovery periods (10 to 15 seconds) between sets do not allow for maximum recovery of muscular energy. Less than 10 seconds of recovery time between sets in a 12- to 20-minute workout may make it more aerobic due to the demands on the metabolic systems. Exercise for both strength and endurance is usually achieved through circuit training, where the athlete continues from one exercise to another without stopping between sets.

The preparation (off-season) cycle for a plyometric program should involve general gross motor exercises, such as skipping for coordination or simple jumping, without specific skill training such as change of direction. As the preseason cycle approaches, exercises should become more specific to the sport.

If the sport itself is specific to plyometric training—as in long jumping, high jumping, triple jumping, and pole vaulting—plyometrics can be carried through the in-season cycle. However, for sports dominated by vertical jumping, such as basketball and volleyball, it may be advisable to reduce the amount of plyometric training to a level consistent with the development of the athlete. For example, a professional basketball team that plays a schedule of three or more games a week with constant travel may find it impossible to train with plyometric jumping exercises during the season. On the other hand, the U.S. men's national volleyball team was known to conduct plyometric training of up to 400 jumps while training during the season because they played a limited match schedule. Common sense must play a role in determining whether the athlete should continue plyometrics in-season.

Time Per Session

Actual exercise time in a beginning plyometric program should be 20 to 30 minutes. An additional 10 to 15 minutes each should be devoted to a warm-up and a cool-down that emphasize stretching and low-intensity movement activities. Warm-ups can start with passive stretching and walking and then progress to skipping, light jogging, and side-to-side movements, using big arm swings to warm up the shoulders. Cool-downs should focus on low-stress activities, such as light jogging, stretching, and walking. Advanced athletes may do longer workouts in order to perform longer drills, requiring greater recovery.

Length of Cycle

The length of time spent in any single training cycle depends on the days per week available before the start of the season. With beginning athletes, the emphasis should be on skill development, not on progression to higher-intensity exercises. Four to six weeks of a basic plyometric program is advised to ensure that athletes can properly execute the mechanics of plyometric activities before they attempt higher volumes and intensities of exercise. If time allows, a 12- to 18-week cycle is recommended. This is compatible with the off-season and preseason cycles of training discussed in the volume section.

Safety

The most important safety consideration to remember is that more is not necessarily better. If a workout has been accomplished with apparent ease, go back to the drawing board for future workouts. Don't impulsively add more exercises that day just because there's no visible fatigue. Remember that quality, not quantity, is the goal in plyometric training.

The abilities and body composition of the individual also affect the safety of training. Large, heavy athletes should not perform single-leg plyometric activities until they have fully adjusted to the stress of plyometric training. It would not be unusual for such athletes to do double-leg jumps for an entire season before developing the necessary strength for more complex activities (standing triple jumps, single-leg hops, and so on). This same conservative philosophy applies to young athletes without strength or jump training experience.

Staying physically healthy is something that many athletes take for granted, but it requires planning. Coaches must make sure that their plyometric training programs do not increase an athlete's chances of injury. Injuries often occur when muscles are tired—at the end of practice or when the coach asks for "just one more." Fatigue takes away from the sharpness of senses, and the athlete is probably just going through the motions of the exercise. Sprained ankles and twisted knees are among the common traumas associated with a lack of control due to excessive fatigue. This is the time when prudence is particularly important.

A final safety consideration concerns the overload principle. In extending this principle to plyometrics, coaches ask, "Should athletes use weights when they jump?" It is not advisable for beginning athletes to use any weighted vests, belts, or bands. Although the earlier European writings describe the use of added weight (up to 10 percent of body weight), this was for elite athletes with years of experience in training and competition. And even these athletes were not continuously subjected to this regimen. Adding weight should be done with caution, only after a long preparation period, and no more than once a week for an 8-week cycle.

PROPER EXECUTION OF PLYOMETRICS

While there are many program design elements to consider with plyometric training, coaches should focus on perfecting the technique jumping and landing mechanics with each training exercise, especially early in the training cycle. If the athlete is allowed to perform the exercise maneuvers improperly, the training will reinforce improper techniques.

Landing Mechanics

The two major reasons why athletes need to use proper technique in landing from a jump are (1) the prevention of injury and (2) the ability to produce power on the takeoff. These are major considerations for all athletes, regardless of age, abilities, and experience.

Two methods can be used to evaluate and practice landing techniques. The first is to have the athlete stand in front of a box or platform landing surface that is elevated 12 to 18 inches in height. The athlete should perform a two-foot takeoff in which he uses a countermovement (dropping the hips) prior to takeoff and should land on top of the box in a controlled fashion. The second method is to have the athlete step from the box or platform, dropping to the ground and absorbing the impact of landing. The coach should observe both of these actions from the side and then from the front of the box or platform. The key points in teaching landing technique include the following:

- Landing on the forefoot and settling to the entire foot; the weight should be evenly distributed over the entire foot. For two-foot landings, the feet should be placed approximately shoulder-width apart, and the athlete should make every attempt to keep the impact evenly shared by each foot. For single-foot landings, the stance foot will land more to the center of the body to help control the center of mass.

- Landing as softly as possible. To control the landing, the athlete should prepare to meet the ground surface by absorbing the impact in the musculature of the thighs and glutes. Inexperienced athletes will often stick the landing. They lock or snap up the joints in the lower extremities and land stiff legged. This usually represents dependence on the quadriceps muscles as the dominant muscle group. By landing in slight flexion, athletes will call into play the hamstring group as well, allowing them to have a more controlled landing.

- Flexing all three joints of the lower extremity. The athlete should land in the ready position or use proper squat technique; the hips are back, and the knees are flexed but do not project over or in front of the toes.

The coach should also observe the athlete from the side to assess proper technique. If the athlete continually lands on the forefoot or with the body excessively forward, the athlete may need to perform additional basic strengthening and balance exercises before pursuing more intense activities.

Additionally, athletes who are quadriceps dominant tend to lock up the knees and land with straight legs. This position is dangerous when it comes to protecting the anterior cruciate ligament of the knee. If the athlete lands in this way, the quadriceps pulls the tibial plateau of the lower leg abruptly forward, putting excessive stress on the ACL. Athletes who learn to control their landings use the hamstrings and glutes to control the impact forces of landing and will dampen or lessen the forces placed on the knee joints and supporting ligaments (eccentric strength).

When observing from the front, the coach can observe whether an athlete is ligament dominant, which was discussed in chapter 7. This refers to those individuals who lack overall leg and hip strength. When they land, they rely on the ligaments on the inside of the knee, namely the medial collateral ligament (MCL), to absorb the impact of landing. This position is known as *genu valgus* or *knock-knees* when the knee collapses to the inside. Thus, the coach must be sure to observe the athlete from the front in order to pinpoint whether this problem is present. If this is detected, the athlete needs to spend more time developing basic leg strength before beginning plyometric training.

At some point, the athlete needs to be evaluated on her ability to perform single-leg landings; this enables the coach to detect side-to-side differences, which reveals if one leg is significantly weaker than the other or if the control in one is impaired versus the other. The assessment that reveals this difference is known as jump and freeze. In this movement, the athlete performs a single-leg linear hop in which she covers 3 feet (91 cm) or more and lands on the same leg she took off on. The coach observes the athlete from the side and front positions again and rates her ability to control this single-leg landing on each foot. If one leg lacks control or if the athlete displays quadriceps or ligament dominance, the athlete should practice in an attempt to correct her technique and should use strength training along with the plyometric training to overcome these issues. Lack of eccentric strength in the lower extremities will manifest itself in proportion to the lack of control the athlete has.

Arm Action

For most athletes, proper arm action during jumping activities comes naturally. However, some athletes need guidance on what to do with their arms during jumps. Especially for maximal efforts, athletes need to use their arms to their advantage. For example, for a basic standing long jump, the athlete's arms should be cocked back before the movement; then, to generate more momentum, the arms should explode forward at the same time that the legs propel the body forward into the jump. The same technique applies to more advanced jumps, such as box jumps, with the arms moving in the direction of desired movement.

One activity that seems to help in reinforcing proper technique is to use a contrast drill to exaggerate the arm activity. The coach stands behind the athlete; the athlete's arms are straight and extended at the shoulders. The coach should grip the athlete's wrists and resist forward motion. The athlete positions himself to execute a jump such as the standing long jump. The athlete will extend the arms at the shoulder, and the coach will hold the athlete's wrists. The athlete attempts to swing both arms forward as the coach resists the move. Once the force approaches maximal, the coach releases the arms by merely pulling the hands away. This allows for a rapid arm movement and will often allow the athlete to sense how much the arms really contribute to the force lifting him from the ground.

◀ SUMMARY ▶

- The most important consideration in implementing and administering a plyometric training program is the athlete. Age, experience, and athletic maturity are all important criteria in establishing and modifying plyometric training.
- The following basic equipment is needed to conduct a plyometric training program: cones, boxes, hurdles, barriers, steps, and weighted objects (such as medicine balls).
- Improving landing mechanics is important both for prevention of injury and for the development of power production for takeoff.
- Focus on the perfection of technique supersedes all other program design considerations for all athletes, regardless of age, abilities, and experience.
- Plyometric exercises can take many forms and may be tailored to the specific skill or sport that the athlete is involved in.

Essential Plyometric Exercises

In this chapter, we turn our attention to the exercises that can be used to manipulate the muscular system in order to create faster movements. This chapter categorizes various plyometric exercises and explains the effects that can be achieved by performing them. Plyometric training can take many forms, including jump training for the lower extremities and medicine ball exercises for the upper extremities. To maximize the benefits of plyometrics, a person must understand not only how to do the exercises, but also how to implement and progress a program. (See chapters 8 and 10 for more information about programs.)

Early jump training exercises were classified according to the relative demands they placed on the athlete. However, all of them can be progressive in nature, and a range of low to high intensity can be used in each type of exercise. The classifications we use in this book are similar to those used by the Europeans in the 1970s. Note, however, that early writings from the Soviet Union classified hops and jumps on the basis of distance rather than type of exercise. Hops were exercises performed for distances less than 30 meters (about 33 yards), while jumps were performed for distances greater than 30 meters. This classification can become confusing, so in this book the words *hop* and *jump* are used interchangeably.

Plyometric drills, regardless of type, have one characteristic in common: For each exercise, gravity and body weight provide the resistive force that must be overcome in order to put the body in motion. This means that ground contact and the forces developed by muscles will provide the stimulus and forces necessary for the athlete to be explosive from the surface. Take away that ground contact and force of gravity acting on the body and you take away the essence of plyometric training. Therefore, it is impossible to use a trampoline or do jumps in a pool and accurately call them plyometrics. With ground contact and body weight being the major forces imposed on the body, it becomes imperative that athletes understand that quality of effort is much more crucial to their development than quantity. When quantity becomes the dominant theme of any training program, athletes run the risk of fatigue and overtraining.

JUMPS IN PLACE

A jump in place is exactly that—a jump completed by landing in the same spot where the jump started. Jumps in this category are also known as jumps on a spot and single- or multiple-response jumps. These exercises are intended to be relatively low in intensity, yet they provide the stimulus for developing a shorter amortization phase by requiring the athlete to rebound quickly from each jump. Jumps in place are done one after another with a short amortization phase.

This category of exercises may include the many footwork drills that do not require the athlete to travel a linear distance. Some of the more interesting footwork drills include low-intensity drills that are performed for short periods of time. They can be manipulated to challenge different energy systems by modifying the length of time they are carried out. For example, the ATP-PC system is challenged during drills lasting up to 10 seconds. This length of time requires the athlete to move as fast as possible to complete the drill. An example might be jumping side to side over a line as quickly as possible for 10 seconds with the movement over and back counting as one repetition. The total number of repetitions completed within the 10-second time frame yields a score. This score can then be compared to those for other athletes or can be used to track improvement by comparing it to a later trial for the same athlete.

Specific footwork drills developed by John Frappier for his training programs are useful examples of the many low-intensity movements that can be used to increase the athlete's reactivity to the ground and to improve the ability to work the feet away from the body's center of gravity. The center of gravity is a biomechanical concept that describes the point in the body about which all levers (the body's limbs) rotate. This is a theoretical concept that changes as the length of the body's levers change. Thus, in the case of an athlete who assumes a piked position, it is possible for the center of gravity to actually lie outside of the body. In the standing athlete, the center of gravity is dependent on body build. The wider the base an athlete assumes, the more stable he becomes. The essence of stability is having the center of gravity over the base of support. However, speed of movement, particularly change of direction, is in many instances dependent on the athlete's ability to have the feet work out from under the center of gravity and then quickly recover.

The first four line drills presented in this section are those developed by Frappier as part of his acceleration program. These drills are low-level, basic-skill patterns that challenge the athlete to move the body quickly and accurately. This is the essence of reactivity, helping the athlete learn to react to the ground as a stimulus. The idea is to perform as if the ground were hot or to practice touch-and-go movements.

Each of the footwork patterns is designed to challenge the athlete's ability to move the feet away from the center of gravity and become briefly unstable. The athlete then regains stability or balance when the feet are once again under the body's center of gravity. This trains the athlete to move quickly and yet be aware of his position in space when performing the drills. This is known as kinesthetic awareness. These are challenging yet easily accomplished exercises that are designed to meet the criteria of plyometric activity—requiring athletes to use the eccentric loading of the legs (stretch-shortening cycle) followed by concentric contractions.

The other 11 exercises are excellent jumps in place.

FOUR SQUARE

LEVEL

Low

EQUIPMENT

Four-square plyometric pattern, foam blocks (optional)

START

The four-square plyometric pattern (figure 9.1) is made up of two lines 48 inches (122 cm) long, crossing at right angles and forming 24-inch (61 cm) squares in each direction. The athlete starts at square number 1 and jumps in the order prescribed.

ACTION

When doing the pattern, the athlete needs to remain facing forward. The athlete should attempt to keep his body's center of gravity in the middle of the area that he is jumping in and should move his lower extremities from square to square as fast as possible. Each time the athlete returns to square 1, count one repetition. If the athlete's foot touches any part of the tape or if he misses a square, the repetition does not count.

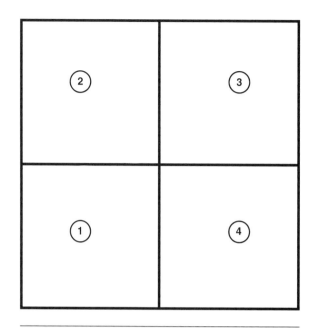

Figure 9.1 Four-square plyometric pattern.

To increase the difficulty of the pattern and increase the intensity of the drill, foam blocks 6 inches (15 cm) high and 24 inches long may be placed on the lines for the athlete to jump over. Center them on the lines separating each square in the direction the athlete will be jumping.

Blocks may be set on top of each other to further increase the difficulty of the task. If an athlete knocks over the foam blocks, the drill is stopped, the blocks are reset, and the athlete starts over.

SAMPLE PROGRAM

This program is intended to be a sample of the type of jumps taken during a workout using the four-square pattern.

As with all of the footwork patterns presented, this is just a sample program that can be reduced, expanded, or changed to fit the overall abilities and needs of the athlete. Users are limited only by their own imagination.

BOTH LEGS

Box 1-2, maximum in 10 seconds

Box 1-2-3, maximum in 15 seconds

Box 1-3-2, maximum in 15 seconds

Box 1-2-3-4, maximum in 20 seconds

SINGLE LEG

Box 1-2, maximum in 10 seconds: R_____, L_____

Box 1-4, maximum in 10 seconds: R_____, L_____

Box 1-3, maximum in 10 seconds: R_____, L_____

Box 4-2, maximum in 10 seconds: R_____, L_____

BOTH LEGS
WITH ONE 6-INCH FOAM BLOCK

Box 1-2, maximum in 10 seconds

Box 1-4, maximum in 10 seconds

LEVEL

Low

EQUIPMENT

Eight-square plyometric pattern, foam blocks (optional)

START

The eight-square plyometric pattern begins with the four squares from the first pattern; four lines are added running from the ends of each straight line at 45-degree angles (figure 9.2). Each of the new lines is 24 inches in length, and these lines cut the squares in half to create four additional "boxes." The numbering for the four new boxes starts in the area of box number 1 with 5. Go up for number 6, across for number 7, and back down to number 8.

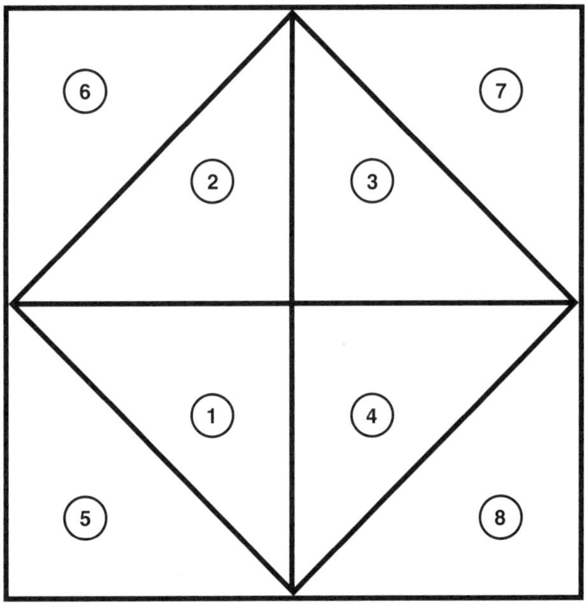

ACTION

The rules that applied for the four-square pattern also apply for the eight-square pattern. Again, the athlete should keep his body facing forward and should make sure that he does not touch any of the lines with his feet.

SAMPLE PROGRAM

BOTH LEGS

Box 1-2, maximum in 10 seconds

Box 1-2-3, maximum in 15 seconds

Box 1-3-2, maximum in 15 seconds

Box 1-4-2, maximum in 15 seconds

Box 1-2-4, maximum in 15 seconds

Box 1-2-3-4, maximum in 20 seconds

Box 1-4-3-2, maximum in 20 seconds

Box 1-3-7-5, maximum in 40 seconds

Box 4-2-6-8, maximum in 40 seconds

SINGLE LEG

Box 1-2, maximum in 5 seconds: R____, L____

Box 1-4, maximum in 5 seconds: R____, L____

Box 1-3, maximum in 5 seconds: R____, L____

BOTH LEGS

Box 1-4-5-8, maximum in 20 seconds

Box 5-6-7-8, maximum in 40 seconds

BOTH LEGS
WITH ONE 6-INCH FOAM BLOCK

Box 1-4, maximum in 15 seconds

Box 5-8, maximum in 30 seconds

Box 4-6, maximum in 30 seconds

Figure 9.2 Eight-square plyometric pattern.

LEVEL

Low

EQUIPMENT

Tape to mark floor

START

This pattern was designed for and named after Anthony Muñoz, former all-pro offensive tackle for the Cincinnati Bengals. Use two 48-inch strips of tape laid on the floor 8 inches (20 cm) apart from inside edge to inside edge. The even-numbered squares on the right side of the formation are 16 inches (41 cm) apart, separated by strips that are 24 inches long. On the left-hand side, square number 1 is 8 inches, square 3 is 16 inches, and square 5 is 24 inches. On each of the squares, the dividing line is also 24 inches long (figure 9.3).

ACTION

The athlete follows the same rules that applied to the four-square and eight-square patterns. The athlete should keep her body facing forward and should not touch any of the lines with her feet.

SAMPLE PROGRAM

BOTH LEGS

Box 1-2 (2 sets), maximum in 5 seconds

Box 1-4 (2 sets), maximum in 5 seconds

Box 2-5 (2 sets), maximum in 5 seconds

Box 2-3-4 (2 sets), maximum in 10 seconds

Box 1-2-3 (2 sets), maximum in 10 seconds

Box 1-2-3-4-5-6 (2 sets), total time

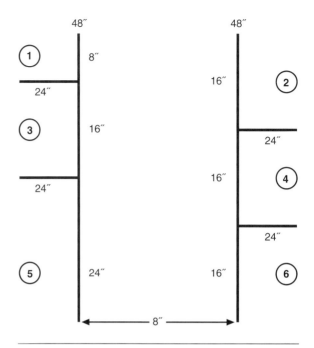

Figure 9.3 Munoz formation.

LEVEL

Low

EQUIPMENT

Tape to mark floor

START

Frappier designed and named this program for Tim Krumrie, all-pro defensive tackle for the Cincinnati Bengals. This pattern resembles a tic-tac-toe board. Take four 48-inch strips of tape and lay out a pattern so that the inside measurement of each square is 16 inches along each side (figure 9.4).

ACTION

Follow the pattern numbering as in the other formations. The athlete keeps his body facing forward and does not touch any of the lines with his feet.

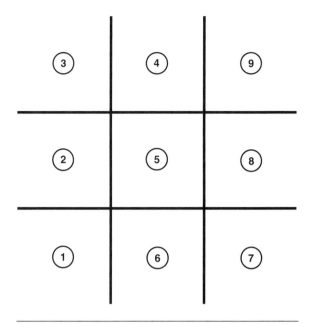

Figure 9.4 Krumrie formation.

SAMPLE PROGRAM

Box 1-5-9 (2 sets), maximum in 5 seconds

Box 7-5-3 (2 sets), maximum in 5 seconds

Box 6-7-6-1 (2 sets), maximum in 15 seconds

Box 6-1-6-7 (2 sets), maximum in 15 seconds

Box 1-2-5-8-9-4, total time

TWO-FOOT ANKLE HOPS

LEVEL

Low

EQUIPMENT

None

SPORTS

Baseball, softball, tennis, volleyball

START

Stand with feet shoulder-width apart and the body in a vertical position.

ACTION

Using only the ankles for momentum, hop continuously in one place (figure 9.5). Extend the ankles to their maximum range on each vertical hop.

Figure 9.5 Two-foot ankle hop.

SINGLE-FOOT SIDE-TO-SIDE ANKLE HOP

LEVEL

Low

EQUIPMENT

No equipment is required but cones placed 3 to 4 feet (91 to 122 cm) apart may be used as borders.

SPORTS

Track and field (jump events, sprints, and throwing events)

START

Stand on one foot. If using cones, stand between the cones.

ACTION

Hop from one foot to the other (figure 9.6). If using cones, land on the right foot next to the right cone, then land on the left foot next to the left cone. Continue hopping back and forth.

Figure 9.6 Single-foot side-to-side ankle hop: *(a)* hop to right side; *(b)* hop to left side.

SIDE-TO-SIDE ANKLE HOP

LEVEL

Low

EQUIPMENT

No equipment is required, but cones may be used as borders.

SPORTS

Baseball, softball, figure skating, tennis

START

Stand with feet shoulder-width apart and the body in a vertical position.

ACTION

Using both feet, jump from side to side (figure 9.7); the jump should cover a span of 2 to 3 feet (61 to 91 cm). Produce the motion from the ankles. Keep the feet shoulder-width apart and land on both feet at the same time.

Figure 9.7 Side-to-side ankle hop: *(a)* hop to right side; *(b)* hop to left side.

TUCK JUMP WITH KNEES UP

LEVEL

Moderate to high

EQUIPMENT

None

SPORTS

Bicycling, diving, weightlifting

START

Stand with feet shoulder-width apart and the body in a vertical position; do not bend at the waist.

ACTION

Jump up, bringing the knees up to the chest and grasping the knees with the hands (figure 9.8) before the feet return to the floor. Land in a standing vertical position. Repeat the jump immediately.

Figure 9.8 Tuck jump with knees up.

TUCK JUMP WITH HEEL KICK

LEVEL

Moderate

EQUIPMENT

None

SPORTS

Downhill skiing, figure skating, gymnastics

START

Stand with the feet shoulder-width apart, the body in a straight vertical position, and the arms by your sides.

ACTION

Keeping the knees pointed down (still in line with the body), jump and kick the buttocks with the heels (figure 9.9). Repeat the jump immediately. This is a quick-stepping action from the knees and lower legs. Swing the arms up as you jump.

Figure 9.9 Tuck jump with heel kick.

SPLIT-SQUAT JUMP

LEVEL

Moderate

EQUIPMENT

None

SPORTS

Soccer, volleyball, weightlifting

START

Spread the feet far apart, front to back, and bend the front leg 90 degrees at the hip and 90 degrees at the knee (figure 9.10a).

ACTION

Jump up, using the arms to help lift, and hold the split-squat position (figure 9.10b). Land in the same position and immediately repeat the jump.

 TIP Try for complete extension of the legs and hips when you jump. Remember that the ankle, knee, hip, and trunk all play a vital role in achieving maximal height when jumping and in achieving speed when running.

Figure 9.10 Split-squat jump: *(a)* starting position; *(b)* jump with split-squat position.

SPLIT SQUAT WITH CYCLE

LEVEL

High

EQUIPMENT

None

SPORTS

Bicycling, figure skating, ice hockey

START

Standing upright, spread the feet far apart, front to back, and bend the front leg 90 degrees at the hip and 90 degrees at the knee (figure 9.11a).

ACTION

Jumping up, switch leg positions—the front leg kicks to the back position, and the back leg bends up and comes through to the front (figure 9.11b). While bringing the back leg through, try to flex the knee so that it comes close to the buttock. Land in the split-squat position (figure 9.11c) and jump again immediately.

Figure 9.11   Split squat with cycle: *(a)* starting position; *(b)* jump; *(c)* landing.

SPLIT-PIKE JUMP

LEVEL

High

EQUIPMENT

None

SPORTS

Figure skating, gymnastics

START

Stand in the athletic position with the feet shoulder-width apart.

ACTION

Jump up and lift the legs so that they are spread in a V position at the hips at the height of the jump (figure 9.12). The legs should be maintained in a straight position throughout the jump. Return to the starting position and repeat.

Figure 9.12 Split-pike jump.

STRAIGHT-PIKE JUMP

LEVEL

High

EQUIPMENT

None

SPORTS

Diving

START

Stand with the feet shoulder-width apart and the body straight.

ACTION

Jump up and bring the legs up together in front of the body; flexion should occur only at the hips (figure 9.13). Attempt to touch your toes at the peak of the jump. Return to the starting position and repeat.

Figure 9.13 Straight-pike jump.

SPLIT-SQUAT JUMP WITH BOUNCE

LEVEL

Moderate

EQUIPMENT

None

SPORTS

Soccer, volleyball, weightlifting, basketball

START

Spread the feet shoulder-width apart, side to side. Then spread the feet far apart, front to back, and bend the front knee to 90 degrees.

ACTION

From the split position, perform two small pulses, maintaining the split position. Then perform the jump as in the regular split-squat jump. Pulse two times before performing each subsequent jump.

HIP-TWIST ANKLE HOP

LEVEL

Low

EQUIPMENT

None

SPORTS

Downhill skiing

START

Stand with feet shoulder-width apart and the upper body in a vertical position.

ACTION

Hop up and twist from the hips, turning the legs in a 180-degree arc. On the next hop, turn the legs to return to the starting position. Continue turning the legs from side to side on each hop. The upper body does not turn; the movement comes from the hips and legs.

STANDING JUMPS

A standing jump usually begins from an athletic position and emphasizes a maximal effort in either a horizontal or vertical direction. These efforts may be singular or multiple, and the athlete should use a fully elongated arm swing in order to develop as much force into the ground as possible. These jumps are particularly good for developing start speed and acceleration of the body.

STANDING JUMP-AND-REACH

LEVEL

Low

EQUIPMENT

An object suspended overhead, or a wall with a target marked

SPORTS

Diving, swimming, volleyball

START

Stand with feet shoulder-width apart.

ACTION

Squat slightly (figure 9.14a) and explode upward, reaching for a target or object (figure 9.14b). Do not step before jumping.

Figure 9.14 Standing jump-and-reach: *(a)* drop and arm swing; *(b)* jump.

STANDING LONG JUMP

LEVEL

Low

EQUIPMENT

A soft landing surface, such as a mat or sandpit

SPORTS

Baseball, softball, swimming, track and field (sprints)

START

Stand in a semisquat with feet shoulder-width apart.

ACTION

Using a big arm swing and a countermovement (flexing) of the legs (figure 9.15a), jump forward as far as possible (figure 9.15b).

Figure 9.15 Standing long jump: (a) drop and arm swing; (b) jump.

STANDING LONG JUMP WITH SPRINT

LEVEL

Moderate to high

EQUIPMENT

A mark 10 meters (or yards) from the end spot of the jump; a mat, grass surface, or sandpit for landing (optional)

SPORTS

Ice hockey, track and field (jumping events and sprints)

START

Stand in a semisquat with feet shoulder-width apart.

ACTION

Using a big arm swing, jump forward as far as possible (figure 9.16a). On landing, sprint forward approximately 10 meters (figure 9.16b). Try to keep from collapsing on the landing; land fully on both feet, then explode into a sprint.

 TIP Think *touch and go* when executing hops and jumps. You want to get off the landing surface as fast as possible.

Figure 9.16 Standing long jump with sprint: (a) jump forward; (b) sprint.

STANDING LONG JUMP WITH LATERAL SPRINT

LEVEL

Moderate to high

EQUIPMENT

Two marks, 10 meters to either side of a landing pit

SPORTS

Football

START

Stand in a semisquat with feet shoulder-width apart.

ACTION

Using a big arm swing, perform a standing long jump. Land on both feet, trying to stay upright. Immediately sprint laterally (right or left) for 3 meters (figures 9.17a and b).

Figure 9.17 Standing long jump with lateral sprint: *(a)* landing; *(b)* lateral sprint.

STANDING JUMP OVER BARRIER

LEVEL

Low to moderate

EQUIPMENT

One cone or hurdle

SPORTS

Baseball, softball, basketball, football

START

Stand with feet shoulder-width apart.

ACTION

Bending only at the hips (figure 9.18a), bring the knees up to jump over the barrier (figure 9.18b). Don't let the knees turn sideways or split apart to clear the object.

Figure 9.18 Standing jump over barrier: *(a)* drop the hips; *(b)* jump over cone.

LEVEL

Moderate

EQUIPMENT

A mark 40 meters from the start

SPORTS

Track and field (jumping events)

START

Stand with one foot slightly in front of the other.

ACTION

Use three steps (left-right-left or right-left-right) in a continuous motion to simulate a takeoff (figure 9.19, *a-c*). Complete the three steps with a quick-quicker-quickest rhythm, then explode vertically off the last one (figure 9.19*d*). Emphasize the action of takeoff and make the motion crisp. As soon as you land after the jump, step right into the next sequence of steps. Continue for 40 meters.

Figure 9.19 1-2-3 drill: *(a)* first step; *(b)* second step; *(c)* third step; *(d)* explode.

STRADDLE JUMP TO CAMEL LANDING

LEVEL

Moderate

EQUIPMENT

A mat or flexible barrier

SPORTS

Figure skating

START

Stand with one foot in front of the other at an angle to the side of the mat or barrier (figure 9.20a).

ACTION

Using an action similar to a straddle high jump, plant the takeoff foot at an angle to the

Figure 9.20 Straddle jump to camel landing: *(a)* starting position; *(b)* landing.

barrier and use a straight-leg swing of the lead leg to lift the body over the mat. This turns the front of your body so it straddles the mat. Land on the foot that cleared the mat first, and let the trailing leg swing over and in a straight line behind you (figure 9.20b). Hold your arms out to the side for balance as if you were a figure skater on skates.

SINGLE-LEG LATERAL JUMP

LEVEL

Moderate to high

EQUIPMENT

Small barrier (optional)

SPORTS

Ice hockey, soccer

START

Stand on your right foot (figure 9.21a).

ACTION

Jump up but push sideways to the left off the ground and land on your right foot (figure 9.21b). Immediately push off sideways to the right, landing on the right foot again. Continue pushing off from and landing on your right foot for the prescribed repetitions. Repeat this exercise using the other leg.

Figure 9.21 Single-leg lateral jump: *(a)* starting position; *(b)* jump.

LATERAL JUMP OVER BARRIER

LEVEL

Low to moderate

EQUIPMENT

One cone or hurdle

SPORTS

Soccer

START

Stand alongside the object to be cleared (figure 9.22a).

ACTION

Jumping vertically but pushing sideways off the ground, bring the knees up to jump sideways over the barrier (figure 9.22b).

Figure 9.22 Lateral jump over barrier: *(a)* starting position; *(b)* jump.

LATERAL JUMP WITH TWO FEET

LEVEL

Low

EQUIPMENT

None

SPORTS

Baseball, softball

START

Stand with feet shoulder-width apart.

ACTION

Swing the leg on the side to which you are going to jump across the stationary leg. Swing the same leg out to the other side and jump in that direction as far as possible, landing on both feet. Then jump back to the starting position by reversing the process.

STANDING TRIPLE JUMP

LEVEL

High

EQUIPMENT

A mat or sandpit

SPORTS

Track and field (sprints)

START

Stand with feet shoulder-width apart, 3 to 6 meters from a sandpit or other soft landing surface such as a mat (distance depends on ability).

ACTION

Push off both feet simultaneously (figure 9.23a) and extend through the hips to land on one foot (hop; figure 9.23b); then push from this foot forward to land on the other foot (step; figure 9.23c); then jump from that foot, extending the feet forward as far as possible and landing with both feet in the pit or on a mat (figure 9.23d).

Figure 9.23 Standing triple jump: (a) first step; (b) hop landing; (c) step landing; (d) jump.

STANDING TRIPLE JUMP WITH BARRIER JUMP

High

A barrier (a line of cones or a mat) just in front of a sandpit

Track and field (sprints)

Stand with feet shoulder-width apart, 3 to 6 meters from a sandpit (distance depends on ability).

Push off both feet simultaneously (figure 9.24a) and extend through the hips to land on one foot (hop; figure 9.24b); then push from this foot forward to land on the other foot (step; figure 9.24c); then jump from that foot over the barrier (figure 9.24d), extending the feet forward as far as possible.

Figure 9.24 Standing triple jump with barrier jump: *(a)* push off both feet; *(b)* land on one foot; *(c)* land on other foot; *(d)* jump over barrier.

MULTIPLE HOPS AND JUMPS

Multiple hops and jumps combine the skills developed by performing jumps in place and standing jumps. These exercises require a controlled, maximal effort to perform one movement after another. Multiple hops and jumps are best performed over a distance of less than 30 meters (or yards). For proper technique, athletes should focus on having a brief ground contact time between attempts and using a powerful arm swing to assist at takeoff. These exercises consist of repeated, moderate to maximal efforts. Advanced forms of multiple jumps can also be found under the heading Box Drills.

HEXAGON DRILL

LEVEL

Low

EQUIPMENT

A hexagon with 24-inch sides formed with tape on the floor

SPORTS

Figure skating, soccer, squash, racquetball, tennis

START

Stand in the center of the hexagon with feet shoulder-width apart.

ACTION

Jump across one side of the hexagon and back to center, then proceed around each side of the hexagon (figure 9.25). This may be done for a specific number of complete trips around the hexagon or for a total time.

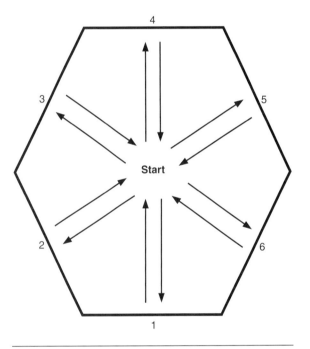

Figure 9.25 Hexagon drill.

FRONT CONE HOP

LEVEL

Low

EQUIPMENT

A row of 6 to 10 cones or small barriers (8 to 12 inches [20 to 30 cm] tall) set up approximately 3 to 6 feet (91 to 183 cm) apart

SPORTS

Baseball, softball, downhill skiing, tennis

START

Stand with feet shoulder-width apart at the end of the line of barriers (with their length spread out before you).

ACTION

Keeping the feet shoulder-width apart, jump over each barrier (figure 9.26), landing on both feet at the same time. Use a double-arm swing and work to decrease the time spent on the ground between each barrier.

Figure 9.26 Front cone hop.

DIAGONAL CONE HOP

LEVEL

Low

EQUIPMENT

A row of 6 to 10 cones or small barriers (8 to 12 inches tall) staggered approximately 3 to 4 feet apart

SPORTS

Downhill skiing

START

Stand with feet together at the end of the line of barriers.

ACTION

Keeping the ankles together, jump in a zigzag fashion across the barriers (figure 9.27), moving down the line. Land on the balls of the feet at the same time, and use a double-arm swing to stabilize the body movement.

Figure 9.27 Diagonal cone hop.

CONE HOP WITH CHANGE-OF-DIRECTION SPRINT

Moderate

A partner and a row of 6 to 10 cones placed 3 to 4 feet apart with the last two cones placed to form a Y

Football, soccer, tennis

Stand with feet shoulder-width apart in the athletic position.

Perform two-foot hops over the row of cones. As you clear the last cone (figure 9.28a), your partner points to one of the far cones. Sprint to that cone immediately after landing from the last hop (figure 9.28b).

Figure 9.28 Cone hop with change-of-direction sprint: (a) land over last cone; (b) sprint in direction indicated by partner.

LATERAL CONE HOP

LEVEL

Moderate

EQUIPMENT

Three to five cones lined up 2 to 3 feet apart. Distance depends on ability.

SPORTS

Basketball, ice hockey, in-line skating, speedskating, tennis, wrestling

START

Stand with feet shoulder-width apart at the end of the line of cones (with cones stretched out to one side).

ACTION

Jump sideways down the row of cones, landing on both feet (figure 9.29a). In clearing the last cone, land on the outside foot (figure 9.29b) and push off to change direction (figure 9.29c), then jump two-footed back down the row of cones sideways. At the last cone, push off again on the outside foot and change directions. Keep movement smooth and even, trying not to pause when changing directions.

Figure 9.29 Lateral cone hop: (a) jump over cones; (b) at last cone, land on outside foot; (c) push off outside foot to change direction.

CONE HOP WITH 180-DEGREE TURN

LEVEL

Moderate

EQUIPMENT

A line of four to six cones spaced 2 to 3 feet apart

SPORTS

Soccer

START

Stand next to the line of cones, with your feet even with the first cone (figure 9.30a).

ACTION

Jump and, while in the air, turn 180 degrees (figure 9.30b) so that you land facing the opposite direction (figure 9.30c). Continue to jump and turn in the air down the entire line of cones.

Figure 9.30 Cone hop with 180-degree turn: (a) starting position; (b) jump and turn 180 degrees in the air; (c) land facing the opposite direction.

RIM JUMP

LEVEL

Low to moderate

EQUIPMENT

A high object such as a basketball goal or the crossbar on a football goalpost

SPORTS

Basketball, volleyball, weightlifting

START

Stand under the high object with feet shoulder-width apart.

ACTION

Jump continuously, reaching with the hands and trying to reach the object on every jump (figure 9.31). Time on the ground should be minimal, and each jump should be at least as high as the one before.

Figure 9.31 Rim jump.

DOUBLE-LEG HOPS

LEVEL

Moderate

EQUIPMENT

None

SPORTS

Figure skating, football, in-line skating, speedskating, swimming, track and field (sprints)

START

Stand with feet shoulder-width apart.

ACTION

Squat down (figure 9.32a) and jump as far forward as possible (figure 9.32b). Immediately after touching down, jump forward again. Use quick double-arm swings and keep landings short. Do in multiples of three to five jumps.

Figure 9.32 Double-leg hops: *(a)* drop position; *(b)* jump.

SINGLE-LEG HOPS

LEVEL

High

EQUIPMENT

None

SPORTS

Ice hockey, track and field (sprints), wrestling

START

Stand on one leg (figure 9.33a).

Figure 9.33 Single-leg hops: *(a)* starting position; *(b)* jump.

ACTION

Push off the standing leg and jump forward (figure 9.33b), landing on the same leg. Use a strong leg swing to increase jump length and strive for height. Immediately take off again and continue for 10 to 25 meters. Perform this drill with the other leg for symmetrical development. Beginning athletes will use a straighter jump leg; advanced athletes should try to pull the heel toward the buttocks during the jump.

HURDLE (BARRIER) HOP

LEVEL

Moderate to high

EQUIPMENT

Hurdles or barriers (12 to 36 inches [30 to 91 cm] high) set up in a row, spaced according to athlete ability. Barriers should be able to collapse if the athlete makes a mistake.

SPORTS

Rugby, track and field (sprints)

START

Stand at the end of the line of barriers (figure 9.34a).

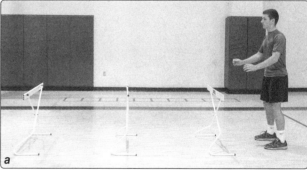

Figure 9.34 Hurdle (barrier) hop: *(a)* starting position; *(b)* jump over hurdle.

ACTION

Jump forward over the barriers, keeping the feet together (figure 9.34b). Movement comes from the hips and knees; keep the body vertical and straight, and do not let the knees move apart or to either side. Use a double-arm swing to maintain balance and to gain height.

STANDING LONG JUMP WITH HURDLE HOP

LEVEL

Moderate to high

TIP
Perform these exercises as if each jump is the highest and the best that you've ever done. Think of every effort as the last one. Maximal effort in training makes your effort in competition look easy.

EQUIPMENT

Three to six hurdles 18 to 42 inches (46 to 107 cm) high placed 8 to 12 feet (2.4 to 3.6 m) apart. Use hurdle heights that are challenging yet allow the athlete to perform the jumps by spending a minimal amount of time on the ground.

SPORTS

Basketball, netball, swimming, track and field (jumping events), volleyball

START

Stand with feet shoulder-width apart in the ready position (figure 9.35a).

ACTION

Perform a standing long jump from a two-foot start (figure 9.35b). After landing approximately 18 inches in front of the hurdle (figure 9.35c), jump vertically over the hurdle (figure 9.35d). Continue moving forward over the remaining hurdles by repeating a standing long jump followed by a vertical jump over each hurdle. Use a double-arm swing to maximize both the long and vertical (hurdle) jumps.

Figure 9.35 Standing long jump with hurdle hop: (a) starting position; (b) standing long jump; (c) landing in front of hurdle; (d) jumping over hurdle.

WAVE SQUAT

LEVEL

High

EQUIPMENT

External resistance ranging from a 6-pound medicine ball to a barbell with 60 percent of the athlete's body weight

SPORTS

Basketball, diving, football, track and field (sprints), volleyball

START

Start in a quarter-squat position with weight resting on the shoulders (figure 9.36a). Feet should be shoulder-width apart.

ACTION

Start moving forward by performing three double-leg hops with the resistance on the shoulders, flexing the knees to approximately 130 degrees (figure 9.36b). On the fourth jump, descend to a 90-degree position of knee flexion (figure 9.36c) and perform a maximal vertical jump (figure 9.36d). Perform the sequence several times for maximal effort.

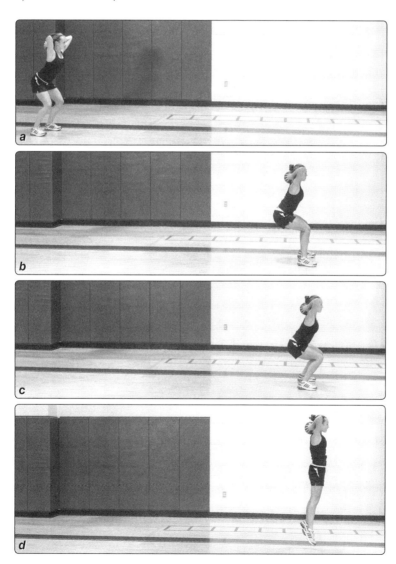

Figure 9.36 Wave squat: (a) starting position; (b) double-leg hop; (c) 90-degree knee flexion; (d) maximal vertical jump.

LEVEL

Moderate to high

EQUIPMENT

Bleachers or stadium steps

SPORTS

Bicycling, downhill skiing, track and field (jumping events), weightlifting, wrestling

START

Stand in a quarter-squat position at the bottom of the bleachers; hands are on the hips or the back of the neck, and feet are shoulder-width apart (figure 9.37a).

Figure 9.37 Stadium hops: *(a)* starting position; *(b)* jump.

ACTION

Jump to the first bleacher (figure 9.37b) and continue up for 10 or more jumps. Make the landings light and quick; movements should be continuous up the stairs without pauses. Generally, athletes should be able to take two bleachers at a time.

ZIGZAG DRILL

LEVEL

Moderate to high

EQUIPMENT

Two parallel lines, 24 to 42 inches apart and 10 meters long

SPORTS

Basketball, diving, football, track and field (sprinting), volleyball

START

Stand balanced on one foot on a line.

ACTION

Jump from one line to the other (figure 9.38) in a continuous forward motion for 10 meters, always taking off and landing on the same foot. Do not "double hop" at the touchdown.

Figure 9.38 Zigzag drill: *(a)* jump from one line; *(b)* land on other line on same foot; *(c)* jump back to first line.

OLYMPIC HOPS

LEVEL

Moderate

EQUIPMENT

A 10- to 20-yard stretch of surface

SPORTS

Downhill skiing, in-line skating, rugby, wrestling

START

Assume a deep-squat position (figure 9.39a) with the upper body straight and the hands held behind the head with fingers interlocked.

ACTION

Initiate a small hop with the body in a vertical posture and both feet coming off the ground (figure 9.39b). Hip and knee movement should be less than full extension. Maintain the squat position throughout the hop execution so that you use the hips and adductors to initiate and continue the movement.

Figure 9.39 Olympic hops: *(a)* deep-squat starting position; *(b)* hop.

DEPTH JUMPS

Depth, or drop, jumps use the athlete's body weight and gravity to impose force against the ground. This force must be overcome in order for the athlete to demonstrate that she has the strength and power to react to this ground force. Ground reaction forces are the key to the development of power within the athlete. The time spent on the ground is the negative in plyometric drills, and all athletes should attempt to be off the ground as quickly as possible. This is the essence of speed and power development.

Because depth jumps are intended to be of a prescribed intensity, an athlete should never jump from the top of a box to add even greater height and ultimately more force to the jump. Rather, the athlete should attempt to step off the box into space before dropping to the ground. Controlling the height dropped helps accurately measure intensity and also helps reduce overuse problems.

Depth jumps are very stressful on the body and very technically demanding. Therefore, several exercises can be used as precursor exercises to help the athlete learn the components of the depth jump simply and effectively. The following drills will facilitate the learning curve of beginning or novice athletes.

DROP AND FREEZE

LEVEL

Low

EQUIPMENT

A box or landing surface 18 to 24 inches high

SPORTS

Soccer, basketball, volleyball, mixed martial arts

START

Stand on the box with both feet close to the front edge of the box.

ACTION

Place one foot over the edge of the box and pull up the toe to lock the ankle. Slightly flex the other knee and use it to push out over the edge of the surface (figure 9.40a). Attempt to drop the

Figure 9.40 Drop and freeze: *(a)* step off box; *(b)* land on both feet.

exact distance that you are off the ground. Land on both feet (figure 9.40b), with the knees flexed, and immediately stop any further downward motion. This freezing action will help to build eccentric strength and develop control in the landing of all plyometric activities.

LEVEL

Low to moderate

EQUIPMENT

A box 6 to 12 inches high with a top surface no smaller than 24 inches square

SPORTS

Diving, netball

START

Stand on the ground with feet shoulder-width apart, facing a box.

ACTION

Squat slightly and, using the double-arm swing (figure 9.41a), jump from the ground onto the box (figure 9.41b).

Figure 9.41 Jump to box: (a) flex knees and swing arms; (b) jump onto box.

LEVEL

Low

EQUIPMENT

An object suspended at the peak of the athlete's jump

SPORTS

Diving

START

Stand in a staggered stance, front to back.

ACTION

Take a short step forward with the preferred foot and quickly bring the back foot together with the front foot (a step-close technique). Then jump vertically, reaching for the suspended object.

DEPTH (DROP) JUMP

LEVEL

Low to moderate

EQUIPMENT

A box 12 inches high

SPORTS

Gymnastics, netball, volleyball, weightlifting

START

Stand on the box, with toes close to the front edge.

ACTION

Step from the box (figure 9.42a) and drop to land on both feet (figure 9.42b). Try to anticipate the landing and spring up as quickly as you can (figure 9.42c). Keep the body from settling on the landing, and make the ground contact as short as possible.

Figure 9.42 Depth (drop) jump: (a) step from box; (b) drop landing; (c) jump.

DEPTH JUMP OVER BARRIER

LEVEL

High

EQUIPMENT

A 12- to 42-inch box and a barrier 28 to 36 inches high, placed about 3 feet from the box

SPORTS

Diving

START

Stand on the box, with feet shoulder-width apart.

ACTION

Step off the box (figure 9.43a) and, after landing (figure 9.43b), jump over the barrier (figure 9.43c).

Figure 9.43 Depth jump over barrier: (a) step off box; (b) landing; (c) jump over barrier.

DEPTH JUMP TO RIM JUMP

LEVEL

Moderate

EQUIPMENT

A box 12 to 42 inches high placed in front of an elevated marker such as a basketball hoop

SPORTS

Basketball

START

Stand on the box, with toes close to the edge and facing the high object.

ACTION

Step off the box (figure 9.44a) and land on both feet (figure 9.44b). Immediately jump up, reaching with one hand toward the marker (figure 9.44c), and then do repeated jumps, alternating hands and trying to reach the object each time. Time on the ground should be very short, and each jump should be as high as the one before. Perform three to five rim jumps after each depth jump.

Figure 9.44 Depth jump to rim jump: (a) step off box; (b) drop down; (c) jump to target.

LEVEL

High

EQUIPMENT

A box 12 to 42 inches high, a basketball, and a basketball goal

SPORTS

Basketball

START

Stand on the box, with toes close to the edge, and hold a ball in front of you.

ACTION

Step off the box (figure 9.45a) and land on both feet (figure 9.45b). Explode up and forward while extending your arms and the ball up (figure 9.45c). Try to stuff the ball in the basket, or at least touch the rim.

Figure 9.45 Depth jump with stuff: *(a)* step off box; *(b)* drop down; *(c)* jump up and stuff ball.

DEPTH JUMP WITH LATERAL MOVEMENT

EQUIPMENT
A partner and a box 12 to 42 inches high

SPORTS
Tennis

START
Stand on the box, with toes close to the edge, facing your partner (figure 9.46a).

ACTION
Step off the box and land on both feet (figure 9.46b). As you land, your partner points to the right or left (figure 9.46c); sprint in that direction for 10 to 12 meters.

Figure 9.46 Depth jump with lateral movement: *(a)* starting position; *(b)* drop down; *(c)* sprint in direction that partner points.

DEPTH JUMP WITH 180-DEGREE TURN

LEVEL

Moderate to high

EQUIPMENT

One or two boxes 12 to 42 inches high

SPORTS

Basketball, figure skating, netball, rugby, track and field (throwing events)

START

Stand on a box, with toes close to the edge.

ACTION

Step off the box (figure 9.47a) and land on both feet (figure 9.47b). Immediately jump up and do a 180-degree turn in the air (figure 9.47c), landing again on both feet. For added difficulty, jump on the box again after doing the turn (figure 9.47d).

Figure 9.47 Depth jump with 180-degree turn: *(a)* step off box; *(b)* land on both feet; *(c)* jump and rotate; *(d)* jump on box.

DEPTH JUMP WITH 360-DEGREE TURN

High

One or two boxes 12 to 42 inches high

Basketball, rugby, track and field (throwing events)

Stand on a box, with toes close to the edge.

Step off the box and land on both feet (figure 9.48*a*). Immediately jump up and do a 360-degree turn in the air (figure 9.48*b*), landing again on both feet (figure 9.48*c*). For added difficulty, land on a second box after doing the turn. This is an advanced drill; it should not be performed by beginners.

Figure 9.48   Depth jump with 360-degree turn: *(a)* land on both feet; *(b)* rotate in the air; *(c)* land again on both feet.

LEVEL

High

EQUIPMENT

A box 12 to 42 inches high

SPORTS

Diving, swimming

START

Stand on the box, with feet shoulder-width apart and toes close to the edge (figure 9.49a).

ACTION

Step off the box and land on both feet (figure 9.49b). Immediately after landing, jump as far forward as possible (figure 9.49c), again landing on both feet.

Figure 9.49 Depth jump to standing long jump: *(a)* starting position; *(b)* drop to ground; *(c)* long jump.

LEVEL

High

EQUIPMENT

A box 12 to 18 inches high

SPORTS

Diving, gymnastics, soccer

START

Stand on the box, with toes close to the edge.

ACTION

Step off the box (figure 9.50a) and land on one foot (figure 9.50b). Then jump as high as possible (figure 9.50c), landing on the same foot. Keep the ground contact as short as possible. For added difficulty, jump to a second box after the jump. This is an advanced drill; it should not be performed by beginners.

Figure 9.50 Single-leg depth jump: *(a)* step off the box; *(b)* land on one foot; *(c)* jump.

LEVEL

High

EQUIPMENT

A box 12 to 42 inches high and a partner with a blocking bag

SPORTS

Football

START

Stand on the box, with toes close to the edge (figure 9.51a). The partner stands facing the box, about 4 feet away.

ACTION

Step off the box and land on both feet (figure 9.51b). On landing, explode into the blocking bag shoulder first (figure 9.51c).

Figure 9.51 Depth jump with blocking bag: (a) starting position; (b) drop down; (c) explode into blocking bag.

LEVEL

High

EQUIPMENT

A box 12 to 42 inches high and a partner with a football

SPORTS

Football, rugby

START

Stand on the box, with toes close to the edge, facing your partner (figure 9.52a).

ACTION

Step off the box and land on both feet (figure 9.52b). Explode up and forward, extending your arms to catch a pass from your partner at the peak of your jump (figure 9.52c).

Figure 9.52 Depth jump with pass catching: (a) starting position; (b) drop down; (c) jump and catch.

DEPTH JUMP WITH BACKWARD GLIDE

LEVEL

High

EQUIPMENT

A box 12 to 42 inches high

SPORTS

Track and field (throwing events)

START

Stand with heels close to the back of the box and with feet shoulder-width apart (figure 9.53a).

ACTION

Step backward off the box and land on both feet (figure 9.53b). Immediately after landing, thrust one leg back and perform a glide step pattern as if shot putting (figure 9.53c).

Figure 9.53 Depth jump with backward glide: (a) starting position; (b) jump down behind box; (c) glide step.

DEPTH JUMP TO PRESCRIBED HEIGHT

LEVEL

Low to moderate

EQUIPMENT

Two boxes of equal height placed 2 to 4 feet apart. Height and distance depend on athlete ability.

SPORTS

Diving, track and field (jumping events), volleyball

START

Stand on one box, with toes close to the front edge and with feet shoulder-width apart, facing the second box.

ACTION

Step off the box, landing on both feet, and jump onto the second box, landing lightly. The jump from the ground should be as quick as possible.

PLYOMETRIC PUSH-UP

LEVEL

High

EQUIPMENT

Padded surface

SPORTS

Track and field throwing events, football

START

Assume the classic push-up position—prone, feet together, and hands shoulder-width apart at the level of the shoulders.

ACTION

Push hard enough against the surface so that the upper body and hands leave the padded surface. The distance will depend on the athlete's upper-body strength. Anticipate the landing and use the arms to land softly and decelerate the upper body. Note: In another version, the athlete assumes a spread-eagle position and uses the arms and legs to propel the entire body from the surface.

INCLINE PUSH-UP DEPTH JUMP

LEVEL

Moderate

EQUIPMENT

Two mats, 3 to 4 inches (7.6 to 10.2 cm) high, placed shoulder-width apart; a box high enough to elevate the athlete's feet above the shoulders when the athlete is in a push-up position

SPORTS

Bicycling, diving, volleyball

START

Face the floor as if you were going to do a push-up, with your feet on the box and with your hands between the mats.

ACTION

Push off the ground with your hands and land with one hand on each mat. Either remove one hand at a time from the mats and place them in the starting position or, for added difficulty, push off the mats with both hands and catch yourself in the starting position.

HANDSTAND DEPTH JUMP

LEVEL

High

EQUIPMENT

A partner and two mats or padded boxes, 3 to 4 inches high, placed shoulder-width apart

SPORTS

Gymnastics

START

Stand between the mats or padded boxes, with a partner standing behind, and do a handstand on the floor (figure 9.54a).

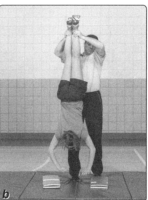

Figure 9.54 Handstand depth jump: *(a)* starting position; *(b)* push off hands; *(c)* land on hands.

ACTION

Push off the floor with both hands (figure 9.54b), landing with one hand on each mat (figure 9.54c). Then push up off the mats and land with your hands in their starting positions. The partner spots for the athlete, ensuring that the body stays vertical.

BOX DRILLS

Box drills combine the essence of both multiple jumps and depth jumps. These drills can range in intensity from fairly low to very high. They serve to develop both horizontal and vertical jumping skills simultaneously. Many box drills can be used as conditioning drills. The jump activities can consist of a few repetitions, or they can go for time intervals as long as 90 seconds. Any box drill can be used to challenge an athlete for shorter intervals and thus involve the phosphocreatine (or PC) energy system; a box drill may also challenge the athlete for longer intervals and thus involve the glycolytic energy system. Box drills are often used to achieve that final training effect necessary to successfully participate in anaerobic sport activity.

30-, 60-, OR 90-SECOND BOX DRILL

LEVEL

Low (30 seconds), moderate (60 seconds), or high (90 seconds)

EQUIPMENT

A box 12 inches high, 20 inches wide, and 30 inches deep

SPORTS

Downhill skiing, football, ice hockey, squash, racquetball, volleyball

START

Stand at the side of the box, with feet shoulder-width apart.

TIP To learn to react faster to ground contact, visualize the ground being hot. You want to spend as little time as you can on the hot surface.

ACTION

Jump onto the box (figure 9.55a), back to the ground on the other side (figure 9.55b), then back onto the box (figure 9.55c). Continue to jump across the top of the box for an allotted time; each touch on top of the box counts as one. Use the following guidelines:

- 30 touches in 30 seconds—Start of training (low intensity)
- 60 touches in 60 seconds—Start of season (moderate intensity)
- 90 touches in 90 seconds—Championship season (high intensity)

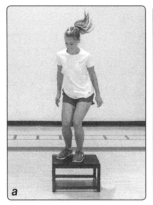

Figure 9.55 30-, 60-, or 90-second box drill: *(a)* jump onto box; *(b)* land on other side; *(c)* jump back onto box.

SINGLE-LEG PUSH-OFF

LEVEL

Low

EQUIPMENT

A box 6 to 12 inches high

SPORTS

Bicycling, netball, rowing, tennis

START

Stand on the ground and place one foot on the box, with the heel close to the closest edge (figure 9.56a).

ACTION

Push off of the foot on top of the box to gain as much height as possible by extending through the entire leg and foot (figure 9.56b). Land with the same foot on top of the box and push off again. Use a double-arm swing for height and balance.

Figure 9.56 Single-leg push-off: (a) starting position; (b) push-off action.

ALTERNATING PUSH-OFF

LEVEL

Low

EQUIPMENT

A box 6 to 12 inches high

SPORTS

Bicycling, diving, soccer

START

Stand on the ground and place one foot on the box, with the heel close to the closest edge.

ACTION

Push off of the foot on the box to gain as much height as possible by extending through the entire leg and foot; land with the feet reversed (the box foot lands a split second before the ground foot). Use a double-arm swing for height and balance.

LEVEL

Low

EQUIPMENT

A box 12 to 24 inches high

SPORTS

Cricket, in-line skating, speedskating, tennis

START

Stand to one side of the box, with the left foot raised onto the middle of the box (figure 9.57a).

ACTION

Using a double-arm swing, jump up and over to the other side of the box (figure 9.57b), landing with the right foot on top of the box and the left foot on the floor (figure 9.57c). This drill should be done in a continuous motion, shuffling back and forth across the top of the box.

Figure 9.57   Side-to-side box shuffle: *(a)* starting position; *(b)* jump over box; *(c)* land on other side.

SCORPION STEP-UP

LEVEL

Moderate

EQUIPMENT

A 12- to 18-inch box

SPORTS

Baseball, basketball, in-line skating, tennis

START

Stand with feet shoulder-width apart next to the box.

ACTION

Step with the outside (lead) leg across the body to the top of the box (figure 9.58a); bring the back leg up to the top of the box (figure 9.58b). Next, step down with the lead leg going behind the support leg to the ground (figure 9.58c) and then land on both feet. Repeat this motion from the other side of the box. Continue for 30 seconds.

  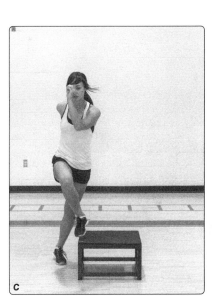

Figure 9.58 Scorpion step-up: (a) perform crossover step onto box; (b) bring other foot onto box; (c) step down with lead leg.

FRONT BOX JUMP

LEVEL

Low to moderate

EQUIPMENT

A box 12 to 42 inches high (depending on athlete ability)

SPORTS

Diving, netball

START

Stand facing the box, with feet shoulder-width apart (figure 9.59a).

ACTION

Figure 9.59 Front box jump: *(a)* starting position; *(b)* jump onto box.

Jump up and land softly with both feet on the box (figure 9.59b). Step back down and repeat. For a more advanced exercise, hop down from the box and immediately jump back onto it. Use a variety of box heights, starting with 12-inch boxes and building up to 42 inches over time.

MULTIPLE BOX JUMP

LEVEL

Moderate to high

EQUIPMENT

Three to five boxes of the same height placed in a row (box height selected according to athlete ability)

SPORTS

Ice hockey, rowing, weightlifting, wrestling

START

Stand with feet shoulder-width apart at the end of the row of boxes with their length spread out before you.

ACTION

Figure 9.60 Multiple box jump.

Jump onto the first box, then off on the other side (figure 9.60), onto the second box, then off, and so on down the row. After jumping off the last box, walk back to the start for recovery.

LATERAL BOX JUMP

LEVEL

Low to moderate

EQUIPMENT

A single box (or a row of three to five boxes) 12 to 42 inches high

SPORTS

Bicycling, figure skating, track and field (sprints)

START

Stand at the side of the box, with feet shoulder-width apart.

ACTION

Jump onto the box (figure 9.61a) and back to the ground on the other side (figure 9.61b). The exercise can be done with a single box or as a continuous movement across a line of three to five boxes of the same height (jumping to the ground between boxes).

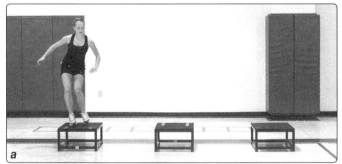 

Figure 9.61   Lateral box jump: *(a)* jump onto box; *(b)* jump off on other side.

PYRAMIDING BOX JUMP

LEVEL

Moderate to high

EQUIPMENT

Three to five boxes of increasing height, evenly spaced 2 to 3 feet apart

SPORTS

Gymnastics, rugby

START

Stand with feet shoulder-width apart, looking down the row of boxes.

ACTION

Jump onto the first box, then off on the other side, onto the second box (figure 9.62), then off, and so on down the row. After finishing the sequence, walk back to the start for recovery, or immediately hop back down the row of boxes.

Figure 9.62 Pyramiding box jump.

LATERAL STEP-UP

LEVEL

Low

EQUIPMENT

A box 6 to 12 inches high

SPORTS

Baseball, softball, in-line skating, speedskating, swimming, wrestling

START

Standing to the side of the box, place the foot closest to the box on top (figure 9.63a).

ACTION

Use the leg on the box to raise the body until the leg is extended (figure 9.63b), then lower to the starting position. Don't push off the foot on the ground; use the bent leg to do all the work. Perform the exercise using both legs.

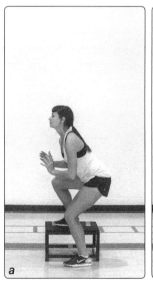

Figure 9.63 Lateral step-up: *(a)* starting position; *(b)* on box.

MULTIPLE BOX-TO-BOX SQUAT JUMPS

LEVEL

High

EQUIPMENT

A row of boxes of the same height (box height selected according to athlete ability)

SPORTS

Rowing, volleyball, weightlifting, wrestling

START

Stand in a deep-squat position with feet shoulder-width apart, looking down the row of boxes; hands should be clasped behind the head (figure 9.64a).

ACTION

Jump to the first box (figure 9.64b), landing softly in a squat position. Maintaining the squat position, jump off the box on the other side and immediately onto and off of the following boxes. Keep the hands on the hips or behind the head.

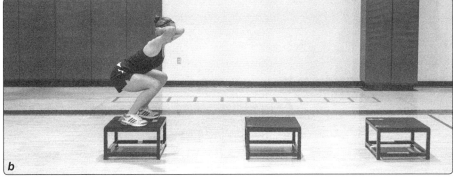

Figure 9.64 Multiple box-to-box squat jumps: *(a)* starting position; *(b)* jump onto box.

MULTIPLE BOX-TO-BOX JUMP WITH SINGLE-LEG LANDING

LEVEL

High

EQUIPMENT

A row of boxes 6 to 12 inches high. Increase the height to 18 to 24 inches after a period of time.

SPORTS

Downhill skiing, track and field (jumping events and sprints)

START

Stand on one foot, looking down the row of boxes (figure 9.65a).

ACTION

Jump onto the first box (figure 9.65b), landing on the takeoff foot, then jump to the floor, landing on the same foot. Continue in this fashion down the row of boxes. Repeat the exercise using the other leg. This is a strenuous exercise; the athlete must be in top form, and strict concentration is needed to prevent injury.

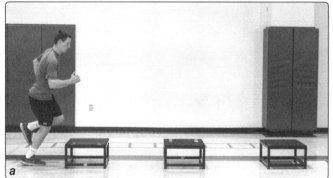 

Figure 9.65 Multiple box-to-box jump with single-leg landing: *(a)* starting position; *(b)* jump on box.

BOUNDING

Bounding drills are exaggerated running movements that help develop a specific aspect of the stride cycle. These drills are used to develop and improve stride length and frequency, and they are typically performed for distances greater than 30 yards or meters. When considering the positioning of the limbs, remember that long levers tend to move slower than short levers. Thus, regarding the forces being generated by the limbs, short levers will generally be quicker but generate less force, whereas long levers will generate more force but more slowly. To increase efficiency, runners should flex the lower extremities to form the shortest radius that the thigh is forced to move through.

SKIPPING

LEVEL

Low

EQUIPMENT

None

SPORTS

Cricket, warm-up

START

Stand comfortably.

ACTION

Lift the left leg with the knee bent 90 degrees while also lifting the right arm with the elbow bent 90 degrees (figure 9.66). As these two limbs come back down, lift the opposite limbs with the same motion. For added difficulty, push off the ground for more upward extension.

Figure 9.66 Skipping.

SIDE SKIPPING WITH BIG ARM SWING

LEVEL

Low

EQUIPMENT

None

SPORTS

Warm-up

START

Stand with feet together.

ACTION

This exercise looks like a jumping jack. Slide step to the side, swinging the arms up and over the head (figure 9.67a). As you push to bring the feet back together, the arms come back down and cross in front of the body (figure 9.67b). Keep performing this extended side step and arm swing for a prescribed distance (about 40 to 50 meters).

Figure 9.67 Side skipping with big arm swing: (a) spread arms and bound; (b) bring feet together and cross arms.

POWER SKIPPING

LEVEL

Low

EQUIPMENT

None

SPORTS

Warm-up

START

Stand comfortably.

ACTION

Hold both arms out in front of you at shoulder height. Moving forward in a skipping motion, raise the leading knee toward the chest, attempting to touch the foot with the hands (figure 9.68). Repeat the motion with the opposite leg and continue skipping for the prescribed distance.

Figure 9.68 Power skipping.

BACKWARD SKIPPING

LEVEL

Low

EQUIPMENT

A mark 20 to 30 meters from the start

SPORTS

Track and field (jumping events)

START

Stand on one foot.

ACTION

Skip backward (figure 9.69) for 20 to 30 meters. Coordinate the arm swing with the skip to add to the backward propulsion.

Figure 9.69 Backward skipping.

LEVEL

Moderate to high

EQUIPMENT

A 30-meter mark

SPORTS

Baseball, softball, bicycling, wrestling

START

Spread the feet apart, front to back, and bend the front leg 90 degrees (figure 9.70a).

ACTION

Jumping up and forward, switch legs (figure 9.70b). As you bring the back leg through, try to touch the buttock. Land in the split-squat position and immediately do another cycle, continuing for a prescribed distance (about 30 meters). Each push from the ground has to propel the body forward. This is an advanced drill.

Figure 9.70 Moving split squat with cycle: *(a)* starting position; *(b)* bound.

LEVEL

Moderate to high

EQUIPMENT

None

SPORTS

Baseball, softball, cricket, track and field (jumping events and sprints)

START

Jog into the start of the drill to increase forward momentum. As you jog, start the drill with the right foot forward and the left foot back.

ACTION

This drill is simply an exaggerated running action. Push off with the left foot (figure 9.71a) and bring the leg forward with the knee bent and the thigh parallel to the ground. At the same time, reach forward with the left arm (figure 9.71b). As the right leg comes through, the right leg extends back and remains extended for the duration of the push-off. Hold this extended stride for a brief time, then land on the left foot. The right leg then drives through to the front bent position, the left arm reaches forward, and the left leg extends back. Make each stride long, and try to cover as much distance as possible.

Figure 9.71 Alternate bounding with single-arm action: (a) start of bound; (b) bounding.

ALTERNATE BOUNDING WITH DOUBLE-ARM ACTION

Moderate to high

None

Baseball, softball, bicycling, track and field (jumping events and sprints)

Jog into the start of the drill to increase forward momentum. As you jog, start the drill with the right foot forward and the left foot back.

Push off with the left foot and bring the leg forward with the knee bent and the thigh parallel to the ground. At the same time, bring both arms forward with great force to help propel the body forward (figure 9.72a). As the left leg comes through, the right leg extends back and remains extended for the duration of the push-off (figure 9.72b). Hold this extended stride for a brief time, quickly bring both arms behind the body, then land on the left foot. The right leg then drives through to the front bent position, the arms come forward, the left leg extends back, and the arms move back. This drill is an exaggerated running action; make each stride long, and try to cover as much distance as possible.

Figure 9.72 Alternate bounding with double-arm action: *(a)* start of bound; *(b)* bounding.

COMBINATION BOUNDING WITH SINGLE-ARM ACTION

LEVEL

Moderate to high

EQUIPMENT

None

SPORTS

Track and field (jumping events)

START

Stand on one foot.

ACTION

In combination bounding, you bound on one foot in a set sequence (right-right-left or left-left-right). Bound from one foot (figure 9.73a), then the same foot (figure 9.73b), and then the other foot (figure 9.73c). The right arm moves forward with the left foot, and vice versa. Continue bounding by repeating the cycle.

Figure 9.73 Combination bounding with single-arm action: *(a)* first bound; *(b)* second bound; *(c)* third bound.

COMBINATION BOUNDING WITH DOUBLE-ARM ACTION

ACTION

In combination bounding, you bound on one foot in a set sequence (right-right-left or left-left-right). Bound from one foot (figure 9.74a), then the same foot (figure 9.74b), and then the other foot (figure 9.74c). Swing both arms forward very quickly on each bound in order to keep the body balanced and keep the motion of the bound smooth.

Figure 9.74 Combination bounding with double-arm action: *(a)* first bound; *(b)* second bound; *(c)* third bound.

SINGLE-LEG BOUNDING

LEVEL

High

EQUIPMENT

None

SPORTS

Track and field (jumping events and sprints)

START

Stand on one foot.

ACTION

Figure 9.75 Single-leg bounding: *(a)* bound from one foot; *(b)* landing.

Bound from one foot (figure 9.75a) as far forward as possible (figure 9.75b), using the other leg and the arms to cycle in the air for balance and to increase forward momentum. Advanced athletes should try to touch the heel of the bounding foot to the buttocks with each bound. Continue bounding for a prescribed distance (about 40 meters). This drill should be performed on both legs for equal strength.

COMBINATION BOUNDING WITH VERTICAL JUMP

LEVEL

High

EQUIPMENT

None

SPORTS

Track and field (jumping events)

START

Stand on one foot.

ACTION

Figure 9.76 Combination bounding with vertical jump: *(a)* step together; *(b)* jump.

Do a combination bounding sequence (right-right-left or left-left-right), then follow immediately with a strong vertical jump. On the third bound, bring the nonbounding foot up to meet the bounding foot (figure 9.76a) so that the jump is off both feet (figure 9.76b). Use a double-arm swing to assist in lifting you vertically. As soon as you land from the vertical jump, complete another bounding sequence.

MEDICINE BALL EXERCISES

In theory, plyometrics for the upper extremities are not different than those for the lower extremities, so treat them the same. The exception is that you are working from a more mobile base with smaller muscles in the upper body. Elastic strength in the upper body and trunk is just as dependent upon stretching rapidly and using the recoil property of muscle as the legs.

DROP PUSH-UP

LEVEL

High

EQUIPMENT

Medicine ball

SPORTS

Basketball, gymnastics, rowing, wrestling

START

Start in push-up position with the legs and arms shoulder-width apart. Place the medicine ball on the ground between your hands.

ACTION

Maintaining your body position, place both hands on top of the ball (figure 9.77a). In a quick movement, pull both hands off the ball to their respective sides (figure 9.77b). Keeping your body in a straight line, drop to the ground surface, push vigorously away from the surface, and place the hands back on top of the ball.

Figure 9.77 Drop push-up: *(a)* hands on ball; *(b)* hands beside ball.

CHEST PASS

LEVEL

Moderate

EQUIPMENT

Medicine ball and partner

SPORTS

Football, basketball

START

Stand facing a partner approximately 10 feet (3 m) away; hold the ball in front of your chest with your elbows back and out.

Figure 9.78   Chest pass.

ACTION

Snap the ball off your chest to your partner (figure 9.78) while stepping forward into the motion. The backs of your hands should come together on the follow-through.

RUSSIAN TWIST

LEVEL

Moderate

EQUIPMENT

Medicine ball

SPORTS

Baseball, squash/racquetball, tennis, track and field (throwing events)

START

Sit with your knees bent, your feet apart, and your back at a 45-degree angle to the floor. Hold the ball in front of your chest with arms at full extension and parallel to your thighs.

Figure 9.79   Russian twist.

ACTION

Rotate your upper body to one side as far as you can (figure 9.79). Keeping your arms in the same plane, turn back the other way, moving from side to side. Do not let the ball touch the ground at any point in the movement.

LUNGE SQUAT WITH TOSS

LEVEL

Moderate

EQUIPMENT

Medicine ball and partner

SPORTS

Basketball, netball, track and field (throwing events)

START

Stand facing a partner approximately 10 feet away. Hold the ball on your chest with your hands on each side of the ball.

Figure 9.80 Lunge squat with toss.

ACTION

Step forward (figure 9.80) and push the ball rapidly from your chest toward the partner. Land in a lunge position with your upper body perpendicular to your front thigh. Your back knee should be lower than your front knee. Do not let the front knee bend past 90 degrees or let your upper body collapse forward. Push back (recovery step) off your front foot to return to the starting position.

WOODCHOPPER

LEVEL

Moderate

EQUIPMENT

Medicine ball

SPORTS

Baseball/softball, squash/racquetball, tennis

START

Stand with feet shoulder-width apart holding a medicine ball in both hands. Lift the medicine ball overhead to the right so it is over your right shoulder.

Figure 9.81 Woodchopper.

ACTION

Lower the medicine to the left, bringing it beside your left hip as you rotate around the torso (figure 9.81). Return to the starting position and repeat. After completing all repetitions to the left, reverse the movement, lifting the medicine ball over the left shoulder and bringing it down beside the right hip.

SINGLE-LEG SQUAT

LEVEL

Moderate

EQUIPMENT

Medicine ball, sturdy platform or weight bench about knee high

SPORTS

Figure skating, gymnastics, track and field (jumping events)

START

Stand in front of a sturdy platform or weight bench. Hold the medicine ball in both hands behind your head. Balance on one foot and reach the other foot back to rest on the platform.

ACTION

Slowly bend the standing knee (figure 9.82). Keep the back knee bent. Hold in the bottom position for a few seconds then return to the starting position. Complete the number of repetitions then switch legs.

Figure 9.82 Single-leg squat.

OVERHEAD SIT-UP TOSS

LEVEL

High

EQUIPMENT

Medicine ball and partner

SPORTS

Diving, gymnastics, rowing, swimming

START

Sit with your back at a 45-degree angle to the floor and with your feet flat on the floor. Position your hands so they are slightly above your head in a position to catch the ball.

ACTION

Have a partner, standing 6 to 10 feet away, toss the medicine ball to a position slightly above your head and into your hands (figure 9.83a). When you catch the ball, allow your body to rock back and allow the ball to touch the ground behind you (figure 9.83b). Flex your trunk forward rapidly and roll up to throw the ball from approximately the same position in which you caught it.

Figure 9.83 Overhead sit-up toss: (a) catch the ball; (b) rock back and touch the ball to the ground.

V-SIT GIANT CIRCLES

LEVEL

Moderate

EQUIPMENT

Medicine ball

SPORTS

Basketball, netball, volleyball

START

Sit in a V-sit position with the legs spread in a V and the medicine ball held above your head with the arms extended.

ACTION

To complete a circle, lower the ball in one direction toward one of your feet (figure 9.84a). Swing the ball across the front of your body and over each toe. Elevate the ball from the second foot to the starting position (figure 9.84b).

Figure 9.84 V-sit giant circle: *(a)* lower ball to foot; *(b)* swing across body back to starting position.

FRONT TOSS

LEVEL

Low

EQUIPMENT

Medicine ball

SPORTS

Basketball, swimming, wrestling

START

Stand with the ball held between your feet.

ACTION

Jump up with the ball (figure 9.85a), then use your legs to toss the ball to yourself while in the air (figure 9.85b). After catching it, drop the ball to the ground between your feet and repeat.

Figure 9.85 Front toss: *(a)* jump with ball between feet; *(b)* toss ball from legs while in the air.

LEVEL

Moderate

EQUIPMENT

Medicine ball

SPORTS

Soccer

START

Stand with the ball held between your heels.

ACTION

Use the heel of one foot to flick the ball up and over your back and shoulders (figure 9.86a); then catch the ball in front of your body (figure 9.86b). This toss requires a quick flexion of the knee and considerable effort from the hamstring muscles.

Figure 9.86 Heel toss: *(a)* flick ball up; *(b)* catch ball in front of body.

LEVEL

Low

EQUIPMENT

Medicine ball

SPORTS

Baseball, softball, diving, gymnastics, squash, racquetball

START

Sit on the floor with your legs and the ball straight in front of you.

Figure 9.87 Over-under.

ACTION

Lift your right leg and pass the ball under it from the inside (figure 9.87). Then pass the ball over the top of your right leg, under your left leg from the inside, and over the top of your left leg (so the ball makes a figure eight around your legs).

TRUNK ROTATION

Figure 9.88 Trunk rotation.

LEVEL

Low

EQUIPMENT

Medicine ball

SPORTS

Rowing, squash, racquetball, tennis, track and field (throwing events), weightlifting

START

Sit on the floor with your legs spread and with the ball behind your back.

ACTION

Rotate to the right, pick up the ball (figure 9.88), bring it around to your left side, and replace it behind your back (so the ball makes a circle around your body). Repeat for the prescribed number of times and then reverse directions.

UNDERHAND THROW

LEVEL

Low

EQUIPMENT

Partner and medicine ball

SPORTS

Gymnastics, ice hockey, swimming

START

Stand in a squat position, holding the ball close to the ground (figure 9.89a); the partner should be about 3 meters away.

ACTION

Keeping your back straight, rise straight up and throw the ball up and out to the partner (figure 9.89b), using your legs to provide momentum.

Figure 9.89 Underhand throw: *(a)* starting position; *(b)* throw.

PULL-OVER PASS

Low

EQUIPMENT

Partner and medicine ball

SPORTS

Basketball, soccer, tennis

START

Lie on your back with your knees bent, holding the ball on the floor behind your head (figure 9.90a); the partner should stand at your feet.

ACTION

Keeping your arms extended, pass the ball to your partner (figure 9.90b). To increase the intensity, your partner can back up and require you to throw farther.

Figure 9.90 Pull-over pass: (a) starting position; (b) pass.

OVERHEAD THROW

LEVEL

Low to moderate

EQUIPMENT

Medicine ball and partner

SPORTS

Baseball, softball, cricket, soccer, swimming

START

Stand while holding a medicine ball overhead.

ACTION

Step forward (figure 9.91a) and bring the ball sharply forward with both arms (figure 9.91b), throwing it to a partner or over a specific distance.

Figure 9.91 Overhead throw: (a) step forward; (b) throw ball to partner.

LOW-POST DRILL

LEVEL

Moderate

EQUIPMENT

Partner, medicine ball, and basketball goal

SPORTS

Basketball

START

Stand with your back to the basket, about a meter to the front or side of the basket.

ACTION

Your partner starts the drill by throwing you the ball in the low-post position. Catch the ball (figure 9.92a), pivot (figure 9.92b), and jump to touch the ball against the goal (figure 9.92c). Immediately after landing, jump to touch the goal with the ball a second time. Finally, pivot back toward your partner (figure 9.92d) and pass the ball to him (figure 9.92e).

Figure 9.92 Low-post drill: (a) catch throw; (b) pivot to goal; (c) touch ball to goal; (d) pivot back to partner; (e) throw ball.

SIDE THROW

LEVEL

Low to moderate

EQUIPMENT

Medicine ball and partner or large solid barrier

SPORTS

Baseball, softball, cricket

START

Holding a medicine ball on your right, stand with feet shoulder-width apart.

ACTION

Swing the ball farther to the right and then forcefully reverse directions to the left and release. You may toss the ball to a partner or throw it against a solid barrier (e.g., a gym wall).

BACKWARD THROW

LEVEL

Moderate

EQUIPMENT

Partner and medicine ball

SPORTS

Rowing, swimming

START

Stand about 3 meters in front of your partner, facing the same direction and holding the ball in front of you.

ACTION

Holding the ball between your legs (figure 9.93a), squat down and then toss the ball up and over your head to your partner (figure 9.93b). Be careful to bend your knees, bend from your hips, and keep your back straight.

Figure 9.93 Backward throw: *(a)* squat with ball between legs; *(b)* toss ball over head to partner.

KNEELING SIDE THROW

LEVEL

Moderate

EQUIPMENT

Partner and medicine ball

SPORTS

Baseball, softball, track and field (throwing events), wrestling

START

Kneel with your partner about 3 meters to the side and hold the ball to the other side with both hands at hip level (figure 9.94a).

ACTION

Twist your upper body and arms together and throw the ball to your partner (figure 9.94b).

Figure 9.94 Kneeling side throw: (a) starting position; (b) throwing ball to partner.

QUARTER-EAGLE CHEST PASS

LEVEL

Moderate to high

EQUIPMENT

Four partners, coach, and medicine ball

SPORTS

Basketball, football, netball, rugby, volleyball

START

Assume a ready position with a partner in front of you, in back of you, and to each side.

ACTION

When the coach calls out "right" or "left," quickly turn your body a quarter turn and pass the ball to the person facing you (figure 9.95). The drill continues for 10 to 12 passes.

Figure 9.95 Quarter-eagle chest pass.

POWER DROP

LEVEL

High

EQUIPMENT

Partner, box 12 to 42 inches high, and medicine ball

SPORTS

Basketball, football, gymnastics, track and field (throwing events), volleyball

START

Lie supine on the ground with your arms stretched up over your chest. The partner stands on the box, holding the medicine ball at arm's length.

ACTION

The partner drops the ball (figure 9.96). Catch the ball and immediately propel the ball back to the partner. Repeat.

Figure 9.96 Power drop.

MEDICINE BALL SLAM

LEVEL

High

EQUIPMENT

Medicine ball

SPORTS

Basketball

START

Stand in athletic position, holding a medicine ball, feet more than shoulder-width apart.

ACTION

Swing the medicine ball to the left side (figure 9.97) and slam it to the ground. Pick up the medicine ball and repeat to the other side.

Figure 9.97 Medicine ball slam.

CATCH AND PASS WITH JUMP-AND-REACH

LEVEL

High

EQUIPMENT

Partner, box 12 to 42 inches high, medicine ball, and high object such as a basketball goal

SPORTS

Basketball, football, volleyball

START

Stand on the box, with feet shoulder-width apart and with toes close to the edge (figure 9.98a).

ACTION

Step off the box and land on both feet (figure 9.98b). Explode up and forward, extend your arms, and catch a pass from your partner (figure 9.98c). On landing (figure 9.98d), explode up again and reach for the high object with the medicine ball.

Figure 9.98 Catch and pass with jump-and-reach: *(a)* start on box; *(b)* drop and land; *(c)* jump and catch; *(d)* land with ball.

SUMMARY

- The seven classifications of lower-extremity plyometric exercises include jumps in place, standing jumps, multiple hops and jumps, depth jumps, box drills, bounding, and medicine ball exercises.

- Although specific drills may be most beneficial to athletes in a given sport, coaches can choose from the provided plyometric exercises those that will likely benefit any athlete, regardless of the sport.

Plyometric Training in a Comprehensive Conditioning Program

Many people wonder whether resistance training or other modes of training can be safely and effectively integrated into the same workout as plyometric training. The answer is yes, but only for athletes who are experienced in weight training and have also been through basic jump training. In this chapter, we review techniques for combining plyometrics with other modes of training in order to optimize the performance adaptations that athletes can achieve.

INTEGRATIVE TRAINING

Strength and conditioning specialists, coaches, fitness professionals, and even youth coaches often strive to integrate various types of conditioning into safe, age-appropriate, effective, and enjoyable programs for athletic development.[1,2,3,4] Integrative training programs are plans designed to help athletes optimize athletic performance by incorporating both general and specific strength and conditioning activities into training; these programs are also focused on enhancing both fitness- and skill-related components of performance. The vital elements of integrative training include the integration of safe and effective plyometric training through education and instruction by qualified professionals who understand the physical demands of program design.[3,5]

For an example of an integrative training program, see the sample program for soccer in chapter 11.

COMPLEX TRAINING

Early European writings labeled the combination of resistance and jump training as *complex training.* Complex training occurs when the athlete alternates weight training and plyometrics within the same workout session. (For an example, see week 2 of the sample program for long jumpers in chapter 11.) A study done at Southern Cross University in Lismore, Australia, suggested that training programs that include both heavy weightlifting and plyometric exercises "may enhance the use of elastic strain energy or facilitate the stretch reflex to a greater extent than does maximal power training."[6] In this study, maximal power training consisted of doing jumps and bench press exercises on special machines designed to allow for maximal power development during these activities. Although this study did not look directly at combined or complex weight training and plyometric training, it did validate the idea of combining these activities to achieve maximal results. No doubt more research in this area needs to be done; however, the results tend to support the effectiveness of performing exercises in this way.

Another study conducted at the University of Utah included 48 male subjects. This study found that those who trained using a combination of squat exercises and plyometric exercises over a six-week period increased their vertical jump significantly (10.67 cm) compared to those who trained on squats (3.30 cm) or plyometrics (3.81 cm) alone.[7] The researchers concluded that the athletes who stand to benefit most from combined training programs are those competing in short-term power events. The specified events included basketball; volleyball; alpine ski racing; sprint events in cycling; and sprinting, jumping, and throwing events in track and field.

Researchers also believed that when athletes use a combined squat–plyometric program, neuromuscular adaptations occur earlier in a training cycle (within the first four weeks); therefore, an athlete should be careful to avoid overtraining. Coaches need to carefully monitor the athlete's response to training intensity and ensure sufficient recovery between workouts. The athlete may also experience a quicker rise in performance when doing this form of training. This makes it extremely useful for athletes who have a shorter time to prepare for competition because of their scheduling (e.g., professional tennis players).

Combining strength movement exercises (such as squats) with speed movements (such as the depth jump, double-leg hop, or standing triple jump) can be a very effective way to stimulate the neuromuscular system and provide variety for the athlete. The human body appears to have an arousal mechanism that is stimulated with maximal or near maximal lifting, and the athlete can take advantage of this situation when using plyometric exercises as well. The body appears to remain in this arousal or heightened state of excitement for a short window of time at the conclusion of a heavy set. By immediately adding a plyometric activity, the athlete can take advantage of this physiological state and use it to perform higher-quality plyometric drills.

Combining the bench press with the power drop (a medicine ball exercise) is an example of complex training for the upper extremities. Other examples of complex training might include squats combined with hurdle hops. Lat pulls or pull-over lifts can be combined with variations of the overhead medicine ball throw. The use of the Romanian deadlift combined with overhead medicine ball throws from a glute-ham device is excellent for developing strength in the low back and hip extensor.

In complex training, the volume of plyometric exercises should be reduced to a number that is easily workable between sets of the particular lift. For instance, an athlete might alternate six sets of half squats with five sets of standing triple jumps; next, the athlete could alternate five sets of double-leg hops with five sets of depth jumps from an 18-inch box. This method of training can be used with any of the major weight lifts—squats, inverted leg presses, split squats, bench presses, power cleans, snatches, and push presses. As a general rule, integrating two major lifts with plyometrics during a workout should yield maximum results. Trying to do any more than this usually requires too much time and brings the threat of fatigue and overtraining.

Finally, remember that this form of training should always be preceded by a basic strength phase of training. This type of training is an advanced form and works best for athletes who have a training base and history to fall back on. Proper execution of the lifts and the jump drills is extremely important, and this is the wrong time to try to teach basic lifting techniques.

USING PLYOMETRICS WITH OTHER TRAINING

Jump training and upper-body plyometrics are relevant to many sports. Gymnastics, diving, volleyball, and jumping events in track and field are all arenas where success depends on the athlete's ability to explode from the standing surface and generate vertical velocity, linear velocity, or both in order to achieve the desired result.

But plyometrics is not a panacea in athletic conditioning. It does not exist in a vacuum, nor should it be thought of as a singular form of training. Instead, plyometrics is the icing on the cake—to be used by athletes who have prepared their tendons and muscles (through resistance training) for the tremendous impact forces imposed in high-intensity plyometrics.

Anaerobic conditioning, in the form of sprint or interval training, is essential to developing the stride patterns required in proper plyometric bounding. The explosive reactions of sprinting or of movement drills that require changes of direction can be performed as part of interval training (repeated efforts with measured recovery periods).

Done together, resistance training and anaerobic training help prepare the athlete's body for plyometrics. In turn, plyometric training enhances the athlete's ability to perform in resistance exercise and anaerobic activity—a true partnership in athletic training.

Resistance Training

Resistance training is the ideal counterpart to plyometric training because it helps prepare the muscles for the rapid impact loading of plyometric exercises. In resistance training, the athlete works to develop the eccentric phase of muscle contraction by first lowering the body or weight and then overcoming the weight using a concentric contraction. Plyometric training can be successfully integrated with resistance training by immediately imposing a speed-strength task on muscles that have been subjected to pure strength movements such as those in weightlifting (as discussed earlier regarding complex training).

Open-chain resistance training (using machines that isolate a single joint) is useful for developing strength in specific muscle groups. However, athletes who use plyometrics also need to perform closed-chain exercises that involve multijoint activities, such as free weight exercises using barbells, dumbbells, and medicine balls. These exercises, which are generally performed with the feet fixed to the ground as in squatting, are more functional for athletes, allowing them to assume positions specific to their sports when they exercise. Closed-chain exercises have proven themselves to have much higher carryover value than isolated-joint exercises in developing athletic ability.

The more intense the plyometric exercises become, the more crucial the need for strength. As mentioned earlier, some of the early European literature spoke of the need for athletes to be able to squat 2.5 times their body weight before undergoing a training program. There is no doubt that those authors had a high-intensity program in mind—with a goal that might be unreasonable for the average high school or age group athlete. However, a strength requirement is part and parcel of plyometric training at all levels.

The parameters used to determine if an athlete is strong enough to begin a plyometric program may center more on testing of functional strength (including power) than on the traditional one-repetition maximum (1RM) squat that measures pure strength. One such test has been used by a number of practitioners in plyometric training programs. As a test of power more than strength, it may have more direct applicability. For the test, weight equal to 60 percent of the athlete's body weight is placed on a squat bar, and the athlete is asked to perform five repetitions in five seconds, tested against a stopwatch. If the athlete cannot do so, the emphasis of the athlete's training should be on a resistance training program, and the intensity of the plyometric training program should remain low to moderate.

Poor strength in the lower extremities results in loss of stability when landing, and high-impact forces are excessively absorbed by the soft tissues of the body. Early fatigue also becomes a problem for athletes without adequate leg strength. Together, these factors will result in the deterioration of performance during exercise and an increased chance for injury (as in any overuse situation).

Anaerobic, Sprint, and Interval Training

Plyometrics trains two anaerobic energy systems—the creatine phosphate system and the lactic acid system. The creatine phosphate system depends on energy stores that already exist in the muscles. Plyometric exercises that last a mere 4 to 15 seconds deplete the energy stores. In a program designed to train the creatine phosphate system, a considerable amount of rest or recovery should be allotted between exercises; the emphasis is on quality of work, not quantity. The lactic acid threshold is reached when the muscles' energy stores have been exhausted by the creatine phosphate system. Exercise that proceeds past the point of using the energy stores will tax the lactic acid threshold. Exercise bouts at near-maximal effort that last around 30 to 90 seconds are appropriate for training that system.

In general, jumps in place, standing jumps, and depth jumps are short-duration activities used to train the creatine phosphate system. Multiple jumps, box drills, and particularly bounding can qualify as exercises for training the lactic acid threshold.

Training the creatine phosphate system is beneficial for athletes involved in sports that require quick bursts of power with long recovery periods between performances, such as the long jump or triple jump. Training the lactic acid threshold is helpful for athletes in sports such as football or volleyball, where activity is fairly prolonged and rest periods are more infrequent.

Sprint and interval training are running programs that require the athlete to perform high-quality efforts in training for a certain amount of time (usually around 30 to 90 seconds) with prescribed recovery periods. This type of training is closely related to plyometric training of the lactic acid threshold, but sprints are used instead of multiple jumps, box drills, or bounding exercises.

Circuit Training

One of the many benefits of plyometric training is that it can be organized into circuits with other types of training. By moving from station to station (see figure 10.1), the athlete can do a variety of exercises that stress the vertical or linear components (or both) of various movement patterns. For coaches, circuit training also serves the purpose of group management very well. Entire teams can be involved in a circuit of plyometric exercises, thus ensuring some uniformity of exercise application and intensity levels.

By using circuits, athletes can perform activities of even greater duration than with anaerobic, sprint, or interval training. This may move the level of cardiovascular

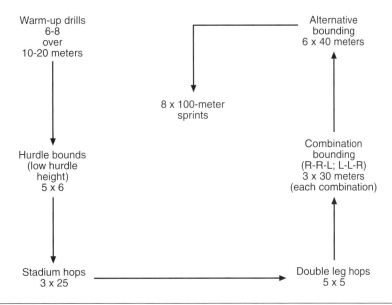

Figure 10.1 Sample circuit.

stress toward the point where improvement in aerobic conditioning occurs, resulting in increased stamina. The cumulative effect of circuit training is considerable, so the recovery period should be at least two days.

◆ SUMMARY ▷

- Integrative training programs are plans designed to help athletes optimize athletic performance by incorporating both general and specific strength and conditioning activities into training; these programs are also focused on enhancing both health- and skill-related components of physical fitness.

- The cornerstone of integrative training is the integration of safe and effective plyometric training through education and instruction by qualified professionals who understand the physical demands of program design.

- With proper program design, plyometric training can be integrated into most other training modes.

Sport-Specific Plyometric Training Programs

Plyometric training is very specific in nature but very broad in applicability. These exercises are an essential part of training programs for all sports. However, successfully incorporating the exercises into a program depends on many factors. Designing a training program for any sport requires a philosophical approach that is consistent with the demands of that specific sport. The coach or conditioning specialist has to develop an understanding of the biomechanics of each sport. In this way, the designer of the program will understand the forces involved in being successful in each activity.

The conditioning specialist should begin this process by conducting a needs analysis for each sport or athlete. A needs analysis involves examining the fitness requirements of the activity and the fitness needs of the athlete involved in the sport. When designing a training program, the conditioning specialist must consider the physiological and biomechanical requirements of the sport, as well as the requirements for the position of the player within the sport. The requirements can vary quite a bit for different positions (e.g., baseball catcher versus baseball pitcher). In addition, performing a needs analysis for athletes will help identify deficits that limit peak performance. These deficits can then be targeted with corrective plyometric exercises before the athlete progresses to advanced plyometric training. A physiological analysis will help ensure that the training program addresses the areas of strength, flexibility, power, endurance, and speed required to be successful in the sport. A biomechanical analysis will help the program designer choose training activities that develop the athlete in the manner most specific to the sport. For example, looking at the mechanics of sprinting will reveal a need for drills that specifically target the hip extensors, including the hamstrings.

Once the needs analysis has been carried out, a philosophy or approach to the development of the athlete must be put in place. Inexperienced conditioning specialists often want to teach everything they know within a week of being introduced to a new athlete. This approach can lead to frustration, overtraining, and eventually injury for the athlete. After years of working with athletes in this area, a coach learns that patience and careful planning are much more likely to result in positive outcomes. The following are the steps that coaches should build into their philosophy of training.

Step 1: Consider the Athlete

This simple category includes some very important considerations. Look at the athlete's age, gender, physical and mental maturity, and athletic experience, including the years in sport participation as well as the years of exposure to physical training. Failure to adequately consider these characteristics of the athlete will lead to frustration and less-than-optimal results from the training program.

Step 2: Assess and Test the Athlete

Based on the needs analysis, field tests should be conducted to reveal where the athlete stands compared to others of the same age, gender, and skill level. Tests that yield objective data that can be compared to normative data give the best picture of where the athlete stands. This information can also be used to measure individual or team progress, providing a way to identify the athlete's progress as a result of the training program. Many teams have back-to-camp testing requirements, and the athlete's progress in a training program can help ensure that the player is ready to return to his sport and start off with positive results.

Step 3: Consider the Time Frame or Cycle

The majority of training programs are designed for the off-season—the time of the year when players have a fairly long break between sport seasons. The off-season period can range from 4 weeks to 9 months. This downtime can be the most crucial in an athlete's overall development. As an example, the time between an athlete's freshman and sophomore years of both high school and college seems to be critical in the physical development of the young athlete. It is not uncommon to see meteoric changes in a young athlete's physical development during these periods, particularly in the areas of body mass, strength, speed, and power. Whatever the time frame or cycle, careful planning will result in a positive progression of the athlete's development.

Step 4: Select the Time in the Training Year

The best strategy is to plan on a long-term program. Look at the full 12 months of the training year and decide when the athlete's training opportunities exist. This way, the plan can define the athlete's training program for the present, and then when the next opportunity arises, the next cycle can dovetail with the previous training in order to maximize results.

Step 5: Design the Program

For training, the most basic need of athletes is to improve their work capacity. This term refers to the development of basic strength, muscular endurance, anaerobic endurance (unless the sport is an endurance activity), and power.

This is where conditioning specialists should earn their money: the selection of exercises that will develop the skills necessary to be successful in an individual sport. To improve work capacity, athletes must do the foundational work that serves as the base on which to impose skill-specific drills such as plyometric training. Never forget the relationship between strength and plyometrics in establishing work capacity. Strength development is imperative to facilitating plyometric training and vice versa.

This is the stage that results in the day-to-day details of training, including the number and order of exercises, the volume (sets and reps), and the intensity. These choices will determine the athlete's level of success.

SAMPLE PROGRAM FOR FOOTBALL

American football features a high number of participants with various skill sets. Football is one of the most demanding sports in the United States, and it presents multiple opportunities and problems. Based on our recommended approach, the first step in the development of this program is considering the athletes.

Step 1: Consider the Athlete

Football players can be divided into groups by position. This may lead to a total of nine subgroups: quarterbacks, running backs, receivers, tight ends, offensive linemen, defensive linemen, linebackers, defensive backs, and kickers. Further subgroups could be created, such as dividing defensive linemen into defensive ends and interior linemen. However, for a high school situation, a coach could use three basic groups: (1) offensive and defensive linemen, (2) linebackers and running backs, and (3) receivers and defensive backs (this group would also include quarterbacks and kickers).

A needs analysis may differ for each football coach, but most will likely determine that players need a skill set that includes general strength, speed, and power; this can then be expanded to include starting speed, lateral movement, change of direction, and anaerobic endurance.

Because football is the essence of a team sport, training programs applied to the team workout will be directed to the mean. The goal will be to move the average abilities of the team forward. The younger players (freshmen and sophomores) will have the greatest differences in size, experience, body shape, and so on. Positions will naturally separate the players according to size, speed, mass, and movement skills.

Step 2: Assess and Test the Athlete

The following tests are appropriate for evaluating the physical skills of the American football player: 3RM back squat, backward medicine ball throw (15 pounds), 10-yard sprint time, 90-second box test, 300-yard shuttle.

Step 3: Consider the Time Frame or Cycle

For simplicity's sake, we will consider the off-season or interim time to be the period between the end of the school year and the start of football practice. We will assign a 12-week period to the off-season program.

Step 4: Select the Time in the Training Year

The time of year for the training program is during the summer vacation period for most schools. The training period will be divided into three cycles of 4 weeks in duration.

Step 5: Design the Program

Now the specific exercises and variables for the training program must be considered. In the case of young athletes, learning movement skills is crucial, and the work capacity factor must be at the forefront. As an example, the following program provides a potential template for the first cycle.

CYCLE I
Off-Season Training Program

Warm-Up

Perform as a set of 10 reps:

Front lunge	Front plank, 60 seconds
Reverse lunge	Side plank (R, L), 45 seconds each side
Side-to-side lunge	Medicine ball pull-over sit-up
Drop step lunge	Medicine ball alternating toe touch
Crossover lunge	Hip roll

Strength Program

Single-leg squat with body weight. Perform this while standing on a box at least 36 inches (91 cm) from the ground. Place one heel at the back edge of the box and the toe of the other foot on the flat surface of the box. Lower the body until the full range of knee flexion is accomplished. Raise the body and repeat the squat for 6 reps, then switch to the other leg. By the end of the 12-week cycle, the athlete should be able to perform 4 sets of 6 reps.

Javorek complex. This is a series of lifts with an Olympic barbell done consecutively until the entire series is completed. Each lift is carried out for 6 repetitions and extended to 4 sets of 6 reps over time.

1. High pull
2. Muscle snatch
3. Front squat with push press
4. Bent-over row
5. Romanian deadlift

General strength lift series. The intent of this series of lifts is to build general strength throughout the body and to enhance muscular endurance while requiring the athlete to move through a multitude of technical movements.

1. Back squat, 3 × 8
2. Incline bench press, 3 × 8
3. Step-up, 2 × 6 (18-inch box)

Plyometric drills.

Jump to box (36-inch box)

Side-to-side box shuffle (12-inch box), 30 seconds

Scorpion step-up (12-inch box), 30 seconds

30-second box drill (12-inch box)

This template can be expanded or extended for the subsequent 4-week cycles to complete the 12-week off-season program.

SAMPLE PROGRAM FOR BASKETBALL

Unlike American football, basketball features a more limited number of participants with relatively similar skill sets. Basketball is one of the most demanding interval-related sports. Basketball players can benefit greatly from both the mechanical and physiological adaptations achieved through plyometric training. As with American football, the first step in the development of this program is considering the athlete.

Step 1: Consider the Athlete

James is a 16-year-old basketball player with 1 year of varsity experience. He has had 2 years of resistance training in the weightlifting class taught by the high school football coach. He has sprained an ankle in the past, but he is healthy at this time.

Step 2: Assess and Test the Athlete

For an evaluation based on vertical jumping ability, the coach has James complete the following tests:

1. **Standing jump-and-reach.** Standing on both feet, James reaches as high as he can on a wall; the height is marked on the wall. Then James jumps

off both feet and reaches as high on the wall as he can; again the height is marked. The difference between the two marks is recorded.

2. **Jump from box.** James does a depth jump from an 18-inch box. After he lands, he jumps up and reaches as high on the wall as he can; the height of the touch is recorded.

3. **Three-step vertical jump.** James takes three steps, and on the final step (which should be with his preferred foot), he jumps up and reaches as high on the wall as he can; the height of the jump is marked.

4. **Three-repetition maximum parallel squat.** James determines the maximum amount of weight he can lift three times when doing a back squat. To do the squat, James stands with his back to a barbell that is resting on a rack at shoulder height; he lifts the barbell to rest on his shoulders, bends at the hips and knees until his thighs are parallel to the floor, and returns to the starting position, repeating three times.

5. **Five-repetition, 5-second parallel squat at 60 percent body weight.** James performs five squats with a barbell that is weighted with an amount equal to 60 percent of his body weight. He attempts to do the squats within 5 seconds.

The test results dictate the type and direction of the program. For James, tests 4 and 5 indicate adequate strength because his 3RM squat was 1.5 times his body weight, and he could squat five times in 5 seconds with 60 percent of his body weight. If these scores had been below standard (e.g., he could squat only 75 percent of his body weight and took 7.5 seconds to complete five squats at 60 percent of his body weight), this would indicate that resistance work is still a major requirement of training or even a prerequisite to undergoing high-intensity plyometrics. Strength work alone might enable James to increase his vertical jump if he were deficient.

Tests 1, 2, and 3 demonstrate James' present vertical jumping ability and provide data that can be used to measure his progress at the end of the program. James reached 21 inches in the standing jump-and-reach, 18 inches in the jump from box, and 20 inches in the three-step vertical jump, indicating that he isn't any better off on one foot than two.

Step 3: Consider the Time Frame or Cycle

James' program will be for 4 weeks. The sample program has been condensed from a normal periodized training year to demonstrate the preparation, progression, and performance variables involved in program design. At the end of this cycle, James will be retested to check for progress.

Step 4: Select the Time in the Training Year

James will follow this program during the month of September, before the onset of the basketball season. This is the time when most high school athletes in winter sports begin to make an effort to get in shape.

Step 5: Design the Program

In this sample 4-week program, each week is planned according to three variables: preparation, progression, and performance.

Remember, this is a hypothetical program. The following schedule pertains only to James.

WEEK 1

Preparation: Use high-volume, low-intensity resistance training and low-intensity plyometrics to allow the body's soft tissues to adjust to the stress of jumping and the impact of landing.

Progression: Include enough variety to challenge the athlete to learn new skills.

Performance: Focus on proper landing techniques and the use of the arms in performing low-intensity exercises. Make sure the athlete understands the concept of the amortization phase.

Monday, Wednesday, Friday: Weight Training

Parallel squat with 70 percent 1RM (one-repetition maximum, or 70 percent of the maximum weight James is able to lift one time), 3 × 12

Split squat with 50 percent of body weight, 3 × 10 each leg

Inverted leg press (8RM), 4 × 8

Push press (front) (8RM), 4 × 8

Shrug pull (5RM), 4 × 5

Tuesday: Plyometrics

Two-foot ankle hop, 1 × 10

Side-to-side ankle hop, 2 × 20

Hip-twist ankle hop, 2 × 20

Split-squat jump, 2 × 10 each leg

Standing jump-and-reach, 1 × 6

Thursday: Plyometrics

Two-foot ankle hop, 1 × 10

Side-to-side ankle hop, 2 × 20

Hip-twist ankle hop, 2 × 20

Rim jump, 2 × 10

Single-leg push-off (from a 12-inch box), 2 × 20

Alternating push-off (from a 12-inch box), 2 × 20

WEEK 2

Preparation: Use resistance training to stress basic strength in the lower extremities.

Progression: Integrate higher levels of intensity into plyometric exercises. This adds complexity and intensity to the resistance training.

Performance: Remember that quality, not quantity, is the key in performing plyometric exercises.

Monday: Plyometrics

Front box jump (18-inch box), 3 × 10

Standing jump over barrier (36 inches), 1 × 10

Double-leg hop, 3 × 3

Rim jump, 2 × 10

Two-foot ankle hop, 3 × 10

Tuesday: Weight Training

Front squat (8RM), 3 × 8

Inverted leg press (8RM), 4 × 8

Push press (front) (8RM), 2 × 8

High pull (8RM), 2 × 8

Wednesday: Weight Training

Back squat with 70 to 80 percent 1RM, 5 × 5

Thursday: Plyometrics

Side-to-side ankle hop, 3 × 10

Single-leg push-off, 3 × 10

Front box jump (18-inch box), 3 × 10

Rim jump, 3 × 10

Standing triple jump, 1 × 5

Friday: Weight Training

Repeat Tuesday's workout but replace the push press with the behind-the-neck push press.

WEEK 3

Preparation: Emphasize heavy plyometric work. Use resistance training as a form of recovery.

Progression: Focus on building basic strength in those muscle groups associated with plyometric exercises for vertical jumping. Continue to build on both volume and intensity.

Performance: Emphasize quality of effort by applying time and distance goals. (For example, how quickly can the athlete accomplish 10 repetitions of the side-to-side box shuffle? How far can the athlete travel when performing standing triple jumps?)

Monday: Plyometrics

Depth jump (from 18-inch box), 3 × 10

Standing jump over barrier (18 to 24 inches), 3 × 10

Double-leg hop, 3 × 5

Single-leg hop over cone, 3 × 10

Side-to-side ankle hop, 3 × 10

Tuesday: Weight Training

Front squat, 3 × 8

Inverted leg press, 4 × 8

Behind-the-neck push press, 3 × 8

Stiff-knee clean, 3 × 5

Wednesday: Weight Training

Prone hamstring curl (concentric: raise weight with both legs; eccentric: lower weight with one leg), 3 × 8

Back squat with 85 to 90 percent 1RM, 5 × 5

Thursday: Plyometrics

Front box jump (18-inch box), 3 × 10

Standing triple jump, 1 × 3

Lateral cone hop (12 to 18 inches), 3 × 10

Alternating push-off, 3 × 10

Rim jump, 3 × 10

Friday: Weight Training

Repeat Tuesday's workout but substitute split squats for front squats.

WEEK 4

Preparation: Emphasize low-volume, high-intensity exercises. Neuromuscular preparation is directed toward maximal efforts with full recovery in both plyometrics and weight training.

Progression: The challenge is to work toward maximal efforts in plyometrics. Maximal vertical efforts with minimal ground contact time are a must.

Performance: Resistance training as well as plyometrics should now be focused on power. The concept of maximal force applied rapidly is the key to developing the vertical jump.

Monday: Plyometrics

Depth jump (from 18-inch box), 3 × 10

Standing jump over barrier (18 to 24 inches), 3 × 10

Single-leg hop over cone, 3 × 10

Double-leg hop, 3 × 10

Tuesday: Weight Training

Quarter squat, 5 × 3

Inverted leg press, 5 × 5

Hamstring curl, 3 × 8

Front squat to push press, 5 × 3

Wednesday: Plyometrics

Depth jump to 24-inch box or higher, 3 × 10

Alternating push-off, 3 × 10

Lateral jump over cone (12 to 18 inches), 3 × 10

Rim jump, 3 × 10

Thursday: Weight Training

Repeat Tuesday's workout but add 5 × 3 power cleans from the thigh hang position.

Friday: Retest

In our theoretical model of training, the results of the retesting might look like this: To check for improvement, James is tested again on the tasks that he did at the beginning of the cycle. After completing the 4-week training, James scores 22 inches for the standing jump-and-reach, 22.5 inches for the jump from box, and 23 inches for the three-step vertical jump. As the training year continues, James should try to maintain his improved vertical jumping ability and perhaps increase it even more. Future workouts will be designed according to his new goals.

High-Level Plyometric Training

As a former point guard and shooting guard at the college and NBA level, this professional basket-ball player is a physically gifted athlete who used plyometric training to enhance his athletic talent. During his initial evaluation, he is able to jump to a 48-inch platform from a dead standing start, so there is no doubt that he possesses a great deal of natural leaping ability. Plyometrics designed to build on his natural ability can help him prepare for training camp. This is a crucial time for the professional athlete, because this is when he literally earns his job.

Single Plyometric Workout

- Hurdle hop (42-inch hurdles spaced approximately 4 feet apart), 5 × 6
- Hurdle hop (42-inch hurdles spaced approximately 12 feet apart), 6 × 3. This exercise requires the athlete to perform a standing long jump to an area just in front of the hurdle and then perform a vertical jump over the hurdle. He repeats this for the entire number of hurdles.
- Box-to-box depth jump (from a 42-inch box to a 42-inch box), 4 × 10
- Variations of the Frappier footwork patterns
- Standing triple jump, 5 × 1

Keep in mind that this young man is a gifted, mature, and physically well-developed male athlete. He is a former collegiate All-American and has had several years of experience in the NBA. He was able to tolerate this volume and high intensity largely because of his maturity and ability.

SAMPLE PROGRAM FOR SOCCER

Soccer is a sport that places particular demands on the lower extremities and trunk. Speed and agility are valuable assets for those who play the forward positions. Stability, balance, and acceleration are the skills most needed by defensive players. Because soccer is one of the most demanding sports in terms of anaerobic cardiovascular endurance, plyometric drills are a natural complement to training for these athletes.

Step 1: Consider the Athlete

Brooke is a 17-year-old female soccer player who is preparing to leave for an NCAA Division I college program. Before she leaves for college, Brooke wants to develop skills that will impress her college coaches. She has 12 weeks to prepare for her introduction to the collegiate level of competition. She is still involved in summer club playing, but she thinks that she needs to do extra work if she is going to make the desired impression on the college coaches.

Step 2: Assess and Test the Athlete

Brooke is 5 feet 9 inches tall and weighs 137 pounds. She has lifted on an irregular basis in the past. Her background also includes experience in performing basic plyometric training.

1. **Standing jump-and-reach.** Brooke has a standing jump-and-reach score of 15 inches.
2. **Maximum squat.** Brooke is able to do a 95-pound maximum squat for three reps.
3. **Bench press.** Testing for a 1RM score in the bench press provides some indication of Brooke's basic upper-body strength. Her maximum effort is 55 pounds.
4. **T-test.** This test is performed on a T that is 10 yards across the top and has a 10-yard stem. The athlete starts at the base of the stem. She runs forward, then shuffles to the right or left along the top of the T until she touches both ends. The athlete then returns to the middle and backpedals along the stem to the original starting position. Brooke's score is 10.2 seconds. The average score for the collegiate female soccer player is 10.8 seconds.
5. **Sit-up test for 30 seconds.** Throw-ins in soccer are a function of core strength, and this test is an indicator of the need for trunk strengthening. Brooke completes 20 sit-ups in 30 seconds.

All of the scores indicate that Brooke is a young athlete who has been able to compete at the high school level because of her soccer skills and speed. Being quick and skillful would make her a candidate for recruiting; however, survival at the next level is going to require strength, power, and physical stamina.

Step 3: Consider the Time Frame or Cycle

Brooke has 3 months in which to develop her overall physical strength and endurance. Her continued desire to play soccer during this time might become a conflict. However, she is willing to split her workout days, ensuring that she will spend 3 days per week training with the weights and plyometrics.

Step 4: Select the Time in the Training Year

Brooke will use this program during the summer months after graduation from high school until she reports to her university for school and practice. Each cycle can fit well into a 4-week block.

Step 5: Design the Program

The basic needs of this athlete are general strength and power development with specific emphasis on developing the vertical jump, core strength, and both upper- and lower-body strength.

Day 1

Hamstring curl, 3 × 12
Leg press, 3 × 10
Lat pull-down, 3 × 12
Shoulder press, 3 × 10

Bench press, 3 × 10
Back hyperextension, 2 × 12
Torso rotation, 3 × 8

Core Strength: Medicine Ball Work

Sit-up, straight arm (15 reps)
Pull-over pass (15 reps)
Alternate toe touch (10 reps each side)
Side throw (15 reps each side)

Backward throw (15 reps)
Front toss (10 reps)
Heel toss (10 reps)

Day 2

Split squat, 2 × 10 each side
Dumbbell press, 2 × 10
Front squat to shoulder press, 3 × 6
Frappier footwork patterns, up to 2 1/2
    minutes total time, four-square pattern
    (any combination of squares may be
    used)

Front cone hop, 5 × 6
Lateral cone hop, 3 × 6 each direction
Single-leg push-off (12-inch box), 1 × 30
    seconds
Side-to-side box shuffle (12-inch box),
    1 × 30 seconds

Day 3

Repeat day 1.

Progression: The goal is to advance Brooke into more dynamic activities that will challenge her yet provide continuous strength gains.

Day 1

Front squat, 3 × 8
Lunge, 2 × 10 both legs
Push press, 3 × 8

Seated row, 3 × 8
Incline bench press, 3 × 8
Dumbbell pull-over, 3 × 10

Core Strength: Medicine Ball Work

Repeat this circuit twice:

Overhead sit-up toss (15 reps)
Pull-over pass (15 reps)
Hip crunch (15 reps)
Russian twist (10 reps)
Side throw (15 reps each side)
Hip roll (10 reps each side)

Backward throw (10 reps)
Front toss (15 reps)
Heel toss (10 reps)

Day 2

Lat pull-down, 3 × 10; each set followed by 10 reps of overhead throw

Bench press, 3 × 8; each set followed by 12 reps of power drop

Heel toss with medicine ball, 3 × 10

Hexagon drill, 3 sets

Lateral hurdle (12-inch) hops (hop down, back, and down without stopping), 3 × 3

Depth jumps (18-inch box), 3 × 10

30-second box drill (12-inch box), 3 sets

Skipping, 3 × 20 yards

Power skipping, 3 × 20 yards

Single-leg hops, 3 × 20 yards

Day 3

Repeat day 1.

WEEKS 9 TO 12

Performance: Power development becomes the main focus of this final cycle. Lifting loads should be reduced to 30 to 60 percent of 1RM so that the bar can be moved rapidly. This allows for maximal power development through the full range of motion. As often as possible, plyometric drills should be related to the specific movements in soccer.

The intensity of this third cycle is very high and will depend on Brooke's ability to gain strength and demonstrate an adequate level of adaptation to the plyometric training. If she fails to do so, the exercise intensity will be lowered, and lower-level plyometrics will be substituted.

Day 1

5-5-5 squat, 4 sets

Push press, 4 × 5

High pull (clean grip), 4 × 5

Single-leg squat, 4 × 5 each leg

Depth jump (18-inch box), 3 × 8

Depth jump with 180-degree turn (18-inch box), 2 × 8 both directions

Hurdle hop (24-inch), 5 × 6

60-second box drill, 1 set

Day 2

Core Strength: Medicine Ball Work

Repeat this circuit twice:

Sit-up pass (25 reps)

Pull-over pass (25 reps)

Diagonal toss (20 reps each side)

Trunk rotation (12 reps each side)

Hip roll (20 reps each side)

Repeat this circuit three times:

Overhead throw (15 reps for maximum distance)

Backward throw (10 reps for maximum distance)

Front toss (20 reps)

Heel toss (15 reps)

Plyometric Drills

Skipping, 3 × 30 yards

Power skipping, 3 × 30 yards

Alternate bounding with single-arm action, 3 × 30 yards

Double-leg hop, 5 × 5

Day 3

Repeat day 1.

SAMPLE PROGRAM FOR VOLLEYBALL

Volleyball features highly-skilled athletes whose success in competition is related to their ability to jump and land properly. Volleyball athletes use high-intensity jumping in the majority of their sport and skill training, so special considerations should be made to ensure that the addition of plyometrics are optimized for these athletes.

Step 1: Consider the Athlete

Tiann is a 14-year-old female volleyball player who has been released from physical therapy treatment with a referral for a diagnosis of patellofemoral pain syndrome. Tiann is an elite volleyball player who has ambitions of trying out for her high school's volleyball team in the next few months.

During the initial evaluation by the strength coach, Tiann mentions her older sister, who is also a volleyball player, and her mother. Both have a history of ACL injury. The patient reports increased knee pain with running, jumping, and lateral cutting while playing volleyball. Objective findings during the initial evaluation include the following: decreased posterior chain strength (hamstrings and glutes), apparent loose joints with knee hyperextension (bends backward), and limited control during jumping and landing, which is also evident as knock-knee alignment during double- and single-leg squats. The strength coach recalls reading in a recent news article that females who demonstrated increased knock-kneed landing mechanics not only had increased risk for patellofemoral pain, but also for ACL injury. Based on this patient's poor landing mechanics and her familial history of ACL injuries, the strength coach determines that Tiann's deficits could put her at risk to sustain a future ACL injury and also limit her performance. These deficits in her technical performance of plyometric exercises should be the initial focus of her assessment and training.

Step 2: Assess and Test the Athlete

Strength coaches must understand potential familial or genetic links in combination with neuromuscular imbalances—as evidenced from increased knee valgus motion and knock-kneed position during landing—in order to recognize and screen patients who may be predisposed to ACL injury. The case of the 14-year-old volleyball player referred to preventative training is an example of someone who should be recognized for both her familial predisposition (maternal and sibling) and biomechanical risk for a severe and debilitating ACL injury. Accordingly, this potential high-risk athlete would likely benefit from more in-depth risk assessment and a targeted preventative program to improve jumping and landing mechanics that will likely resolve her patellofemoral pain, as well as reduce the risk of an ACL injury in the future.

As outlined in chapter 7, the tuck jump assessment allows strength coaches and trainers to easily identify and target neuromuscular deficits that limit an athlete's jumping performance and likely increase the risk of injury. Identifying deficits in neuromuscular control can be done by conducting functional tests, including the tuck jump assessment and two-dimensional video analysis. In addition, the coach should evaluate other risk factors such as reduced hamstring strength in athletes who maintain high-risk landing mechanics. Standard two-dimensional analysis using a standard video camera is a great tool that strength coaches can use to screen and evaluate athletes for the risk of ACL injury. The coach should watch for knock-kneed landings during vertical jumps, side-to-side jumps, and box jumps. Strength coaches can use this information from screening and assessments to educate athletes on their functional deficits, then use this information to guide exercise progression.

Step 3: Consider the Time Frame or Cycle

Tiann has 2 months in which to address her deficits and progress her programming so that she is physically prepared to initiate her volleyball season.

Step 4: Select the Time in the Training Year

Tiann has no other physical training commitments during this preseason period and can dedicate her training to these goals.

Step 5: Design the Program

The basic needs for this volleyball player are to correct deficits and improve power development with specific emphasis on vertical jump and core strength. End-stage progressions should move to volleyball-specific drills that will transition her directly into sport practices.

WEEKS 1 TO 3

Tuck jump with thighs parallel, 10 to 20 jumps or 5 to 20 seconds

Lunge jump, 5 to 10 jumps or 5 to 15 seconds

Deep-squat jump, 10 to 20 repetitions

Single-leg forward–backward box speed hop, 10 to 25 repetitions or 5 to 15 seconds

Alternate bounding with single-arm action, 10 to 50 meters

Lateral box jump, 10 to 30 seconds

Single-leg forward hop over barrier, 6 to 12 sets

Lateral jump over barrier, 6 to 12 sets

Box drop to athletic position, 5 to 10 repetitions

Box depth jump single forward, 5 to 15 repetitions

Box depth jump with backward glide, 8 to 15 repetitions

Box jump single, 10 to 20 repetitions

Medicine ball (6 to 15 pounds) chest pass sit-up, 2 or 3 sets of 25+, last set to fatigue

Marine crunch (throw-down), 2 or 3 sets of 25+, last set to fatigue

Partner standing trunk rotation, 2 or 3 sets to fatigue in both directions

Chest pass from back, 2 or 3 sets of 25+

Medicine ball slide, 2 or 3 sets of 10 to 20 repetitions

WEEKS 4 TO 6

Tuck jump with heel kick, 10 to 20 jumps or 5 to 20 seconds

Cycled lunge jump, 10 to 20 jumps or 5 to 20 seconds

Deep-squat jump, 10 to 20 repetitions

Double-leg vertical power jump, 10 to 15 jumps or 5 to 15 seconds

Single-leg lateral box speed hop, 10 to 25 repetitions or 5 to 15 seconds

Combination bounding with single-arm action, 10 to 50 meters

Double- or single-leg zigzag hop, 6 to 12 sets

Forward–backward hop over barriers, 6 to 10 sets

Hurdle hop, 6 to 10 sets

Box depth jump double/single leg forward, 5 to 10 repetitions

Box depth jump with medicine ball chest pass, 10 to 15 repetitions

Box depth jump with medicine ball catch, 10 to 15 repetitions

Box depth jump with forward long jump, 8 to 15 repetitions

Box jump for speed, 5 to 20 seconds

Pull-over crunch with medicine ball, 2 or 3 sets of 25+, last set to fatigue

Seated 45-degree trunk twist, 2 or 3 sets to fatigue

Side throw kneeling or standing, 2 or 3 sets of 25+

Two-hand supine backward throw, 2 or 3 sets of 20

Two-hand overhead throw, 2 or 3 sets of 20

WEEKS 7 TO 9

Tuck jump with abdominal crunch, 10 to 20 jumps or 5 to 20 seconds

Single-leg vertical power jump, 5 to 10 jumps or 5 to 10 seconds

Double-leg speed hop, 3 to 5 hops for short duration or up to 30 meters for long duration

Lateral lunge with single-leg box support, 10 to 30 seconds

Forward hop over barriers with middle lateral box, 6 to 10 sets

Multidirectional barrier hop, 6 to 10 sets

Forward barrier hop with medicine ball dunk, 8 to 15 sets

Hurdle hop with box contacts, 8 to 15 sets

Box depth jump forward and backward, 5 to 10 repetitions

Box depth jump with maximum medicine ball throw, 10 to 15 repetitions

Box depth jump with spin dunk, 10 to 15 repetitions

Box depth jump with medicine ball catch and redirect dunk, 10 to 15 repetitions

Box depth jump with 180-degree spin, 8 to 15 repetitions

Single-leg power box step, 8 to 15 repetitions for both legs

Seated 45-degree lateral catch, 2 or 3 sets of 25+, last set to fatigue, both sides

Medicine ball spin and dunk, 10 to 20 repetitions or 10 to 30 seconds

Two-hand forward underhand throw, 2 or 3 sets of 20

Jump throw, 2 or 3 sets of 20

WEEKS 10 TO 12
Preseason Integration Exercises

Defensive Spin Reaction

Equipment

Volleyballs, 30- to 42-inch box, coach

Duration

20 to 30 balls, 3 to 5 sets

Starting Position

The athlete stands in an athletic position, facing 90 degrees away from the coach, who is standing on the box.

Movement

When the coach on the box gives a ball call, the athlete quickly spins 90 degrees to face the coach. The coach should hit the ball to within one quick step and reach of the athlete. The athlete passes the ball to the target and quickly resets to the athletic position facing 90 degrees away from the coach. Repeat until the cart of volleyballs is empty. The coach should use tip and roll shots to make sure the athlete is not on her heels and is staying on her toes.

Box Depth Joust Shuffle Block Drill

Equipment

Four boxes, three coaches, three volleyballs, volleyball net

Duration

10 to 30 repetitions

Starting Position

Coaches are on top of the boxes at the ends and middle of the net. The athlete is on top of a box in the middle of the court on the opposite side of the net from the coaches.

Movement

The athlete drops off the box and quickly jumps up to joust with the middle coach. As the athlete is coming down from the joust jump, the coach will cue the athlete on which direction she should go. The athlete takes a large crossover step in that direction and blocks the hit by that coach.

Box Depth Jump (Maximum) With Directional Dig

Equipment

One box 12 to 30 inches high, coach, volleyball

Duration

10 to 30 repetitions

Starting Position

The athlete stands on the box, facing the coach.

Movement

The athlete drops off the box and performs a maximum vertical jump. After landing in athletic position, the athlete goes to get the ball hit by the coach. The coach should hit a ball that the athlete can reach with one step and a dive.

Multidirectional Barriers to Cue to Ball Reaction

Equipment

11 barriers (5 set up straight ahead, 3 going to the right and left of each side), two volley-balls, three coaches

Duration

10 to 20 repetitions

Starting Position

The athlete faces straight ahead toward the five barriers.

Movement

The athlete quickly hops straight ahead over the five barriers. When the athlete is on the ground and ready to go over the fifth barrier, the coach should indicate a direction. The athlete executes a 90-degree spin in that direction. After the 90-degree spin, the athlete goes over the final three barriers. At the end of the three barriers, the coach tosses a low ball that requires the athlete to go to the ground. The athlete should concentrate on a quick full extension, not going to her knees.

SAMPLE PROGRAM FOR BASEBALL

In the past, old-school baseball had the reputation of valuing three skills—throwing, hitting, and running—not necessarily all in the same player. Typically, professional baseball teams drafted players based on an athlete having at least one of these skills. Today, the value of athleticism seems to be growing in professional baseball, and multiskilled players are receiving the attention and playing time.

One thing that is consistent across the board is the need for trunk strength. Looking at the number of injuries in major-league baseball among hitters and pitchers, the oblique muscle strain is one injury that might be minimized by paying attention to the development of core strength. Trunk strength has a direct relationship to swinging the bat and ultimately to bat speed.

Step 1: Consider the Athlete

Jerry is a 23-year-old professional baseball player. He has been on the road for several months after the baseball season. Vacation, business interests, and so on, have consumed much of his time. He has now decided to put serious time into getting ready for spring ball. He has been lifting on his own and has a fair level of strength development. As a first baseman, he is not expected to possess great sprint speed. He is, however, expected to produce hits and runs.

Step 2: Assess and Test the Athlete

In this case, the client is a physically gifted athlete who has been through a long season of playing competitive baseball games. The most important thing is that the athlete wants to be subjected to a training program of 6 weeks duration with the goal of preparing him for spring training. The ultimate assessment will be his performance in that baseball camp plus his current strength and power performance.

Step 3: Consider the Time Frame or Cycle

Jerry has 6 weeks to get ready. The training specialist must develop a program that will maximize the benefits without resulting in overtraining or injury.

Step 4: Select the Time in the Training Year

The time is preseason and will lead up to the beginning of spring training.

Step 5: Design the Program

WEEKS 1 TO 3

Preparation: This program will include several variations of complex training because of the short time interval available for training. This training will have a special emphasis on developing core or trunk strength. Given Jerry's reputation as a hitter, the program must emphasize those areas that will get the majority of stress once he sets foot in camp.

Progression: This program will be divided into two cycles of 3 weeks each. The first 3 weeks will include resistance training exercises and plyometric drills that emphasize fundamental movements. Many of the exercises are grouped together based on muscle group or total-body function. The second cycle will emphasize sport-specific drills as well as plyometric activities to increase speed of movement. The medicine ball drills for core strength are changed every 2 weeks.

Day 1

Front squat, 3 × 8; followed by 3 × 8 push press

Inclined hammer curl, 3 × 10; followed by 3 × 10 biceps pull-down on the lat machine

Chest press on the machine, 3 × 8; followed by 3 × 8 seated row

Core Strength: Medicine Ball Work (First 2 Weeks)

Repeat this circuit twice:

  Trunk rotation (10 reps each direction)

  Alternating toe touch (10 reps each side)

  Hip roll (10 reps each direction)

  Offset push-up (10 each side)

Repeat this circuit twice:

  Seated toe touch (15 reps)

  Sit-up toss (15 reps)

  Bridge with both feet on medicine ball
   (15 reps)

  Superman arch (15 reps)

Day 2

Back squat, 3 × 10; each set to be followed by 1 × 10 jumps to the box (24-inch box)

Behind-the-neck press, 3 × 6; each set to be followed by 1 × 10 overhead medicine ball throws at maximum effort

Lat pull-down, 3 × 10; each set to be followed by 1 × 10 medicine ball pull-over tosses

Torso rotation, 3 × 8; each set to be followed by 1 × 12 reps of side throws and 12 over-and-back throws (each side)

Same medicine ball work as day 1.

Day 3

Step-up, 3 × 10; each set to be followed by 1 × 10 side lunges (each side), followed by 1 set of walking L lunges over a distance of 20 yards

Hang clean, 4 × 6; each set to be followed by a set of 6 hurdle jumps (30-inch hurdle)

Lateral hurdle hop (18-inch hurdle), 3 × 3, to be repeated five times

Hexagon drills (each drill includes three trips around the hexagon), 5 sets

Hamstring curl, 4 × 6; these sets to be followed by 3 × 30 yards of heel kick running

Same medicine ball work as day 1.

Core Strength Program Progression (Next 3 Weeks)

The core strength program should change after the first 3 weeks and should include the following for the next 2 weeks.

Repeat this circuit three times:

  Alternating toe touch (15 reps each side)

  Hip roll (15 reps each direction)

  Sit-up pass (25 reps)

  Power drop (25 reps)

Repeat this circuit three times:

  Russian twist (15 reps)

  Single-leg bridging (15 reps each leg)

  Standing side throw (20 reps each side)

  Push-up with hands on the ball (15 reps)

WEEKS 4 TO 6

The final 3 weeks of training will include more sport-specific and speed-of-movement drills, along with functional resistance training.

Day 1

Multi-hip machine work (working hip flexion, extension, abduction, and adduction), 3 × 12
Lateral change-of-direction drills for maximal effort, 1 × 10

The player practices hitting a soft-tossed baseball into a net with the Frappier resistance cords attached to the player's hips and arms. The cords are removed immediately after the player hits 40 to 50 balls, and he hits freely for another 40 to 50 balls. This represents a form of contrast training that helps improve trunk rotation speed.

Core Strength: Medicine Ball Work

Use the core strength program progression for weeks 3 and 4, then progress to the following program for weeks 5 and 6.

Day 2

Four-way lunge (front, 45-degree, side, and crossover), 1 × 10
Frappier footwork drills (approximately 20 minutes of various routines)
Medicine ball drills for core strength
Interval speed running workout on treadmill (approximately 1 hour in length)

Day 3

Repeat day 1.

Core Strength Program Progression (Final 2 Weeks)

The final 2 weeks of core strength exercises using the medicine ball are as follows:

Repeat this circuit twice:

Alternate toe touch (10 reps each side)
Superman toss (15 reps)
Diagonal toss (15 reps each side)
Walkabout (30 seconds)

Repeat this circuit three times:

Trunk rotation (15 reps each side)
Hip roll (15 reps each direction)
Russian twist (15 reps each side)
Over-and-back toss (20 reps)
Standing diagonal throw (12 reps)

SAMPLE PROGRAM FOR TENNIS

This program is designed for a younger athlete, Chris, who is 13 years of age. The program will give Chris the opportunity to develop movement and exercise skills that will help him accomplish greater strength gains once he has physically matured. Load or intensity of resistance is less of a priority at this stage of his athletic development. The emphasis is on developing core or trunk strength as well as lower- and upper-extremity strength. Developing strength in these areas will enable Chris to improve his ability to move quickly in a lateral direction on the tennis court. The plyometric drills are aimed at stressing those neuromuscular pathways that will also improve this skill.

Step 1: Consider the Athlete

Chris is a 13-year-old tennis player with several years of experience playing at the junior level, and he has a sectional ranking in the top 10 players of his age. He has had little to no resistance training in his background. He has never been involved in a serious conditioning program prior to this.

Step 2: Assess and Test the Athlete

1. **Hexagon drill.** Standing in the center of the hexagon with his feet shoulder-width apart, Chris begins jumping from the center across the front edge of the hexagon, and he continues around each side until he has made three round trips. He must return to the center after each jump to the outside and will be timed with a stopwatch from start to conclusion of the three cycles. Chris should be facing forward throughout the cycle of jumps.

2. **20-yard sprint.** Chris is timed in a 20-yard maximal sprint on a flat surface. This sprint can be performed from a split-step or standing start position.

3. **T-test.** Using a T that is marked as 10 yards across the top with a 10-yard stem, Chris starts at the base of the stem and runs forward to the top of the T. He then shuffles to his left and touches a cone placed 5 yards away, shuffles to his right all the way across the top of the T (10 yards), then shuffles back to the middle. At this point, Chris backpedals back to the start. His total time is recorded.

4. **Medicine ball overhead throw.** Using a 4-kilogram (8.8 pound) medicine ball, Chris takes one step and uses two hands to throw the ball from over his head as far as he can. The distance that the ball travels (from a start line to the point where the ball lands) is measured and recorded.

The test results will dictate the type of program Chris is best suited for. This picture can be complicated by the fact that he is nearing puberty and has never used strength training before. Learning the techniques of squatting, lunges, and other total-body lifts will enhance the young athlete's abilities even though he is not lifting heavy weights. The load (amount of weight) lifted is not nearly as crucial in his development as is the need to learn skills of movement. Therefore, the program should focus on submaximal plyometric drills that can be supplemented with strength exercises of high volume and low intensity (load).

Chris records a score of 11.5 seconds for the hexagon (60th percentile) and 3.2 seconds for the 20-yard sprint (70th percentile). On the T-test, Chris had a score of 11.4 seconds, and he threw the medicine ball 16 feet.

These scores are typical of a ranked junior tennis player at this age. Because tennis is a sport that is so heavily weighted toward the skill of stroke production, athleticism is often overlooked or viewed as secondary to the skills of the game itself. As with all sports, however, the rise in athletic ability of the participants is becoming obvious. Several articles have been published in tennis publications indicating that those individuals entering the professional ranks are becoming taller and heavier. This relates to the speed and force that can be applied during stroke patterns. Bigger and faster athletes are going to hit the ball harder, serve faster, and cover the court better.

The scores recorded indicate that Chris needs to improve in several areas of athletic ability. He needs to develop start speed, lateral change of direction, and core strength (as indicated by the short distance of his medicine ball throw).

Step 3: Consider the Time Frame or Cycle

Chris is an example of a young athlete who is subject to the demands of a time-consuming schedule of practice and competition. He really has no off-season. He doesn't participate in other sports, and his school studies and tennis take up all of his available time. His slow time for tennis is in the fall between October and November.

Step 4: Select the Time in the Training Year

This program will be designed to fit into a 6-week period. It will consist of a 2-week preparation period that will focus on improving core strength. The next 2 weeks will feature submaximal and low- to moderate-intensity plyometric exercises. Finally, the performance period should consist of 2 weeks of moderate- to high-intensity training, particularly for the lower extremities, that still takes into consideration the age and abilities of this athlete.

Step 5: Design the Program

Each of the 6 weeks is planned according to three variables: preparation, progression, and performance.

WEEK 1

Preparation: Use medicine ball exercises to develop core and lower-extremity strength. This time frame should call for high-volume, low-intensity resistance training. For athletes in this age group, the most important goal is learning the skilled movements associated with resistance training. Because of the age of this particular athlete, the intensity of the resistance should be less of a priority.

Progression: Add exercises as tolerated, always aiming for a minimum of 10 to 15 repetitions per exercise. Resistance training for the young athlete should move from simple to more complex movements. The progression should also be from general to specific.

Performance: Execution, execution, execution! The young athlete must be made aware of the proper positioning and movements of each exercise. Do not take anything for granted when working with an athlete of this age. A lot can be accomplished to help the athlete establish proper fundamentals of training.

Remember, with athletes this age, attention span may become an issue. Try to keep the workouts crisp and moving right from one exercise to the next. Recovery is not as crucial for this type of athlete, especially when using lighter resistance aimed at developing a basic strength base.

Monday and Friday: Resistance Training Exercises

Squats with 6- to 8-pound medicine ball held on shoulders behind head, 3 × 10

Split squats with 6- to 8-pound medicine ball held on shoulders, 2 × 10

Chest press with 10- to 12-pound dumbbells, 2 × 12

Pull-over with 10- to 12-pound medicine ball, 2 × 12

Seated row (12RM), 2 × 12

Wednesday: Plyometrics

Krumrie footwork pattern

- 1-2 for 5 seconds
- 1-6 for 5 seconds
- 1-2-5-1 for 10 seconds
- 9-8-5-9 for 10 seconds
- 1-5-7-5-1 for 15 seconds
- 9-5-3-5-9 for 15 seconds

Hexagon drill, 3 × 3 circuits

Two-foot ankle hop, 4 × 10 yards

Jump to box (12- to 18-inch box), 4 × 5

Preparation: Continue to emphasize basic strength and stability with the resistance training exercises.

Progression: Advance to more complex movements.

Performance: Continue to emphasize proper alignment and relationships between each segment of the exercise, trunk position, and tempo of exercise so that each is performed under control.

Monday and Friday: Resistance Training

Perform 3 × 10 repetitions for each of the previous exercises (from week 1) set up in a circuit pattern. Allow 30 to 45 seconds between each exercise for recovery.

Wednesday: Plyometrics

Krumrie footwork pattern
- 1-2 for 5 seconds
- 1-6 for 5 seconds
- 1-2-3-1 for 10 seconds
- 1-6-9-1 for 10 seconds
- 1-5-7-1 for 10 seconds
- 9-5-3-9 for 10 seconds
- 1-2-5-6-1 for 15 seconds
- 9-8-5-6-9 for 15 seconds

Two-foot ankle hop, 5 × 10 yards

Standing long jump, 6 reps

Side-to-side box shuffle, 3 × 30 seconds

Preparation: Continue to build strength in such a way that the athlete learns to stabilize and control the body.

Progression: Introduce overhead lifting movements that force the athlete to control movements initiated with the legs and finished with the arms.

Performance: Focus on initiation of a total-body movement with the legs exerting force against the ground.

Monday and Friday: Resistance Training

Push-up (body weight), 3 × 10

Front squat with 8- to 10-pound medicine ball, 3 × 10

Dumbbell press with 8- to 10-pound dumbbells, 3 × 10

Lat pull-down to the front (12RM), 2 × 12

Split squat (10RM), 2 × 10 each leg

Core Strength: Medicine Ball Work

Use a 6- to 8-pound medicine ball.

Trunk rotation, 2 × 10 each direction

Pull-over pass, 2 × 15

Sit-up toss, 2 × 15

Lateral toss, 2 × 15 each side

Overhead throw, 3 × 10

Wednesday: Plyometrics

Hexagon drill for time, 2 sets

Side-to-side ankle hop, 3 × 20 seconds

Hip-twist ankle hop, 3 × 20 seconds

Standing long jump, 1 × 5

Front cone hop (8- to 12-inch cone), 5 × 6

Lateral cone hop (8- to 12-inch cone),
3 × 3

WEEKS 5 AND 6

Preparation: Core or trunk strength should have a major emphasis at this point. Chris has been gaining in exercise skill and should now begin to experience actual physiological gain as well. One of the major demands of the sport of tennis is anaerobic endurance. The program should reflect this as a major goal.

Progression: Volume and frequency of exercise continue to rise in an effort to further develop strength as well as local muscular endurance.

Performance: Exercises should become more specific to the sport so that the athlete can get maximum transfer from the weight room to the court. With the goal of improving lateral change of direction, the exercises should emphasize this area.

Monday and Friday: Resistance Training

Push-up (body weight) with three different hand positions (shoulder width, wider, and narrower than shoulders), 3 × 10

Lateral step-up with 8- to 10-pound dumbbells, 2 × 12

Front squat to push press with 10- to 12-pound medicine ball, 3 × 10

Lunge in four directions (front, 45-degree, side, and crossover), 1 × 10

Dumbbell press with 10 to 12 pounds, 3 × 10

Core Strength: Medicine Ball Work

Use a 6- to 10-pound medicine ball.

Pull-over and touch toes, 1 × 15

Sit-up, 1 × 15

Pull-over sit-up, 1 × 15

Russian twist, 1 × 15

Hip roll, 1 × 10

Lateral toss, 3 × 15 each side

Wednesday: Plyometrics

Perform a circuit of plyometric training using each of the exercises in weeks 3 and 4. Do five standing long jumps, then perform the hexagon, side-to-side ankle hop, hip twist, front cone hop, and lateral cone hop for 30 seconds each. Repeat this circuit three times, allowing 30 to 90 seconds of rest between bouts.

SAMPLE PROGRAM FOR MIXED MARTIAL ARTS

Athletes who participate in mixed martial arts (MMA) come in various genders, sizes, and ages. In general, speed of movement, stability, strength, and balance are crucial elements to be considered. At Olympic or professional levels of competition, most athletes will be physically and chronologically mature.

For these athletes, sparring and practice competitions take up the majority of their time and effort. Practice or training sessions are usually focused on combat techniques. These athletes are highly motivated, have high tolerance for exercise stress, and will usually be eager to try novel approaches to their training.

Step 1: Consider the Athlete

John is a 25-year-old MMA athlete who has been fighting for 2 years. He is 6-foot-4 and 220 pounds and was a collegiate football player who turned to MMA after college. He is physically well developed and has multiple years of weight training experience. He has been focusing on improving his wrestling and boxing skills during the majority of his practice sessions. He is now looking for a program that will help him become more ballistic in his kicking techniques.

Step 2: Assess and Test the Athlete

John has a history of knee injuries to his right knee. He states that the knee is fine now and is fully rehabbed from two prior surgeries, the last one performed 2 years ago.

Otherwise, he states that he has been bench pressing 315 pounds and squatting 385 pounds for sets of 3. He prefers to do his weight training at his dojo (training facility) along with the specialty exercises he performs for his sport (ropes, kettlebells, and so on).

The one test used to assess the strength and function of the surgically intervened knee is a single-leg squat performed in front of a squat rack so that John can grab a supporting stanchion if he needs to balance or support himself. The test is performed on a box that is 3 inches high. The box is placed in front of the squat rack. John stands with one heel placed at the back edge of the box. The toe of the other foot is on the back side of the box so that it can slide vertically down and up. From this position, John performs a single-leg squat, down to full flexion and back up to standing. He is asked to repeat this for 6 repetitions.

John was observed from the front and the side as he performed the squats. For his surgical leg, it was noted that his knee collapsed to the inside (medially) when he descended to the squat position, and the knee demonstrated a wobble on the ascent. Both observations are indications of weakness in the quadriceps and hamstrings. This area will demand attention before John undertakes a high-intensity, high-volume plyometric training program.

After assessments of John's range of motion and flexibility, he is deemed to be normal and fit in all areas other than his surgical knee, where functional strength seems to be the questionable factor.

Step 3: Consider the Time Frame or Cycle

John lives out of the area and is willing to devote only a single day each week to plyometric training. He can drive to the facility to spend 2 hours training once a week.

Step 4: Select the Time in the Training Year

John allows himself 2 weeks to recover before any serious competitions or matches (fights).

He is willing to do the plyometric training at any time during the year other than his recovery periods before his matches. It is decided that plyometric training for John will be conducted on Tuesday afternoons.

Step 5: Design the Program

This workout is designed to be performed once a week over a 2-hour period. Maximum recovery should be allowed between sets of exercises. This program is intended for the mature, well-developed, and experienced athlete. A strength base is an imperative part of attempting to benefit from this type of training. Before beginning this program, an athlete should be able to squat at least 1.5 times his body weight and be able to successfully perform 10 plyometric clap push-ups. Consideration must also be given to the fact that a specific weakness has been identified in the athlete's physical makeup.

EXERCISES

This workout should be preceded by a thorough and complete warm-up routine. The warm-up must include both static and dynamic stretching followed by movement drills or low-level plyometric drills to prepare the muscles, tendons, and ligaments for the highly challenging workout.

Single-Leg Squat

This exercise should be performed three times per week for 2 weeks (4 sets of 6) before starting the plyometric training program. John will do these on his own at his dojo and also when he comes to the facility once per week.

Olympic Hop

Perform Olympic hops for 6 × 20 yards. Each individual hop should cover approximately 3 feet (91 cm) on each effort.

Skater Hop

Perform 4 to 6 sets of 10 reps to each side.

Set two cones 4 to 5 feet (122 to 152 cm) apart and two cones inside of these 1 to 2 feet (30 to 61 cm) apart. The athlete begins by hopping from side to side, directing himself at the outside cones for 6 reps each way. At the moment the athlete lands on the sixth rep, he immediately hops toward the inside cones and goes side to side as fast as he can for a set of 10 reps. Repeat this drill 4 to 6 times.

Split-Squat Jump

Perform 5 or 6 sets of 10 reps.
The athlete performs a split-squat jump moving forward down a mat surface. After alternating legs, the athlete performs a front kick. He lands in a controlled fashion and begins the next series of split-squat jumps.

Neider Press

Perform 4 to 6 sets of 40-second intervals. Allow a 120-second recovery period between sets.

The athlete assumes an athletic ready stance while holding a 25- to 45-pound weight plate with arms extended at a 90-degree angle from the shoulders. He moves the weight by bringing it to the chest, then extends the arms rapidly away from the body on a 45-degree angle as quickly as possible.

90-Second Box Drill

Use a 12-inch-high box, preferably 20 inches (51 cm) wide and 30 inches (76 cm) deep to provide an adequate landing surface. The athlete stands to the side of the box and jumps to the top of the box, landing on both feet. He immediately jumps off the other side of the box. After landing on the surface, the athlete immediately reverses his direction back to the top of the box and continues moving side to side for 90 seconds. The goal is at least 90 counts (a count is recorded each time both feet hit the top of the box).

Hurdle Hop

Perform 6 sets of 6 to 10 reps.

The athlete starts in a position facing six hurdles set at 36 to 42 inches (91 to 107 cm) in height. Using a rapid arm swing, the athlete jumps vertically up and over the first hurdle. On feeling his feet touch the ground, the athlete immediately attempts to reverse the direction and clear the next hurdle. He repeats this movement for the full line of hurdles.

Box-to-Box Depth Jump With 180-Degree Turn

Perform 4 sets of 10 to 12 repetitions.

SAMPLE PROGRAM FOR SWIMMING

In this case, the goal is to develop a program that will increase power in the upper extremities and help develop the stabilizing muscles of the shoulder. Vertical jumping is an effective form of exercise for swimmers because it emulates thrusting off the wall after a turn in swimming.

Step 1: Consider the Athlete

Kristina is a 17-year-old swimmer. She is ranked high on the age-group and national levels. She has no experience in resistance training and has chronic shoulder pain due to a condition known as multidirectional instability in both shoulders.

Step 2: Assess and Test the Athlete

1. **Push-ups.** The athlete assumes a push-up position with the hands resting on the ground directly under the shoulders; the body is in straight alignment, off the ground from the toes. The tester counts how many push-ups the athlete can perform in 30 seconds.

2. **Overhead medicine ball throw for distance.** The athlete assumes a standing position one step behind a tape line, holding the ball behind the head with both hands. She takes one step forward and throws the ball overhead as far as she can. She must not step on or over the tape line. The tester measures the distance from the tape line to the spot where the ball hits the ground.

3. **Medicine ball chest pass.** The athlete assumes a seated position on a ground surface with her back against the wall and her legs straight out. She holds the ball at midchest with both hands. On command, she attempts to pass the ball out as far as she can. The distance thrown is measured from the heels to the spot where the ball hits the ground.

4. **Sit-ups for time.** This test is a measure of trunk power. The athlete is on her back, her legs are bent, and her feet are resting flat on the floor and are secured by the tester. Her hands are interlocked and placed on the area behind her neck. The athlete is asked to perform as many successful sit-ups (defined as a trunk movement resulting in the elbows touching the thighs) as possible within a 30-second time frame. An appropriate goal would be 30 sit-ups performed in 30 seconds.

5. **Jump-and-reach test.** Swimmers are not particularly known for their leg power and their ability to jump vertically. However, improvement in this area will result in better performances and decreases in overall time. Improved vertical jumping ability can lead to increased power and faster pushes off the wall.

These tests are an indication of the strength and power that Kristina has in the upper extremities, trunk, and legs. As expected, her push-up score is a very low 8; the acceptable score as used by the U.S. Swimming Association is 30. Her medicine ball overhead throw is 12 feet 8 inches, while the average score of other swimmers in her age bracket is 23 feet. Her chest pass score is 8 feet 9 inches, while the average score for other similar athletes is 18 feet 6 inches. Her sit-up score is 22, placing her two standard deviations below the mean score for elite junior swimmers. Her jump-and-reach score is 12 inches, while the average score for female athletes her age is 18 inches.

The overall assessment is that Kristina is deficient in terms of strength and power in the upper extremities. Her multidirectional instability obviously affects her performance on these tests.

The training specialist needs to design a program that will strengthen the shoulders as well as teach the athlete how to exert force rapidly. The metabolism used by swimmers is long-term anaerobic to aerobic; therefore, endurance and stamina are as important to success as raw strength and power. Another important consideration is the amount of practice time devoted to this sport and the athlete's current ability to function in the water.

Step 3: Consider the Time Frame or Cycle

Kristina is at the beginning of her season, which starts just after the Labor Day holiday in September. Her season is pointed entirely toward success in the national competition held in mid-April. She has the ability to work out three times a week until February, when her pool time becomes so extensive that two times per week maximum will be available for dry-land training. Given Kristina's current physical status and test scores, the preparation cycle is crucial to her success this year.

Step 4: Select the Time in the Training Year

With this information and the knowledge that preparation is the key to Kristina having a good chance to perform well throughout the season, the program designer would be well advised to plan carefully and focus on the first 6-week cycle.

Step 5: Design the Program

WEEKS 1 TO 4

Preparation: Because the test scores indicate large deficiencies in upper-extremity strength and power, the program should focus on overcoming just that.

Progression: Moderate- to high-volume, low-intensity resistance training will be used to develop strategic areas of the shoulder in order to help overcome the instability problem. The medicine ball will be a key tool in implementing this program.

Exercise Frequency

Three days a week (Tuesday, Thursday, and Saturday) at the pool.

Limitations

Little to no equipment is available. Basically, the only equipment available is a gymnastics mat (large enough to hold 10 athletes) and medicine balls of weights that vary in 2-pound increments from 6 to 12 pounds.

Exercises

Push-up, 3 × 8. For these push-ups, the athlete is required to touch her chest to the ball in the down position. The purpose of the ball is to provide a target that limits the excursion of the exercises, therefore ensuring completion of them.

Offset push-up, 3 × 5. These push-ups require the athlete to place one hand on the ball and perform the push-up movement. The purpose of placing one hand on the ball is that it forces the athlete to stabilize the shoulder with the hand on the ball to a greater degree (because the ball is a somewhat unstable surface).

Close-grip push-up with both hands on the ball, 3 × 5. This sets up a difficult angle for the arms while also adding the element of instability in order to increase forced stability.

Pull-over pass, 1 × 30

Underhand throw, 1 × 30

Power drop, 2 × 20

Side toss, 2 × 20

Overhead throw, 1 × 15

5-5-5 squat with medicine ball held on the shoulders, 3 sets

Jump squat with medicine ball held on the shoulders, 3 × 8

WEEKS 4 TO 8

Progression: Increase the number of repetitions during the push-up activities by two or three each week. By weeks 4 to 8, add the following:

Walkabout, 1 × 30 seconds. This is performed by assuming the push-up position with one hand on the ball and one hand on the ground. The athlete transfers the on-the-ground hand to the ball so that it rests next to the other hand on the ball. The original hand on the ball then moves to the ground on that side. The alternating of the hands results in the athlete moving across the top of the ball in a "walking" sort of way.

By week 8, the following may also be a possibility:

Medicine ball depth jump, 1 × 10. These are performed by starting in the push-up position with both hands on the ball. The athlete drops from being on the ball to a position where both hands are on the ground with the elbows slightly flexed. By rapidly extending the arms and generating a shoulder push, the athlete jumps from the ground to the starting position.

The latter exercises call into play the rather quick contraction of the stabilizing muscles around the shoulder. This strategy goes back to what the Eastern Europeans called shock training, in which shocking the stabilizers of the shoulder trains them to contract rapidly and function more effectively.

Preparation needs for this type of athlete under these conditions are not a rarity. Indeed, many coaches, athletes, and strength coaches are faced with similar situations. When there is little in the way of resources, equipment, and time, the athlete will suffer unless the coaches can be creative.

Jump to 12-inch box, 3 × 10

Frog jump, 3 × 10. The athlete squats until her hands are flat on the ground with elbows inside the knees. She explodes vertically and streamlines the body, obtaining full body extension with hands and arms over the head.

SAMPLE PROGRAM FOR LONG JUMPING (TRACK AND FIELD)

This program is designed to improve linear jumping.

Step 1: Consider the Athlete

Sean is an 18-year-old college freshman with a personal best of 46 feet in the triple jump. He has high school experience as a triple and long jumper but has had an average career at best. His current status indicates that he has no injuries or physical limitations.

Step 2: Assess and Test the Athlete

Because the goal is improving the linear jump, the athlete's present ability is measured using the following linear tests:

1. **Standing triple jump for distance.** Sean stands on his preferred foot; then he hops, steps, and jumps into a pit. The distance is measured from the start of the jump to the landing.

2. **Five double-leg hops for distance.** Taking off from and landing on both feet at the same time, Sean hops five times to see how much distance he can cover. The distance is measured from the start to the landing on the fifth hop.

3. **Flying 30 meters for time.** To measure the flying 30, the coach needs to mark off 100 meters on the track. The athlete gradually builds up speed over the first 60 meters. He is then timed between the 60- and 90-meter marks. This measures his absolute speed.

4. **One-repetition maximum parallel squat.** Sean determines the maximum amount of weight he can lift one time doing a squat.

5. **Five-repetition, five-second parallel squat at 60 percent body weight.** Sean attempts to perform five squats in five seconds.

Sean's test results will indicate his ability and readiness to undertake a high-intensity plyometric training program. Sean's scores on tests 4 and 5 demonstrate that he meets the basic strength criteria. If he were deficient, weight training would need to be emphasized for 4 to 6 weeks before he undertakes intensive plyometric training.

Tests 1, 2, and 3 show Sean's present linear jumping ability and provide data that can be used to measure his progress at the end of the program. Sean jumped 9.25 meters (30.34 feet) on the standing triple jump, covered 9.9 meters (32.47 feet) on the double-leg hops, and had a time of 3.1 seconds in the flying 30 meters.

Step 3: Consider the Time Frame or Cycle

Sean's program takes place over a 4-week period. The program has been condensed from a normal periodized training year to demonstrate the preparation, progression, and performance variables involved in program design.

Step 4: Select the Time in the Training Year

Normally, a track athlete would begin training at the start of school in the fall. However, Sean will be involved in a crash course of training during the 4 weeks in February. He needs to prepare for the first outdoor meet that takes place at the beginning of March.

Step 5: Design the Program

Each of the 4 weeks is planned according to three variables: preparation, progression, and performance.

WEEK 1

Preparation: Use high-volume, low-intensity resistance training and low-intensity plyometrics to allow the body's soft tissues to adjust to the stress of linear jumping and the impact of landing.

Progression: Emphasize variety in the type of plyometrics used, and review the skills of linear jumping.

Performance: Focus on proper landing techniques and the use of the arms in performing low-intensity exercises. Make sure the athlete understands the concept of the amortization phase.

Monday: Weight Training

Parallel squat with 70 percent 1RM, 3 × 12

Push press (front), 4 × 8

Lat pull, 3 × 8

Split squat with 50 percent body weight, 3 × 10 each leg

Hamstring curl (concentric: raise weight with both legs; eccentric: lower weight with one leg), 3 × 8

Tuesday: Plyometrics

Front cone hop (18 inches), 1 × 10

Single-leg push-off (12-inch box), 2 × 20

Alternating push-off (12-inch box), 2 × 20

30-second box drill, 2 × 30-second segments

Front box jump (12-inch box), 2 × 10

Double-leg hop, 3 × 3

Wednesday: Weight Training

Front squat, 3 × 12

Inverted leg press, 4 × 6

Incline bench press, 3 × 10

Split squat with 50 percent body weight, 3 × 10 each leg

Calf raise, 5 × 12

Thursday: Plyometrics

Front cone hop (18 inches), 2 × 10

Double-leg hop, 3 × 3

Standing triple jump, 1 × 5

Submaximal alternate bounding with double-arm action, 3 × 40 yards

Friday: Weight Training

Repeat Monday's workout but add three sets of 10 shrug pulls.

WEEK 2

Preparation: Weight training should emphasize work for the hip adductors and abductors, as well as the hip flexors and hip extensors.

Progression: Many dynamic jumps should be done while moving across the ground.

Performance: Linear jumping skill includes synchronizing the arms with the lower extremities to maximize efforts.

Monday: Plyometrics and Weight Training

Front cone hop (18 inches), 3 × 10

Double-leg hop, 3 × 5

Standing triple jump over barrier, 1 × 5

Alternate bounding with double-arm action, 3 × 40 yards

Split squat, 3 × 8

Lat pull, 3 × 8

Hamstring curl, 3 × 8

Inverted leg press, 3 × 8

Behind-the-neck press, 3 × 8

Tuesday

Rest

Wednesday: Weight Training

Lunge, 3 × 8
High pull, 3 × 8
Front shoulder raise with dumbbells, 3 × 8

Parallel squat with 80 to 85 percent 1RM, 3 × 8

Thursday: Plyometrics

Stadium hop, 3 × 15
Combination bounding with double-arm action, 3 × 40 yards

Barrier hop (hurdle hop), 5 × 5
Double-leg hop (for distance), 3 × 5

Friday: Weight Training

Lunge, 3 × 8
Lat pull, 4 × 6
Inverted leg press, 5 × 5

High pull, 4 × 4
Front push press, 4 × 5

WEEK 3

Preparation: Resistance training becomes more ballistic; emphasis continues to be placed on performing lifts in positions similar to the joint angles reached in linear jumping.

Progression: Plyometric training becomes more complex yet is task specific. Running speed is a consideration in this phase of training.

Performance: For plyometric training skills, emphasis should be on distance, time, or both.

Monday: Weight Training

Front squat to push press, 4 × 5
Stiff-knee clean, 4 × 4
Inverted leg press, 5 × 3

Split-squat walk (exchange legs and move forward), 4 × 10
Pulley weights hip flexion (to work on knee drive), 3 × 10

Tuesday: Plyometrics

Stadium hop, 3 × 20
Double-leg hop into 40-yard sprint, 5 × 3
Standing long jump (for distance), 3 × 5

Single-leg hop, 3 × 10
Alternate bounding, 3 × 40 yards

Wednesday: Weight Training

Back squat with 90 percent 1RM, 5 × 5

Thursday

Rest

Friday: Plyometrics and Weight Training

Multiple box-to-box squat jump (18- to 24-inch boxes), 5 × 6
Combination bounding, 5 × 40 yards

Alternate bounding with double-arm action, 5 × 60 yards
Depth jump to standing long jump, 3 × 8
Repeat Monday's weight training workout.

WEEK 4

Preparation: Resistance training and plyometrics should now focus on power. Low volume and high intensity are the keys in both forms of training.

Progression: Single-leg activities are of the highest intensity in plyometric training. Along with depth jumps, these become a vital part of development.

Performance: During this cycle, quality of effort will yield maximal distances in the shortest times.

Monday: Plyometrics and Weight Training

Stadium hop, 5 × 20

Barrier hop (hurdle hop), 5 × 5

Combination bounding, 3 × 50 yards

Single-leg bounding, 3 × 40 yards

Long jump with a five-stride approach, 1 × 6

Parallel squat with 90 to 95 percent 1RM, 5 × 3

Hamstring curl, 3 × 8

Inverted leg press, 5 × 3

Overhead squat (snatch grip), 3 × 8

Tuesday

Rest

Wednesday: Weight Training

Power clean from the thigh hang position, 5 × 3

Thursday: Plyometrics

Depth jump to standing triple jump with slide-out landing, 1 × 10

Depth jump to standing long jump, 1 × 10

Alternate bounding with double-arm action (timed with stopwatch), 5 × 40 yards

Combination bounding into sandpit, 5 × 30 yards

Friday: Retest

To check for improvement, Sean is tested again on the tasks that he did at the beginning of the program. After using this 4-week program, Sean scores 10 meters (32.80 feet) on the standing triple jump, covers 10.1 meters (33.13 feet) on the double-leg bounds, and runs the flying 30 meters in 3.0 seconds. As the track season continues, Sean should see an improvement in his linear jumping ability.

◀ SUMMARY ▶

- Plyometric training can be adapted to any sport, and athletes should do exercises that help enhance the movements they perform in their sport.

- The presented programs are samples that have been implemented with actual athletes in their training seasons.

- By mimicking certain movements during plyometric training, athletes can decrease the amortization time for key sport-related activities and become faster and more powerful in movements specific to their sports.

References

Chapter 2

1. Chu, D.A. 1983. Plyometrics: The link between strength and speed. *NSCA J* 5(2): 20-21.

2. Chmielewski, T.L., G.D. Myer, D. Kauffman, and S.M. Tillman. 2006. Plyometric exercise in the rehabilitation of athletes: Physiological responses and clinical application. *J Orthop Sports Phys Ther* 36(5) (May): 308-319.

3. Rassier, D.E., and W. Herzog. 2005. Force enhancement and relaxation rates after stretch of activated muscle fibres. *Proc Biol Sci* 272(1562) (March 7): 475-480.

4. Bobbert, M.F., K.G. Gerritsen, M.C. Litjens, and A.J. Van Soest. 1996. Why is countermovement jump height greater than squat jump height? *Med Sci Sports Exerc* 28(11) (Nov.): 1402-1412.

5. Cordasco, F.A., I.N. Wolfe, M.E. Wootten, and L.U. Bigliani. 1996. An electromyographic analysis of the shoulder during a medicine ball rehabilitation program. *Am J Sports Med* 24(3) (May-June): 386-392.

6. Siff, M. 2004. *Supertraining.* 6th ed. Denver: Supertraining Institute.

7. Chu, D.A. 2001. Plyometrics or not? *Strength and Conditioning Journal* 23(2): 70-72.

8. Swanik, C.B., and K.A. Swanik. 1999. Plyometrics in rehabilitating the lower extremity. *Athlet Ther Today* 4(3): 16-22, 32-33, 63.

9. Wilk, K.E., and C. Arrigo. 1993. Current concepts in the rehabilitation of the athletic shoulder. *J Orthop Sports Phys Ther* 18(1) (July): 365-378.

10. O'Connor, D.P., and J.W. King. 1999. Application of plyometrics to the trunk. *Athlet Ther Today* 4(3): 36-40.

11. Knuttgen, K.G., and W.J. Kraemer. 1987. Terminology and measurement in exercise performance. *Journal of Applied Sports Science* 1(1): 1-10.

12. Kubo, K., H. Kanehisa, D. Takeshita, Y. Kawakami, S. Fukashiro, and T. Fukunaga. 2000. In vivo dynamics of human medial gastrocnemius muscle-tendon complex during stretch-shortening cycle exercise. *Acta Physiol Scand* 170(2) (Oct.): 127-135.

13. Chu, D.A. 1999. Plyometrics in sports injury rehabilitation and training. *Athlet Ther Today* 4(3): 7-11.

14. Radcliffe, J.C., and R.C. Farentinos. 1985. *Plyometrics: Explosive power training.* 2nd ed. Champaign, IL: Human Kinetics.

15. Chu, D.A. 1984. Plyometric exercise. *National Strength Coaches Association Journal* 6(5): 56-62.

16. Potach, D.H., and D.A. Chu. 2000. *Plyometric training.* 2nd ed. Champaign, IL: Human Kinetics.

17. Chu, D.A. 1998. *Jumping into plyometrics.* 2nd ed. Champaign, IL: Human Kinetics.

18. Myer, G.D., K.R. Ford, J.L. Brent, and T.E. Hewett. 2006. The effects of plyometric versus dynamic stabilization and balance training on power, balance, and landing force in female athletes. *J Strength Cond Res* 20(2): 345-353.

19. Irmischer, B.S., C. Harris, R.P. Pfeiffer, M.A. DeBeliso, K.J. Adams, and K.G. Shea. 2004. Effects of a knee ligament injury prevention exercise program on impact forces in women. *J Strength Cond Res* 18(4) (Nov.): 703-707.

20. Myer, G.D., K.R. Ford, and T.E. Hewett. 2004. Rationale and clinical techniques for anterior cruciate ligament injury prevention among female athletes. *J Athl Train* 39(4) (Dec.): 352-364.

21. Hewett, T.E., T.N. Lindenfeld, J.V. Riccobene, and F.R. Noyes. 1999. The effect of neuromuscular training on the incidence of knee injury in female athletes: A prospective study. *Am J Sports Med* 27(6) (Nov.-Dec.): 699-706.

22. Hewett, T.E., A.L. Stroupe, T.A. Nance, and F.R. Noyes. 1996. Plyometric training in female athletes: Decreased impact forces and increased hamstring torques. *Am J Sports Med* 24(6) (Nov.-Dec.): 765-773.

23. Hewett, T.E., G.D. Myer, K.R. Ford, R.S. Heidt Jr., A.J. Colosimo, S.G. McLean, A.J. van den Bogert, M.V. Paterno, and P. Succop. 2005. Biomechanical measures of neuromuscular control and valgus loading of the knee predict anterior cruciate ligament injury risk in female athletes. *Am J Sports Med* 33(4) (Feb. 8): 492-501.

24. Myer, G.D., K.R. Ford, J.P. Palumbo, and T.E. Hewett. 2005. Neuromuscular training improves performance and lower-extremity biomechanics in female athletes. *J Strength Cond Res* 19(1) (Feb.): 51-60.

25. Petersen, W., C. Braun, W. Bock, K. Schmidt, A. Weimann, W. Drescher, E. Eiling, R. Stange, T. Fuchs, J. Hedderich, and T. Zantop. 2005. A controlled prospective case control study of a prevention training program in female team handball players: The German experience. *Arch Orthop Trauma Surg* 125(9): 614-621.

26. Myer, G.D., M.V. Paterno, and T.E. Hewett. 2004. Back in the game: A four-phase return-to-sport program for athletes with problem ACLs. *Rehab Manag* 17(8) (Oct.): 30-33.

27. Cascio, B.M., L. Culp, and A.J. Cosgarea. 2004. Return to play after anterior cruciate ligament reconstruction. *Clin Sports Med* 23(3) (July): 395-408, ix.

28. Wilk, K.E., K. Meister, and J.R. Andrews. 2002. Current concepts in the rehabilitation of the overhead throwing athlete. *Am J Sports Med* 30(1) (Jan.-Feb.): 136-151.

29. Courson, R. 1999. Plyometrics in rehabilitation of the upper extremity. *Athlet Ther Today* 4(3): 25-29, 32-33, 63.

30. Wilk, K.E., M.L. Voight, M.A. Keirns, V. Gambetta, J.R. Andrews, and C.J. Dillman. 1993. Stretch-shortening drills for the upper extremities: Theory and clinical application. *J Orthop Sports Phys Ther* 17(5) (May): 225-239.

31. Davies, G.J., and J.W. Matheson. 2001. Shoulder plyometrics. *Sport Med Arthrosc Rev* 9: 1-18.

32. Lundin, P. 1985. A review of plyometric training. *NSCA J* 7(3): 69-74.

33. Clutch, D., M. Wilton, C. McGown, and G.R. Bryce. 1983. The effect of depth jumps and weight training on leg strength and vertical jump. *Res Q* 54: 5-10.

34. Bosco, C., J.T. Viitasalo, P.V. Komi, and P. Luhtanen. 1982. Combined effect of elastic energy and myoelectrical potentiation during stretch-shortening cycle exercise. *Acta Physiol Scand* 114(4) (April): 557-565.

35. Kilani, H.A., S.S. Palmer, M.J. Adrian, and J.J. Gapsis. 1989. Block of the stretch reflex of vastus lateralis during vertical jumps. *Hum Movement Sci* 8: 247-269.

36. Bosco, C., P.V. Komi, and A. Ito. 1981. Prestretch potentiation of human skeletal muscle during ballistic movement. *Acta Physiol Scand* 111(2) (Feb.): 135–140.

37. Nicol, C., and P.V. Komi. 1998. Significance of passively induced stretch reflexes on Achilles tendon force enhancement. *Muscle Nerve* 21(11) (Nov.): 1546–1548.

38. Voigt, M., P. Dyhre-Poulsen, and E.B. Simonsen. 1998. Modulation of short latency stretch reflexes during human hopping. *Acta Physiol Scand* 163(2) (June): 181–194.

39. Nardone, A., T. Corra, and M. Schieppati. 1990. Different activations of the soleus and gastrocnemii muscles in response to various types of stance perturbation in man. *Exp Brain Res* 80(2): 323–332.

40. Roberts, T.J., R.L. Marsh, P.G. Weyand, and C.R. Taylor. 1997. Muscular force in running turkeys: The economy of minimizing work. *Science* 275(5303) (Feb. 21): 1113–1115.

41. Roberts, T.J. 2002. The integrated function of muscles and tendons during locomotion. *Comp Biochem Physiol A Mol Integr Physiol* 133(4) (Dec.): 1087–1099.

42. Alexander, R.M., and H.C. Bennet-Clark. 1977. Storage of elastic strain energy in muscle and other tissues. *Nature* 265(5590) (Jan. 13): 114–117.

43. Houk, J., and E. Henneman. 1967. Responses of Golgi tendon organs to active contractions of the soleus muscle of the cat. *J Neurophysiol* 30(3) (May): 466–481.

44. Pearson, K., and J. Gordon. 2000. Spinal reflexes. In E.R. Kandel, J.H. Schwartz, and T.M. Jessell (Eds.), *Principles of neural science.* 4th ed. New York: McGraw-Hill. 713–736.

45. Chalmers, G. 2002. Do Golgi tendon organs really inhibit muscle activity at high force levels to save muscles from injury, and adapt with strength training? *Sports Biomech* 1(2) (July): 239–249.

46. McCrea, D.A. 1986. Spinal cord circuitry and motor reflexes. *Exerc Sport Sci Rev* 14: 105–141.

47. Horita, T., P.V. Komi, C. Nicol, and H. Kyrolainen. 2002. Interaction between pre-landing activities and stiffness regulation of the knee joint musculoskeletal system in the drop jump: Implications to performance. *Eur J Appl Physiol* 88(1-2) (Nov.): 76–84.

48. Wilson, G.J., B.C. Elliott, and G.A. Wood. 1991. The effect on performance of imposing a delay during a stretch-shorten cycle movement. *Med Sci Sports Exerc* 23(3) (March): 364–370.

49. Chapman, G., and G. Caldwell. 1985. *The use of muscle strength in inertial loading.* Vol. IX-A. Champaign, IL: Human Kinetics.

50. Ishikawa, M., and P.V. Komi. 2004. Effects of different dropping intensities on fascicle and tendinous tissue behavior during stretch-shortening cycle exercise. *J Appl Physiol* 96(3) (March): 848–852.

51. Bobbert, M.F., P.A. Huijing, and G.J. van Ingen Schenau. 1987. Drop jumping. II. The influence of dropping height on the biomechanics of drop jumping. *Med Sci Sports Exerc* 19(4) (Aug.): 339–346.

52. Ishikawa, M., P.V. Komi, M.J. Grey, V. Lepola, and G.P. Bruggemann. 2005. Muscle-tendon interaction and elastic energy usage in human walking. *J Appl Physiol* 99(2) (Aug.): 603–608.

53. Ishikawa, M., E. Niemela, and P.V. Komi. 2005. Interaction between fascicle and tendinous tissues in short-contact stretch-shortening cycle exercise with varying eccentric intensities. *J Appl Physiol* 99(1) (July): 217–223.

54. Kurokawa, S., T. Fukunaga, A. Nagano, and S. Fukashiro. 2003. Interaction between fascicles and tendinous structures during counter movement jumping investigated in vivo. *J Appl Physiol* 95(6) (Dec.): 2306–2314.

55. Fukunaga, T., Y. Kawakami, K. Kubo, and H. Kanehisa. 2002. Muscle and tendon interaction during human movements. *Exerc Sport Sci Rev* 30(3) (July): 106–110.

56. Fukunaga, T., Y. Kawakami, T. Muraoka, and H. Kanehisa. 2002. Muscle and tendon relations in humans: Power enhancement in counter-movement exercise. *Adv Exp Med Biol* 508: 501–505.

57. Rassier, D.E., and W. Herzog. 2005. Relationship between force and stiffness in muscle fibers after stretch. *J Appl Physiol* 99(5): 1769–1775.

58. Gollhofer, A., V. Strojnik, W. Rapp, and L. Schweizer. 1992. Behaviour of triceps surae muscle-tendon complex in different jump conditions. *Eur J Appl Physiol Occup Physiol* 64(4): 283–291.

Chapter 3

1. Verkhoshanski, Y. 1969. Perspectives in the improvement of speed-strength preparation of jumpers. *Yessis Rev Sov Phys Educ Sports* 4(2): 28–29.

2. Chmielewski, T.L., G.D. Myer, D. Kauffman, and S.M. Tillman. 2006. Plyometric exercise in the rehabilitation of athletes: Physiological responses and clinical application. *J Orthop Sports Phys Ther* 36(5) (May): 308–319.

3. Dursenev, L., and L. Raevsky. 1978. Strength training of jumpers. *Teoriya i Praktika Fizescheskoi Kultury* 10: 62.

4. Myer, G.D., A.D. Faigenbaum, K.R. Ford, T.M. Best, M.F. Bergeron, and T.E. Hewett. 2011. When to initiate integrative neuromuscular training to reduce sports-related injuries and enhance health in youth? *Curr Sports Med Rep* 10(3): 157–166.

5. Myer, G.D., A.D. Faigenbaum, D.A. Chu, J. Falkel, K.R. Ford, T.M. Best, and T.E. Hewett. 2011. Integrative training for children and adolescents: Techniques and practices for reducing sports-related injuries and enhancing athletic performance. *Phys Sportsmed* 39(1) (Feb.): 74–84.

6. Myer, G.D., and A.D. Faigenbaum. 2011. Exercise is sports medicine in youth: Integrative neuromuscular training to optimize motor development and reduce risk of sports related injury. *Kronos* 10(18): 31–48.

7. Sugimoto, D., G.D. Myer, H.M. Bush, M.F. Klugman, J.M. Medina McKeon, and T.E. Hewett. 2012. Compliance with neuromuscular training and anterior cruciate ligament injury risk reduction in female athletes: A meta-analysis. *J Athl Train* 47(6): 714–723.

8. Hewett, T.E., T.N. Lindenfeld, J.V. Riccobene, and F.R. Noyes. 1999. The effect of neuromuscular training on the incidence of knee injury in female athletes: A prospective study. *Am J Sports Med* 27(6) (Nov.-Dec.): 699–706.

9. Hewett, T.E., A.L. Stroupe, T.A. Nance, and F.R. Noyes. 1996. Plyometric training in female athletes: Decreased impact forces and increased hamstring torques. *Am J Sports Med* 24(6): 765–773.

10. Verkhoshansky, V., and V. Tatyan. 1983. Speed-strength preparation of future champions. *Soviet Sports Review* 18(4): 166–170.

11. Adams, T. 1984. An investigation of selected plyometric training exercises on muscular leg strength and power. *Track and Field Quarterly Review* 84(1): 36–40.

12. Bosco, C., and P. Komi. 1979. Potentiation of the mechanical behavior of the human skeletal muscle through prestretching. *Acta Physiologica Scandinavica* 106: 467–472.

13. Asmussen, E., and F. Bonde-Peterson. 1974. Storage of elastic energy in skeletal muscles in man. *Acta Physiologica Scandinavica* 91: 385–392.

14. Holcomb, W., J. Lander, R. Rutland, and G. Wilson. 1996. A biomechanical analysis of the vertical jump and three

modified plyometric depth jumps. *Journal of Strength and Conditioning Research* 10(2): 83–88.

15. Gehri, D., M. Ricard, D. Kleiner, and D. Kirkendall. 1998. A comparison of plyometric training techniques for improving vertical jumping ability and energy production. *Journal of Strength and Conditioning Research* 12(2): 85–89.

16. Holcomb, W., J. Lander, R. Rutland, and G. Wilson. 1996. The effectiveness of a modified plyometric program on power and the vertical jump. *Journal of Strength and Conditioning Research* 10(2): 89–92.

17. Young, W., J. Pryor, and G. Wilson. 1995. Effect of instructions on characteristics of countermovement and drop jump performance. *Journal of Strength and Conditioning Research* 9(4): 232–236.

18. Hewett, T.E., G.D. Myer, K.R. Ford, R.S. Heidt Jr., A.J. Colosimo, S.G. McLean, A.J. van den Bogert, M.V. Paterno, and P. Succop. 2005. Biomechanical measures of neuromuscular control and valgus loading of the knee predict anterior cruciate ligament injury risk in female athletes: A prospective study. *Am J Sports Med* 33(4) (Feb. 8): 492–501.

19. Harman, E., M. Rosenstein, P. Frykman, and R. Rosenstein. 1991. The effects of arms and countermovement on vertical jumping. *National Strength and Conditioning Journal* 13(2): 38–39.

20. Komi, P.V., and C. Bosco. 1978. Utilization of stored elastic energy in leg extensor muscles by men and women. *Med Sci Sports* 10(4) (winter): 261–265.

21. Horita, T., P.V. Komi, C. Nicol, and H. Kyrolainen. 2002. Interaction between pre-landing activities and stiffness regulation of the knee joint musculoskeletal system in the drop jump: Implications to performance. *Eur J Appl Physiol* 88(1-2) (Nov.): 76–84.

22. Kubo, K., Y. Kawakami, and T. Fukunaga. 1999. Influence of elastic properties of tendon structures on jump performance in humans. *J Appl Physiol* 87(6) (Dec.): 2090–2096.

23. Bobbert, M.F., K.G. Gerritsen, M.C. Litjens, and A.J. Van Soest. 1996. Why is countermovement jump height greater than squat jump height? *Med Sci Sports Exerc* 28(11) (Nov.): 1402–1412.

24. Bosco, C., P.V. Komi, and A. Ito. 1981. Prestretch potentiation of human skeletal muscle during ballistic movement. *Acta Physiol Scand* 111(2) (Feb.): 135–140.

25. Bobbert, M.F., P.A. Huijing, and G.J. van Ingen Schenau. 1987. Drop jumping. I. The influence of jumping technique on the biomechanics of jumping. *Med Sci Sports Exerc* 19(4) (Aug.): 332–338.

26. Kubo, K., H. Kanehisa, D. Takeshita, Y. Kawakami, S. Fukashiro, and T. Fukunaga. 2000. In vivo dynamics of human medial gastrocnemius muscle-tendon complex during stretch-shortening cycle exercise. *Acta Physiol Scand* 170(2) (Oct.): 127–135.

27. Bobbert, M.F., P.A. Huijing, and G.J. van Ingen Schenau. 1987. Drop jumping. II. The influence of dropping height on the biomechanics of drop jumping. *Med Sci Sports Exerc* 19(4) (Aug.): 339–346.

28. Wathen, D. 1993. Literature review: Explosive/plyometric exercises. *National Strength and Conditioning Journal* 15(3): 17–19.

29. McNitt-Gray, J.L., D.M.E. Hester, W. Mathiyakom, and B.A. Munkasy. 2001. Mechanical demand on multijoint control during landing depend on orientation of the body segments relative to the reaction force. *J Biomech* 34: 1471–1482.

30. Dufek, J.S., and B.T. Bates. 1990. The evaluation and prediction of impact forces during landings. *Med Sci Sports Exerc* 22(3) (June): 370–377.

Chapter 4

1. Myer, G.D., A.D. Faigenbaum, D.A. Chu, J. Falkel, K.R. Ford, T.M Best, and T.E. Hewett. 2011. Integrative training for children and adolescents: Techniques and practices for reducing sports-related injuries and enhancing athletic performance. *Phys Sportsmed* 39(1) (Feb.): 74–84.

2. American Academy of Pediatrics. 1983. Weight training and weightlifting: Information for the pediatrician. *Physician and Sports Medicine* 11(3): 157–161.

3. Faigenbaum, A.D., W.J. Kraemer, C.J. Blimkie, I. Jeffreys, L.J. Micheli, M. Nitka, and T.W. Rowland. 2009. Youth resistance training: Updated position statement paper from the National Strength and Conditioning Association. *J Strength Cond Res.* 23(5 Suppl) (Aug.): S60–79.

4. Behm, D.G., A.D. Faigenbaum, B. Falk, and P. Klentrou. 2008. Canadian Society for Exercise Physiology position paper: Resistance training in children and adolescents. *Appl Physiol Nutr Metab* 33(3) (June): 547–561.

5. Strong, W.B., R.M. Malina, C.J. Blimkie, S.R. Daniels, R.K. Dishman, B. Gutin, A.C. Hergenroeder, A. Must, P.A. Nixon, J.M. Pivarnik, T. Rowland, S. Trost, and F. Trudeau. 2005. Evidence based physical activity for school-age youth. *J Pediatr* 146(6) (June): 732–737.

6. Myer, G.D., K.R. Ford, J.P. Palumbo, and T.E. Hewett. 2005. Neuromuscular training improves performance and lower-extremity biomechanics in female athletes. *J Strength Cond Res* 19(1) (Feb.): 51–60.

7. Myer, G.D., K.R. Ford, S.G. McLean, and T.E. Hewett. 2006. The effects of plyometric versus dynamic stabilization and balance training on lower extremity biomechanics. *Am J Sports Med* 34(3): 490–498.

8. Nader, P., R. Bradley, R. Houts, S. McRitchie, and M. O'Brien. 2008. Moderate to vigorous physical activity from ages 9 to 15 years. *Journal of the American Medical Association* 300: 295–305.

9. Nyberg, G., A. Nordenfelt, U. Ekelund, and C. Marcus. 2009. Physical activity patterns measured by accelerometry in 6- to 10-yr-old children. *Med Sci Sports Exerc* 41(10): 1842–1848.

10. Faigenbaum, A.D., R.L. Loud, J. O'Connell, S. Glover, and W.L. Westcott. 2001. Effects of different resistance training protocols on upper-body strength and endurance development in children. *J Strength Cond Res* 15(4) (Nov.): 459–465.

11. Ramsay, J., C. Blimkie, K. Smith, S. Garner, J. MacDougall, and D. Sale. 1990. Strength training effects in prepubescent boys. *Med Sci Sports Exerc* 22: 605–614.

12. Pfeiffer, R., and R. Francis. 1986. Effects of strength training on muscle development in prepubescent, pubescent, and postpubescent males. *Phys Sportsmed* 14(9): 134–143.

13. Sailors, M., and K. Berg. 1987. Comparison of responses to weight training in pubescent boys and men. *J Sports Med Phys Fitness* 27(1) (March): 30–37.

14. Sewall, L., and L. Micheli. 1986. Strength training for children. *J Pediatr Orthop* 6: 143–146.

15. Weltman, A., C. Janney, C.B. Rians, K. Strand, B. Berg, S. Tippitt, J. Wise, B.R. Cahill, and F.I. Katch. 1986. The effects of hydraulic resistance strength training in pre-pubertal males. *Med Sci Sports Exerc* 18(6) (Dec.): 629–638.

16. Faigenbaum, A.D., W.J. Kraemer, B. Cahill, J. Chandler, J. Dziaos, L.D. Elfrink, E. Forman, M. Gaudiose, L. Micheli, M. Nitka, and S. Roberts. 1996. Youth resistance training: Position statement paper and literature review. *Strength and Conditioning* 18(6): 62–75.

17. Faigenbaum, A.D., L.D. Zaichkowsky, W.L. Westcott, L.J. Micheli, and A.F. Fehlandt. 1993. The effects of a twice-a-week

strength training program on children. *Pediatric Exercise Science* 5: 339–345.

18. Falk, B., and G. Mor. 1996. The effects of resistance and martial arts training in 6 to 8 year old boys. *Pediatric Exercise Science* 8: 48–56.

19. Myer, G.D., K.R. Ford, J.L. Brent, and T.E. Hewett. 2006. The effects of plyometric versus dynamic balance training on power, balance and landing force in female athletes. *J Strength Cond Res* 20(2): 345–353.

20. Malina, R.M. 2006. Weight training in youth-growth, maturation, and safety: An evidence-based review. *Clin J Sport Med* 16(6) (Nov.): 478–487.

21. Falk, B., and G. Tenenbaum. 1996. The effectiveness of resistance training in children: A meta-analysis. *Sports Med* 22(3) (Sep.): 176–186.

22. Faigenbaum, A.D., and G.D. Myer. 2010. Resistance training among young athletes: Safety, efficacy and injury prevention effects. *Br J Sports Med* 44(1) (Jan.): 56–63.

23. Myer, G.D., C.E. Quatman, J. Khoury, E.J. Wall, and T.E. Hewett. 2009. Youth versus adult "weightlifting" injuries presenting to United States emergency rooms: Accidental versus nonaccidental injury mechanisms. *J Strength Cond Res* 23(7) (Oct.): 2054–2060.

24. Jones, C., C. Christensen, and M. Young. 2000. Weight training injury trends. *Physician and Sports Medicine* 28: 61–72.

25. Plumert, J., and D. Schwebel. 1997. Social and temperamental influences on children's overestimation of their physical abilities: Links to accidental injuries. *J Exp Child Psychol* 67: 317–337.

26. Coutts, A., A. Murphy, and B. Dascombe. 2004. Effect of direct supervision of a strength coach on measures of muscular strength and power in young rugby league players. *Journal of Strength and Conditioning Research* 18: 316–323.

27. Onate, J.A., K.M. Guskiewicz, and R.J. Sullivan. 2001. Augmented feedback reduces jump landing forces. *J Orthop Sports Phys Ther* 31(9) (Sep.): 511–517.

28. Onate, J.A., K.M. Guskiewicz, S.W. Marshall, C. Giuliani, B. Yu, and W.E. Garrett. 2005. Instruction of jump-landing technique using videotape feedback: Altering lower extremity motion patterns. *Am J Sports Med* 33(6): 831–842.

29. Faigenbaum, A.D., G.D. Myer, F. Naclerio, and A. Casas. 2011. Injury trends and prevention in youth resistance training. *Strength and Conditioning Journal* 33(3): 36–41.

30. Myer, G.D., J.L. Brent, K.R. Ford, and T.E. Hewett. 2008. A pilot study to determine the effect of trunk and hip focused neuromuscular training on hip and knee isokinetic strength. *Br J Sports Med* 42(7) (July): 614–619.

31. Myer, G.D., D.A. Chu, J.L. Brent, and T.E. Hewett. 2008. Trunk and hip control neuromuscular training for the prevention of knee joint injury. *Clin Sports Med* 27(3) (July): 425–448, ix.

32. Faigenbaum, A.D., and W.L. Westcott. 2009. *Youth strength training: Programs for health, fitness and sport.* Champaign, IL: Human Kinetics.

33. Chu, D., A. Faigenbaum, and J. Falkel. 2006. *Progressive plyometrics for kids.* Monterey, CA: Healthy Learning.

34. Mediate, P., and A.D. Faigenbaum. 2007. *Medicine ball for all kids: Medicine ball training concepts and program-design considerations for school-age youth.* Monterey, CA: Healthy Learning.

35. Myer, G.D., and E.J. Wall. 2006. Resistance training in the young athlete. *Operative Techniques in Sports Medicine* 14(3): 218–230.

36. Reed, C.A., K.R. Ford, G.D. Myer, and T.E. Hewett. 2012. The effects of isolated and integrated 'core stability' training on athletic performance measures: A systematic review. *Sports Med* 42: 697–706.

37. Heitkamp, H.C., T. Horstmann, F. Mayer, J. Weller, and H.H. Dickhuth. 2001. Gain in strength and muscular balance after balance training. *Int J Sports Med* 22(4) (May): 285–290.

38. Holm, I., M.A. Fosdahl, A. Friis, M.A. Risberg, G. Myklebust, and H. Steen. 2004. Effect of neuromuscular training on proprioception, balance, muscle strength, and lower limb function in female team handball players. *Clin J Sport Med* 14(2) (March): 88–94.

39. Paterno, M.V., G.D. Myer, K.R. Ford, and T.E. Hewett. 2004. Neuromuscular training improves single-limb stability in young female athletes. *J Orthop Sports Phys Ther* 34(6): 305–316.

40. Myer, G.D., K.R. Ford, J.L. Brent, and T.E. Hewett. 2005. The effects of plyometric versus dynamic balance training on landing force and center of pressure stabilization in female athletes. *Br J Sports Med* 39(6): 397.

41. Sjolie, A.N., and A.E. Ljunggren. 2001. The significance of high lumbar mobility and low lumbar strength for current and future low back pain in adolescents. *Spine* 26(23) (Dec. 1): 2629–2636.

42. Bo Andersen, L., N. Wedderkopp, and C. Leboeuf-Yde. 2006. Association between back pain and physical fitness in adolescents. *Spine* 31(15) (July 1): 1740–1744.

43. Adams, K., J.P. O'Shea, K.L. O'Shea, and M. Climstein. 1992. The effect of six weeks of squat, plyometric and squat-plyometric training on power production. *J Strength Cond Res* 6(1): 36–41.

44. Fatouros, I.G., A.Z. Jamurtas, D. Leontsini, T. Kyriakos, N. Aggelousis, N. Kostopoulos, and P. Buckenmeyer. 2000. Evaluation of plyometric exercise training, weight training, and their combination on vertical jumping performance and leg strength. *J Strength Cond Res* 14(4): 470–476.

45. Myer, G.D., J.L. Brent, K.R. Ford, and T.E. Hewett. 2008. A pilot study to determine the effect of trunk and hip focused neuromuscular training on hip and knee isokinetic strength. *Br J Sports Med* 42(7): 614–619.

46. Mandelbaum, B.R., H.J. Silvers, D.S. Watanabe, J.F. Knarr, S.D. Thomas, L.Y. Griffin, D.T. Kirkendall, and W. Garrett, Jr. 2005. Effectiveness of a neuromuscular and proprioceptive training program in preventing anterior cruciate ligament injuries in female athletes: Two-year follow up. *Am J Sport Med* 33(7): 1003–1010.

47. Hewett, T.E., A.L. Stroupe, T.A. Nance, and F.R. Noyes. 1996. Plyometric training in female athletes: Decreased impact forces and increased hamstring torques. *Am J Sports Med* 24(6): 765–773.

48. Petersen, W., C. Braun, W. Bock, K. Schmidt, A. Weimann, W. Dresher, E. Eiling, R. Stange, T. Fuchs, J. Hedderich, and T. Zantop. 2005. A controlled prospective case control study of a prevention training program in female team handball players: The German experience. *Arch Orthop Trauma Surg* 125(9): 614–621.

49. Myklebust, G., L. Engebretsen, I.H. Braekken, A. Skjolberg, O.E. Olsen, and R. Bahr. 2003. Prevention of anterior cruciate ligament injuries in female team handball players: A prospective intervention study over three seasons. *Clin J Sport Med* 13(2) (March): 71–78.

50. Mandelbaum, B.R., H.J. Silvers, D.S. Watanabe, J.R. Knarr, S.D. Thomas, L.Y. Griffin, D.T. Kirkendall, and W. Garrett, Jr. 2005. Effectiveness of a neuromuscular and proprioceptive training program in preventing anterior cruciate ligament injuries in female athletes: Two-year follow-up. *Am J Sports Med* 33(7) (July): 1003–1010.

51. Klugman, M.F., J.L. Brent, G.D. Myer, K.R. Ford, and T.E. Hewett. 2011. Does an in-season only neuromuscular training protocol reduce deficits quantified by the tuck jump assessment? *Clin Sports Med* 30(4): 825–840.

52. Hewett, T.E., T.N. Lindenfeld, J.V. Riccobene, and F.R. Noyes. 1999. The effect of neuromuscular training on the incidence of knee injury in female athletes: A prospective study. *Am J Sports Med* 27(6) (Nov.-Dec.): 699–706.

53. DiStefano, L.J., D.A. Padua, J.T. Blackburn, W.E. Garrett, K.M. Guskiewicz, and S.W. Marshall. 2010. Integrated injury prevention program improves balance and vertical jump height in children. *J Strength Cond Res* 24(2) (Feb.): 332–342.

54. Faigenbaum, A.D., N.A. Ratamess, J. McFarland, J. Kaczmarek, M.J. Coraggio, J. Kang, and J.R. Hoffman. 2008. Effect of rest interval length on bench press performance in boys, teens, and men. *Pediatr Exerc Sci* 20(4) (Nov.): 457–469.

55. Zafeiridis, A., A. Dalamitros, K. Dipla, N. Manou, N. Galanis, and S. Kellis. 2005. Recovery during high intensity intermittent anaerobic exercise in boys, teens and men. *Med Sci Sports Exerc* 37: 505–512.

56. Potach, D.H., and D.A. Chu. 2000. *Plyometric training.* 2nd ed. Champaign, IL: Human Kinetics.

57. Wathen, D. 1993. Literature review: Explosive/plyometric exercises. *National Strength and Conditioning Journal* 15(3): 17–19.

58. Stein, C., and L. Micheli. 2010. Overuse injuries in youth sports. *Physician and Sports Medicine* 38(2): 102–108.

59. Faigenbaum, A.D., and J. Mcfarland. 2006. Make time for less intense training. *Strength and Conditioning Journal* 28(5): 77–79.

60. Kinugasa, T., and A.E. Kilding. 2009. A comparison of post-match recovery strategies in youth soccer players. *J Strength Cond Res* 23(5) (Aug.): 1402–1407.

61. United States Department of Health and Human Services. 2008. Physical activity guidelines for Americans. www.health.gov/paguidelines.

62. Leek, D., J.A. Carlson, K.L. Cain, S. Henrichon, D. Rosenberg, K. Patrick, and J.F. Sallis. 2011. Physical activity during youth sports practices. *Arch Pediatr Adolesc Med* 165(4): 294–299.

63. Pate, R.R., and J.R. O'Neill. 2011. Youth sports programs: Contribution to physical activity. *Arch Pediatr Adolesc Med* 165(4): 369–370.

Chapter 5

1. Hewett, T.E., A.L. Stroupe, T.A. Nance, and F.R. Noyes. 1996. Plyometric training in female athletes: Decreased impact forces and increased hamstring torques. *Am J Sports Med* 24(6): 765–773.

2. Hewett, T.E., T.N. Lindenfeld, J.V. Riccobene, and F.R. Noyes. 1999. The effect of neuromuscular training on the incidence of knee injury in female athletes: A prospective study. *Am J Sports Med* 27(6): 699–706.

3. Hewett, T.E., G.D. Myer, and K.R. Ford. 2005. Reducing knee and anterior cruciate ligament injuries among female athletes: A systematic review of neuromuscular training interventions. *J Knee Surg* 18(1): 82–88.

4. Myer, G.D., D.A. Chu, J.L. Brent, and T.E. Hewett. 2008. Trunk and hip control neuromuscular training for the prevention of knee joint injury. *Clin Sports Med* 27(3): 425–448, ix.

5. Hewett, T.E., and G.D. Myer. 2011. The mechanistic connection between the trunk, hip, knee, and anterior cruciate ligament injury. *Exerc Sport Sci Rev* 39(4): 161–166.

6. Fleming, B.C. 2003. Biomechanics of the anterior cruciate ligament. *J Orthop Sports Phys Ther* 33(8): A13–15.

7. Myklebust, G., and R. Bahr. 2005. Return to play guidelines after anterior cruciate ligament surgery. *Br J Sports Med* 39(3): 127–131.

8. Alentorn-Geli, E., G.D. Myer, H.J. Silvers, G. Samitier, D. Romero, C. Lazaro-Haro, and R. Cugat. 2009. Prevention of non-contact anterior cruciate ligament injuries in soccer players. Part 1: Mechanisms of injury and underlying risk factors. *Knee Surg Sports Traumatol Arthrosc* 17(7): 705–729.

9. Freedman, K.B., M.T. Glasgow, S.G. Glasgow, and J. Bernstein. 1998. Anterior cruciate ligament injury and reconstruction among university students. *Clin Orthop Related Res* 356: 208–212.

10. Ruiz, A.L., M. Kelly, and R.W. Nutton. 2002. Arthroscopic ACL reconstruction: A 5-9 year follow-up. *Knee* 9(3): 197–200.

11. Myer, G.D., and T.M. McCambridge. 2012. STOP anterior cruciate ligament injuries. www.stopsportsinjuries.org/.

12. Hewett, T.E., G.D. Myer, and K.R. Ford. 2006. Anterior cruciate ligament injuries in female athletes. Part 1: Mechanisms and risk factors. *Am J Sports Med* 34(2): 299–311.

13. Myer, G.D., K.R. Ford, and T.E. Hewett. 2004. Rationale and clinical techniques for anterior cruciate ligament injury prevention among female athletes. *J Athl Train* 39(4): 352–364.

14. Hewett, T.E., G.D. Myer, K.R. Ford, R.S. Heidt Jr., A.J. Colosimo, S.G. McLean, A.J. van den Bogert, M.V. Paterno, and P. Succop. 2005. Biomechanical measures of neuromuscular control and valgus loading of the knee predict anterior cruciate ligament injury risk in female athletes: A prospective study. *Am J Sports Med* 33(4): 492–501.

15. Myer, G.D., K.R. Ford, J.P. Palumbo, and T.E. Hewett. 2005. Neuromuscular training improves performance and lower-extremity biomechanics in female athletes. *J Strength Cond Res* 19(1): 51–60.

16. Hewett, T.E., K.R. Ford, and G.D. Myer. 2006. Anterior cruciate ligament injuries in female athletes. Part 2: A meta-analysis of neuromuscular interventions aimed at injury prevention. *Am J Sports Med* 34(3): 490–498.

17. Myer, G.D., K.R. Ford, J.L. Brent, and T.E. Hewett. 2006. The effects of plyometric versus dynamic balance training on power, balance and landing force in female athletes. *J Strength Cond Res* 20(2): 345–353.

18. Myer, G.D., K.R. Ford, S.G. McLean, and T.E. Hewett. 2006. The effects of plyometric versus dynamic stabilization and balance training on lower extremity biomechanics. *Am J Sports Med* 34(3): 445–455.

19. Myer, G.D., K.R. Ford, J.L. Brent, and T.E. Hewett. 2007. Differential neuromuscular training effects on ACL injury risk factors in "high-risk" versus "low-risk" athletes. *BMC Musculoskelet Disord* 8(39): 39.

20. Myer, G.D., K.R. Ford, J.L. Brent, and T.E. Hewett. 2005. The effects of plyometric versus dynamic balance training on landing force and center of pressure stabilization in female athletes. *Br J Sports Med* 39(6): 397.

21. Myer, G.D., D. Sugimoto, S. Thomas, and T.E. Hewett. 2012. The influence of age on the effectiveness of neuromuscular training to reduce anterior cruciate ligament injury in female athletes: A meta-analysis. *Am J Sports Med* 41(1): 203–215.

22. Myer, G.D., B.W. Stroube, C.A. DiCesare, J.L. Brent, K.R. Ford, R.S. Heidt, Jr., and T.E. Hewett. 2013. Augmented feedback supports skill transfer and reduces high-risk injury landing mechanics: A double-blind, randomized controlled laboratory study. *Am J Sports Med* 41(3): 669–677.

23. Boden, B.P., G.S. Dean, J.A. Feagin, and W.E. Garrett. 2000. Mechanisms of anterior cruciate ligament injury. *Orthopedics* 23(6): 573-578.

24. Malinzak, R.A., S.M. Colby, D.T. Kirkendall, B. Yu, and W.E. Garrett. 2001. A comparison of knee joint motion patterns between men and women in selected athletic tasks. *Clin Biomech* 16(5): 438-445.

25. Chappell, J.D., B. Yu, D.T. Kirkendall, and W.E. Garrett. 2002. A comparison of knee kinetics between male and female recreational athletes in stop-jump tasks. *Am J Sports Med* 30(2): 261-267.

26. Ford, K.R., G.D. Myer, and T.E. Hewett. 2003. Valgus knee motion during landing in high school female and male basketball players. *Med Sci Sports Exerc* 35(10): 1745-1750.

27. Zeller, B.L., J.L. McCrory, W.B. Kibler, and T.L. Uhl. 2003. Differences in kinematics and electromyographic activity between men and women during the single-legged squat. *Am J Sport Med* 31(3): 449-456.

28. Hewett, T.E., G.D. Myer, and K.R. Ford. 2004. Decrease in neuromuscular control about the knee with maturation in female athletes. *J Bone Joint Surg Am* 86-A(8): 1601-1608.

29. McLean, S.G., X. Huang, A. Su, and A.J. van den Bogert. 2004. Sagittal plane biomechanics cannot injure the ACL during sidestep cutting. *Clin Biomech* 19: 828-838.

30. Olsen, O.E., G. Myklebust, L. Engebretsen, and R. Bahr. 2004. Injury mechanisms for anterior cruciate ligament injuries in team handball: A systematic video analysis. *Am J Sports Med* 32(4): 1002-1012.

31. Kernozek, T.W., M.R. Torry, H. Van Hoof, H. Cowley, and S. Tanner. 2005. Gender differences in frontal and sagittal plane biomechanics during drop landings. *Med Sci Sports Exerc* 37(6): 1003-1012; discussion 1013.

32. Ford, K.R., G.D. Myer, R.L. Smith, R.M. Vianello, S.L. Seiwert, and T.E. Hewett. 2006. A comparison of dynamic coronal plane excursion between matched male and female athletes when performing single leg landings. *Clin Biomech (Bristol, Avon)* 21(1): 33-40.

33. Hewett, T.E., K.R. Ford, G.D. Myer, K. Wanstrath, and M. Scheper. 2006. Gender differences in hip adduction motion and torque during a single-leg agility maneuver. *J Orthop Res* 24(3): 416-421.

34. Krosshaug, T., A. Nakamae, B.P. Boden, L. Engebretsen, G. Smith, J.R. Slauterbeck, T.E. Hewett, and R. Bahr. 2007. Mechanisms of anterior cruciate ligament injury in basketball: Video analysis of 39 cases. *Am J Sports Med* 35(3): 359-367.

35. Pappas, E., M. Hagins, A. Sheikhzadeh, M. Nordin, and D. Rose. 2007. Biomechanical differences between unilateral and bilateral landings from a jump: Gender differences. *Clin J Sport Med* 17(4): 263-268.

36. Clanton, T.O., J.C. DeLee, B. Sanders, and A. Neidre. 1979. Knee ligament injuries in children. *J Bone Joint Surg Am* 61(8): 1195-1201.

37. Buehler-Yund, C. 1999. *A longitudinal study of injury rates and risk factors in 5 to 12 year old soccer players.* Cincinnati, OH: University of Cincinnati.

38. Andrish, J.T. 2001. Anterior cruciate ligament injuries in the skeletally immature patient. *Am J Orthop* 30(2): 103-110.

39. Shea, K.G., R. Pfeiffer, J.H. Wang, M. Curtin, and P.J. Apel. 2004. Anterior cruciate ligament injury in pediatric and adolescent soccer players: An analysis of insurance data. *J Pediatr Orthop* 24(6): 623-628.

40. Tursz, A., and M. Crost. 1986. Sports-related injuries in children: A study of their characteristics, frequency, and severity, with comparison to other types of accidental injuries. *Am J Sports Med* 14(4): 294-299.

41. Tanner, J.M., and P.S. Davies. 1985. Clinical longitudinal standards for height and height velocity for North American children. *J Pediatr* 107(3): 317-329.

42. Hewett, T.E., F.M. Biro, S.G. McLean, and A.J. Van den Bogert. 2003. *Identifying female athletes at high risk for ACL injury.* Cincinnati, OH: Cincinnati Children's Hospital, National Institutes of Health.

43. Hewett, T.E., G.D. Myer, K.R. Ford, and J.R. Slauterbeck. 2006. Preparticipation physical exam using a box drop vertical jump test in young athletes: The effects of puberty and sex. *Clin J Sport Med* 16(4): 298-304.

44. Ford, K.R., G.D. Myer, and T.E. Hewett. 2007. Increased trunk motion in female athletes compared to males during single leg landing. *Med Sci Sports Exerc* 39(5): S70.

45. Hodges, P.W., and C.A. Richardson. 1997. Contraction of the abdominal muscles associated with movement of the lower limb. *Phys Ther* 77(2): 132-142; discussion 142-144.

46. Hodges, P.W., and C.A. Richardson. 1997. Feedforward contraction of transversus abdominis is not influenced by the direction of arm movement. *Exp Brain Res* 114(2): 362-370.

47. Wilson, J.D., C.P. Dougherty, M.L. Ireland, and I.M. Davis. 2005. Core stability and its relationship to lower extremity function and injury. *J Am Acad Orthop Surg* 13: 316-325.

48. Winter, D.A. 2005. *Biomechanics and motor control of human movement.* New York: John Wiley & Sons.

49. Zatsiorsky, V.M. 1995. *Science and practice of strength training.* Champaign, IL: Human Kinetics.

50. Ireland, M.L. 2002. The female ACL: Why is it more prone to injury? *Orthop Clin North Am* 33(4): 637-651.

51. Myklebust, G., L. Engebretsen, I.H. Braekken, A. Skjolberg, O.E. Olsen, and R. Bahr. 2003. Prevention of anterior cruciate ligament injuries in female team handball players: A prospective intervention study over three seasons. *Clin J Sport Med* 13(2): 71-78.

52. Mandelbaum, B.R., H.J. Silvers, D.S. Watanabe, J.F. Knarr, S.D. Thomas, L.Y. Griffin, D.T. Kirkendall, and W. Garrett, Jr. 2005. Effectiveness of a neuromuscular and proprioceptive training program in preventing anterior cruciate ligament injuries in female athletes: Two-year follow up. *Am J Sport Med* 33(7): 1003-1010.

53. Petersen, W., C. Braun, W. Bock, K. Schmidt, A. Weimann, W. Drescher, E. Eiling, R. Stange, T. Fuchs, J. Hedderich, and T. Zantop. 2006. A controlled prospective case control study of a prevention training program in female team handball players: The German experience. *Arch Orthop Trauma Surg* 125(9): 614-621.

54. Myer, G.D., J.L. Brent, K.R. Ford, and T.E. Hewett. 2008. A pilot study to determine the effect of trunk and hip focused neuromuscular training on hip and knee isokinetic strength. *Br J Sports Med* 42(7): 614-619.

Chapter 6

1. Myer, G.D., D.A. Chu, J.L. Brent, and T.E. Hewett. 2008. Trunk and hip control neuromuscular training for the prevention of knee joint injury. *Clin Sports Med* 27(3) (July): 425-448, ix.

2. Chmielewski, T.L., G.D. Myer, D. Kauffman, and S.M. Tillman. 2006. Plyometric exercise in the rehabilitation of athletes: Physiological responses and clinical application. *J Orthop Sports Phys Ther* 36(5) (May): 308-319.

3. Hewett, T.E., T.N. Lindenfeld, J.V. Riccobene, and F.R. Noyes. 1999. The effect of neuromuscular training on the incidence of knee injury in female athletes: A prospective study. *Am J Sports Med* 27(6) (Nov.-Dec.): 699-706.

4. Mandelbaum, B.R., H.J. Silvers, D.S. Watanabe, J.F. Knarr, S.D. Thomas, L.Y. Griffin, D.T. Kirkendall, and W. Garett, Jr. 2005. Effectiveness of a neuromuscular and proprioceptive training program in preventing anterior cruciate ligament injuries in female athletes: Two-year follow up. *Am J Sports Med* 33(7): 1003-1010.

5. Olsen, O.E., G. Myklebust, L. Engebretsen, I. Holme, and R. Bahr. 2005. Exercises to prevent lower limb injuries in youth sports: Cluster randomised controlled trial. *BMJ* 330(7489) (Feb. 26): 449.

6. Myklebust, G., L. Engebretsen, I.H. Braekken, A. Skjolberg, O.E. Olsen, and R. Bahr. 2003. Prevention of anterior cruciate ligament injuries in female team handball players: A prospective intervention study over three seasons. *Clin J Sport Med* 13(2) (March): 71-78.

7. Petersen, W., C. Braun, W. Bock, K. Schmidt, A. Weimann, W. Dresher, E. Eiling, R. Stange, T. Fuchs, J. Hedderich, and T. Zantop. 2005. A controlled prospective case control study of a prevention training program in female team handball players: The German experience. *Arch Orthop Trauma Surg* 125(9): 614-621.

8. Cheung, K., P. Hume, and L. Maxwell. 2003. Delayed onset muscle soreness: Treatment strategies and performance factors. *Sports Med* 33(2): 145-164.

9. Chu, D.A. 1995. Rehabilitation of the lower extremity. *Clin Sports Med* 14(1) (Jan.): 205-222.

10. Chu, D.A. 1998. *Jumping into plyometrics.* 2nd ed. Champaign, IL: Human Kinetics.

11. Ishikawa, M., T. Finni, and P.V. Komi. 2003. Behaviour of vastus lateralis muscle-tendon during high intensity SSC exercises in vivo. *Acta Physiol Scand* 178(3) (July): 205-213.

12. Voight, M.L., and S. Tippett. 1994. Plyometric exercise in rehabilitation. In W.E. Prentice (Ed.), *Rehabilitation techniques in sports medicine.* 2nd ed. St. Louis: Mosby. 88-97.

13. Connolly, D.A., S.P. Sayers, and M.P. McHugh. 2003. Treatment and prevention of delayed onset muscle soreness. *J Strength Cond Res* 17(1) (Feb.): 197-208.

14. Proske, U., J.E. Gregory, D.L. Morgan, P. Percival, N.S. Weerakkody, and B.J. Canny. 2004. Force matching errors following eccentric exercise. *Hum Mov Sci* 23(3-4) (Oct.): 365-378.

15. Chmielewski, T.L., R.L. Mizner, W. Padamonsky, and L. Snyder-Mackler. 2003. Knee. In G.S. Kolt and L. Snyder-Mackler (Eds.), *Physical therapies in sport and exercise.* Edinburgh: Elsevier Science Limited. 387.

16. Hewett, T.E., G.D. Myer, K.R. Ford, R.S. Heidt, Jr., A.J. Colosimo, S.G. McLean, A.J. van den Bogert, M.V. Paterno, and P. Succop. 2005. Biomechanical measures of neuromuscular control and valgus loading of the knee predict anterior cruciate ligament injury risk in female athletes: A prospective study. *Am J Sports Med* 33(4): 492-501.

17. Myer, G.D., M.V. Paterno, and T.E. Hewett. 2004. Back in the game: A four-phase return-to-sport program for athletes with problem ACLs. *Rehab Manag* 17(8) (Oct.): 30-33.

18. Prapavessis, H., and P.J. McNair. 1999. Effects of instruction in jumping technique and experience jumping on ground reaction forces. *J Orthop Sports Phys Ther* 29(6) (June): 352-356.

19. Onate, J.A., K.M. Guskiewicz, and R.J. Sullivan. 2001. Augmented feedback reduces jump landing forces. *J Orthop Sports Phys Ther* 31(9) (Sep.): 511-517.

20. Myer, G.D., M.V. Paterno, K.R. Ford, C.E. Quatman, and T.E. Hewett. 2006. Rehabilitation after anterior cruciate ligament reconstruction: Criteria based progression through the return-to-sport phase. *J Orthop Sports Phys Ther* 36(6): 385-402.

21. Myer, G.D., M.V. Paterno, K.R. Ford, and T.E. Hewett. 2008. Neuromuscular training techniques to target deficits before return to sport after anterior cruciate ligament reconstruction. *J Strength Cond Res* 22(3) (April 15): 987-1014.

22. Myer, G.D., L.C. Schmitt, J.L. Brent, K.R. Ford, K.D. Barber Foss, B.J. Scherer, R.S. Heidt, Jr., J.G. Divine, and T.E. Hewett. 2011. Utilization of modified NFL combine testing to identify functional deficits in athletes following ACL reconstruction. *J Orthop Sports Phys Ther* 41(6): 377-387.

23. Paterno, M.V., K.R. Ford, G.D. Myer, R. Heyl, and T.E. Hewett. 2007. Limb asymmetries in landing and jumping 2 years following anterior cruciate ligament reconstruction. *Clin J Sport Med* 17(4) (July): 258-262.

24. Paterno, M.V., L.C. Schmitt, K.R. Ford, M.J. Rauh, G.D. Myer, B. Huang, and T.E. Hewett. 2010. Biomechanical measures during landing and postural stability predict second anterior cruciate ligament injury after anterior cruciate ligament reconstruction and return to sport. *Am J Sports Med* 38(10): 1968-1978.

Chapter 7

1. Verkhoshanski, Y. 1969. Perspectives in the improvement of speed-strength preparation of jumpers. *Yessis Rev Sov Phys Educ Sports* 4(2): 28-29.

2. Chu, D.A., A.D. Faigenbaum, and J.E. Falkel. 2006. *Progressive plyometrics for kids.* Monterey, CA: Healthy Learning.

3. Myer, G.D., K.R. Ford, K.D. Barber Foss, C. Liu, T.G. Nick, and T.E. Hewett. 2009. The relationship of hamstrings and quadriceps strength to anterior cruciate ligament injury in female athletes. *Clin J Sport Med* 19(1) (Jan.): 3-8.

4. Myer, G.D., K.R. Ford, J.P. Palumbo, and T.E. Hewett. 2005. Neuromuscular training improves performance and lower-extremity biomechanics in female athletes. *J Strength Cond Res* 19(1) (Feb.): 51-60.

5. Myer, G.D., R.S. Lloyd, J.L. Brent, and A.D. Faigenbaum. In press. What "age" should youth start training. *ACSM's Health and Fitness Journal.*

6. Myer, G.D., K.R. Ford, S.G. McLean, and T.E. Hewett. 2006. The effects of plyometric versus dynamic stabilization and balance training on lower extremity biomechanics. *Am J Sports Med* 34(3): 490-498.

7. Hewett, T.E., G.D. Myer, K.R. Ford, R.S. Heidt Jr., A.J. Colosimo, S.G. McLean, A.J. van den Bogert, M.V. Paterno, and P. Succop. 2005. Biomechanical measures of neuromuscular control and valgus loading of the knee predict anterior cruciate ligament injury risk in female athletes: A prospective study. *Am J Sports Med* 33(4) (Feb. 8): 492-501.

8. Ford, K.R., G.D. Myer, H.E. Toms, and T.E. Hewett. 2005. Gender differences in the kinematics of unanticipated cutting in young athletes. *Med Sci Sports* 37(1) (Jan.): 124-129.

9. McLean, S.G., S.W. Lipfert, and A.J. van den Bogert. 2004. Effect of gender and defensive opponent on the biomechanics of sidestep cutting. *Med Sci Sports Exerc* 36(6) (June): 1008-1016.

10. Ford, K.R., G.D. Myer, and T.E. Hewett. 2003. Valgus knee motion during landing in high school female and male basketball players. *Med Sci Sports Exerc* 35(10) (Oct.): 1745-1750.

11. Chappell, J.D., B. Yu, D.T. Kirkendall, and W.E. Garrett. 2002. A comparison of knee kinetics between male and female recreational athletes in stop-jump tasks. *Am J Sports Med* 30(2) (Mar.-Apr.): 261-267.

12. Myer, G.D., J.L. Brent, K.R. Ford, and T.E. Hewett. 2011. Real-time assessment and neuromuscular training feedback techniques to prevent ACL injury in female athletes. *Strength Cond J* 33(3) (June 1): 21-35.

13. Myer, G.D., K.R. Ford, and T.E. Hewett. 2004. Rationale and clinical techniques for anterior cruciate ligament injury prevention among female athletes. *J Athl Train* 39(4) (Dec.): 352–364.

14. Myer, G.D., K.R. Ford, and T.E. Hewett. 2008. Tuck jump assessment for reducing anterior cruciate ligament injury risk. *Athletic Therapy Today* 13(5): 39–44.

15. Myer, G.D., J.L. Brent, K.R. Ford, and T.E. Hewett. 2008. A pilot study to determine the effect of trunk and hip focused neuromuscular training on hip and knee isokinetic strength. *Br J Sports Med* 42(7) (July): 614–619.

16. Myer, G.D., D.A. Chu, J.L. Brent, and T.E. Hewett. 2008. Trunk and hip control neuromuscular training for the prevention of knee joint injury. *Clin Sports Med* 27(3) (July): 425–448, ix.

17. Paterno, M.V., G.D. Myer, K.R. Ford, and T.E. Hewett. 2004. Neuromuscular training improves single-limb stability in young female athletes. *J Orthop Sports Phys Ther* 34(6): 305–317.

18. Boden, B.P., G.S. Dean, J.A. Feagin, and W.E. Garrett. 2000. Mechanisms of anterior cruciate ligament injury. *Orthopedics* 23(6): 573–578.

19. Ford, K.R., A.J. van den Bogert, G.D. Myer, R. Shapiro, and T.E. Hewett. 2008. The effects of age and skill level on knee musculature co-contraction during functional activities: A systematic review. *Br J Sports Med* 42(7) (July): 561–566.

20. Ford, K.R., G.D. Myer, L.C. Schmitt, A.J. van den Bogert, and T.E. Hewett. 2008. Effect of drop height on lower extremity biomechanical measures in female athletes. *Med Sci Sports Exerc* 40(5): S80.

21. Soderman, K., H. Alfredson, T. Pietila, and S. Werner. 2001. Risk factors for leg injuries in female soccer players: A prospective investigation during one out-door season. *Knee Surg Sports Traumatol Arthrosc* 9(5) (Sep.): 313–321.

22. Knapik, J.J., C.L. Bauman, B.H. Jones, J.M. Harris, and L. Vaughan. 1991. Preseason strength and flexibility imbalances associated with athletic injuries in female collegiate athletes. *Am J Sports Med* 19(1): 76–81.

23. Sell, T.C., C.M. Ferris, J.P. Abt, Y.S. Tsai, J.B. Myers, F.H. Fu, and S.M. Lephart. 2007. Predictors of proximal tibia anterior shear force during a vertical stop-jump. *J Orthop Res* 25(12) (Dec.): 1589–1597.

24. Withrow, T.J., L.J. Huston, E.M. Wojtys, and J.A. Ashton-Miller. 2006. The relationship between quadriceps muscle force, knee flexion, and anterior cruciate ligament strain in an in vitro simulated jump landing. *Am J Sports Med* 34(2) (Feb.): 269–274.

25. Withrow, T.J., L.J. Huston, E.M. Wojtys, and J.A. Ashton-Miller. 2008. Effect of varying hamstring tension on anterior cruciate ligament strain during in vitro impulsive knee flexion and compression loading. *J Bone Joint Surg Am* 90(4) (April): 815–823.

26. Malinzak, R.A., S.M. Colby, D.T. Kirkendall, B. Yu, and W.E. Garrett. 2001. A comparison of knee joint motion patterns between men and women in selected athletic tasks. *Clin Biomech (Bristol, Avon)* 16(5) (June): 438–445.

27. Hewett, T.E., A.L. Stroupe, T.A. Nance, and F.R. Noyes. 1996. Plyometric training in female athletes: Decreased impact forces and increased hamstring torques. *Am J Sports Med* 24(6): 765–773.

28. MacWilliams, B.A., D.R. Wilson, J.D. DesJardins, J. Romero, and E.Y. Chao. 1999. Hamstrings cocontraction reduces internal rotation, anterior translation, and anterior cruciate ligament load in weight-bearing flexion. *J Orthop Res* 17(6) (Nov.): 817–822.

29. Lloyd, D.G., and T.S. Buchanan. 2001. Strategies of muscular support of varus and valgus isometric loads at the human knee. *J Biomech* 34(10): 1257–1267.

30. Myer, G.D., K.R. Ford, J.L. Brent, and T.E. Hewett. 2006. The effects of plyometric versus dynamic balance training on power, balance and landing force in female athletes. *J Strength Cond Res* 20(2): 345–353.

31. Baumhauer, J., D. Alosa, A. Renstrom, S. Trevino, and B. Beynnon. 1995. A prospective study of ankle injury risk factors. *Am J Sport Med* 23(5): 564–570.

32. Paterno, M.V., L.C. Schmitt, K.R. Ford, M.J. Rauh, G.D. Myer, B. Huang, and T.E. Hewett. 2010. Biomechanical measures during landing and postural stability predict second anterior cruciate ligament injury after anterior cruciate ligament reconstruction and return to sport. *Am J Sports Med* 38(10): 1968–1978.

33. Paterno, M.V., K.R. Ford, G.D. Myer, R. Heyl, and T.E. Hewett. 2007. Limb asymmetries in landing and jumping 2 years following anterior cruciate ligament reconstruction. *Clin J Sport Med* 17(4) (July): 258–262.

34. Hewett, T.E., and G.D. Myer. 2011. The mechanistic connection between the trunk, hip, knee, and anterior cruciate ligament injury. *Exerc Sport Sci Rev* 39(4) (Oct.): 161–166.

35. Wilson, J.D., C.P. Dougherty, M.L. Ireland, and I.M. Davis. 2005. Core stability and its relationship to lower extremity function and injury. *J Am Acad Orthop Surg* 13: 316–325.

36. Hodges, P.W., and C.A. Richardson. 1997. Feedforward contraction of transversus abdominis is not influenced by the direction of arm movement. *Exp Brain Res* 114(2) (April): 362–370.

37. Hodges, P.W., and C.A. Richardson. 1997. Contraction of the abdominal muscles associated with movement of the lower limb. *Phys Ther* 77(2) (Feb.): 132–142; discussion 142–144.

38. Winter, D.A. (Ed.). 2005. *Biomechanics and motor control of human movement.* 3rd ed. New York: John Wiley & Sons, Inc.

39. Ireland, M.L. 2002. The female ACL: Why is it more prone to injury? *Orthop Clin North Am* 33(4) (Oct.): 637–651.

40. Zatsiorsky, V.M. 1995. *Science and practice of strength training.* Champaign, IL: Human Kinetics.

41. Zazulak, B.T., T.E. Hewett, N.P. Reeves, B. Goldberg, and J. Cholewicki. 2007. The effects of core proprioception on knee injury: A prospective biomechanical-epidemiological study. *Am J Sports Med* 35(3) (March): 368–373.

42. Krosshaug, T., A. Nakamae, B.P. Boden, L. Engebretsen, G. Smith, J.R. Slauterbeck, T.E. Hewett, and R. Bahr. 2007. Mechanisms of anterior cruciate ligament injury in basketball: Video analysis of 39 cases. *Am J Sports Med* 35(3) (March): 359–367.

43. Olsen, O.E., G. Myklebust, L. Engebretsen, and R. Bahr. 2004. Injury mechanisms for anterior cruciate ligament injuries in team handball: A systematic video analysis. *Am J Sports Med* 32(4) (June): 1002–1012.

44. Myer, G.D., M.V. Paterno, K.R. Ford, and T.E. Hewett. 2008. Neuromuscular training techniques to target deficits before return to sport after anterior cruciate ligament reconstruction. *J Strength Cond Res* 22(3) (April 15): 987–1014.

45. Myer, G.D., M.V. Paterno, K.R. Ford, C.E. Quatman, and T.E. Hewett. 2006. Rehabilitation after anterior cruciate ligament reconstruction: Criteria based progression through the return-to-sport phase. *J Orthop Sports Phys Ther* 36(6): 385–402.

46. Myer, G.D., B.W. Stroube, C.A. DiCesare, J.L. Brent, K.R. Ford, R.S. Heidt, Jr., and T.E. Hewett. 2013. Augmented

feedback supports skill transfer and reduces high-risk injury landing mechanics: A double-blind, randomized controlled laboratory study. *Am J Sports Med* 41(3): 669–677.

47. Stroube, B.W., G.D. Myer, J.L. Brent, K.R. Ford, R.S. Heidt, Jr., and T.E. Hewett. 2012. Effects of task-specific augmented feedback on deficit modification during performance of the tuck-jump exercise. *J Sport Rehabil* 22(1): 7–18.

Chapter 10

1. Nader, P., R. Bradley, R. Houts, S. McRitchie, and M. O'Brien. 2008. Moderate to vigorous physical activity from ages 9 to 15 years. *Journal of the American Medical Association* 300: 295–305.

2. Nyberg, G., A. Nordenfelt, U. Ekelund, and C. Marcus. 2009. Physical activity patterns measured by accelerometry in 6- to 10-yr-old children. *Med Sci Sports Exerc* 41(10): 1842–1848.

3. Myer, G.D., A.D. Faigenbaum, D.A. Chu, J. Falkel, K.R. Ford, T.M. Best, and T.E. Hewett. 2011. Integrative train-ing for children and adolescents: Techniques and practices for reducing sports-related injuries and enhancing athletic performance. *Phys Sportsmed* 39(1): 74–84.

4. Myer, G.D., A.D. Faigenbaum, K.R. Ford, T.M. Best, M.F. Bergeron, and T.E. Hewett. 2011. When to initiate integrative neuromuscular training to reduce sports-related injuries and enhance health in youth? *Curr Sports Med Rep* 10(3): 157–166.

5. Chu, D., A. Faigenbaum, and J. Falkel. 2006. *Progressive plyometrics for kids.* Monterey, CA: Healthy Learning.

6. Lyttle, A., G. Wilson, and K. Ostrowski. 1996. Enhancing performance: Maximal power versus combined weights and plyometrics training. *Journal of Strength and Conditioning Research* 10(3): 173–179.

7. Adams, K., J. O'Shea, K. O'Shea, and M. Climstein. 1992. The effect of six weeks of squat, plyometric and squat-plyometric training on power production. *Journal of Applied Sports Science Research* 6(1): 36–41.

Index

Note: The italicized *f* and *t* following page numbers refer to figures and tables, respectively.

About the Authors

Dr. Donald Chu, PhDPT, ATC, CSCS, FNSCA, is a professor emeritus of kinesiology and physical education at California State University at Hayward, where he taught for more than 20 years. He is director and founder of Athercare Fitness & Rehabilitation in the San Francisco Bay area, which specializes in sport performance training, fitness programs, physical therapy, and clinical psychology.

Dr. Chu has developed an extensive reputation in the field of sport rehabilitation and fitness and conditioning. He pioneered research-supported plyometric training in the Western hemisphere and is revered throughout the strength and conditioning community for enhancing modern sports' most defining athletic factor: power. Chu has been credited with bringing plyometric training to the attention of coaches, athletes, and fellow professionals in sport conditioning through his application of theoretical knowledge into practical demonstrations.

The author of six books, Chu has also written articles in refereed journals and contributed chapters to many books on sports medicine. More than 140,000 copies of his seminal book on the topic, *Jumping Into Plyometrics*, have been sold since 1994. He has presented extensively to professional groups around the world and consulted with athletes and teams at every level—including Olympians and professionals—on the development of training and conditioning programs.

Dr. Chu holds certifications as an athletic trainer (ATC) from the National Athletic Trainers' Association (NATA) and as a certified strength and conditioning specialist (CSCS) from the National Strength and Conditioning Association (NSCA). He has served on the board of directors for both organizations and is a past president of the NSCA. He resides in Alameda, California.

Gregory D. Myer, PhD, FACSM, CSCS,*D is currently the director of research at the Human Performance Laboratory for the Division of Sports Medicine at Cincinnati Children's Hospital Medical Center and is also serving as the senior research advisor to the Micheli Center for Sports Injury Prevention. He also maintains his primary faculty appointment in the departments of pediatrics and orthopaedic surgery in the College of Medicine at the University of Cincinnati and secondary appointments in the athletic training division at Ohio State University. He is a member, lecturer, and honoree of the ACSM, NSCA, and NATA for his breakthrough research, including his defining work on the development of prevention strategies in knee injury. Myer's work in the Human Performance Laboratory allows him to integrate the most advanced research findings into training protocols for athletic development and injury prevention. Dr. Myer works with athletes from preadolescence to professional level and speaks to coaches around the world seeking to update their own training programs.

Dr. Myer is the author of *Strength and Jump Training for Volleyball* and several book chapters related to his research on the biomechanics of sport performance and training for injury prevention. He has also authored over 150 articles in peer-reviewed medical journals. He resides in Cincinnati, Ohio.